Loves Me,
Loves Me Not

Loves Me, Loves Me Not

The Ethics of Unrequited Love

Laura A. Smit

Baker Academic
Grand Rapids, Michigan

Published by Baker Academic
a division of Baker Publishing Group
P.O. Box 6287, Grand Rapids, MI 49516-6287
www.bakeracademic.com

Printed in the United States of America

Library of Congress Cataloging-in-Publication Data
Smit, Laura, 1961–
    Loves me, loves me not : the ethics of unrequited love / Laura A. Smit.
        p. cm.
    Includes bibliographical references and index.
    ISBN 0-8010-2997-X (pbk.)
    1. Love—Religious aspects—Christianity. I. Title.
  BV4639.S635 2005
  241'.4—dc22   2005009762

Contents

Acknowledgments

Thanks to Calvin College for a McGregor Grant in the summer of 2001, which allowed me to do the basic research for this book, and to Calvin's Center for Social Research for a grant in the spring of 2002, which helped with survey coding and data analysis.

Thanks to Andrea Kloostra Bierma, the McGregor fellow who worked with me in the early stages of this project. She read and coded all the survey answers, compiled tapes of film clips that made me look much more media savvy than I really am, helped with most of the interviews, crunched numbers, and mastered chi-square tables.

Thanks to Pat Sturgeon, Laura Geelhoed, and Nancy Naber for heroic typing assistance.

Thanks to the students who took my "Ethics of Romance" classes in January 2002 and January 2003, providing helpful reactions and suggestions.

Thanks to Betsy Cooper, Amy de Jong, Emilie Kao, Rachel Klompmaker, Joel Lautenbach, Sara Lundberg, Richelle Mikes, Bill Smit, Jane Smit, Jim Vanden Bosch, and William Van Geest for reading the manuscript at various stages.

Thanks to Elizabeth Kao Holmlund, who has lost count of how many times she has read this manuscript! It would not have been finished without her help.

Thanks to Dana Gioia for permission to quote his poem "Unsaid," in *Interrogations at Noon* (Saint Paul, MN: Graywolf Press, 2001).

Thanks to Carla Ulbrich for permission to quote the lyrics to "It Reminds Me of You," *Her Fabulous Debut* (Clemson, SC: A Major Record Label, 1999), available at http://www.carlau.com.

7

Acknowledgments

Thanks to Felicia Brady for permission to quote the lyrics to "Move Me," *Magazine Street* (Cambridge, MA: Magazine Street Music, 2001), available at http://www.feliciabrady.com.

Thanks most of all to those who told me their stories, either in writing or in person.

Introduction

Love, unrequited, robs me of my rest:
Love, hopeless love, my ardent soul encumbers:
Love, nightmare-like, lies heavy on my chest,
And weaves itself into my midnight slumbers!

> sung by Lord Chancellor,
> Gilbert and Sullivan's *Iolanthe*

If you find my beloved, tell him this: I am faint with love.

> Song of Solomon 5:8

This is a book about love. Specifically, this is a book about romantic love, the sort of love that makes your pulse race, prompts hours of daydreams, takes away your breath—and your appetite. As Chris Stevens puts it:

> We're talking about the big L, people—*amore,* Cupid's arrow, this crazy thing called love. I'm not talking about this agape kind of love, or this spiritual, Platonic, brotherhood-of-man, hey-I'm-okay-you're-okay kind of deal. I'm talking about Eros, serious grope time, the bonding of hearts and glands, like Tristan and Isolde, Abelard and Heloise.[1]

Sometimes romantic love gets tangled up with other kinds of love, like friendship, affection, or compassion. Sometimes romantic love vanishes after a few days. Sometimes it becomes a lifelong

---

1. Chris Stevens, "Altered Egos," episode 5.04, *Northern Exposure.* I will be citing many examples from popular culture throughout this book, including TV shows, movies, and popular music. Please do not assume that a citation is an endorsement.

obsession. Despite such differences of intensity and duration, there is something that all experiences of romantic love have in common, and that (admittedly nebulous) something is the subject of this book.

One reason romantic love is so difficult to define is that it is very subjective, and our impressions of whether we are in love and whether that love is real change over time. When you look back at the first time you fell in love, you may conclude that it was not really love at all but something else: a crush, an infatuation, lust, or a fantasy. The problem is that you cannot know now how your current experience of love will appear to you from some point in the future. For now, let's just leave it at this: if you believe you are in love, this book is for you.

This is also a book about rejection—not just how to take rejection but also how to give it. Most people will experience both sides during their lifetime. Almost everyone gets rejected in love, and almost everyone rejects someone else.[2] Being a rejector is not a popular position, and being rejected is not a pleasant experience. But there are good and bad ways to handle both. Even if we cannot make rejection fun or easy, we may be able to handle it in more Christlike ways.

---

2. The most significant research on this topic has been done by Roy F. Baumeister and Sara Wotman. Their work is reported in the article "Unrequited Love: On Heartbreak, Anger, Guilt, Scriptlessness, and Humiliation," *Journal of Social and Clinical Psychology* 9 (1990): 165–95; and also in the book *Breaking Hearts: The Two Sides of Unrequited Love* (New York: Guilford Press, 1992). Both the article and the book are based on a survey they administered to their students at Case Western University. This survey asked students to respond anonymously and in writing to two questions, one asking for an account of a time when the student was rejected in love, the second asking for an account of a time when the student rejected someone else. They surveyed 71 students, who produced 134 accounts [sic]. In other words, there were only 7 students who could not tell both stories: 1 had no story of being a rejector; 6 had no story of being rejected. My own research replicated Baumeister and Wotman's study and agrees with their results. I surveyed 84 students, who produced 163 accounts. Of the 5 students who could not tell both stories, 4 had no story of being a rejector, while 1 had no story of being rejected. Many of the illustrations throughout this book are drawn from this collection of anonymous written stories. As the second stage of the study, I conducted in-depth taped interviews with 12 students, with 2 student focus groups, and with 10 never-married alumni/ae of my college who were between the ages of 35 and 50. I began interviewing alumni/ae when I discovered that, although students were good at identifying the pain of unrequited love,

This is *not* a book about relationships. Rather, this is a book about how to handle love apart from a relationship—either when you are in love with someone who does not love you or when you are pursued by someone you do not love.

The goal of this book is to offer tools for disciplined self-examination of our feelings, for accepting responsibility for those things we can control, and for finding grace in those things we cannot control. God meets each of us in the course of our daily life. He is present to us in the people we love most dearly and know most intimately. We must find ways to recognize his presence and receive the gift of his reflection in those we love, even when that love does not bear the fruit for which we hope. We must find ways to be channels of his grace and goodness, even when we are rejecting an offer of romance.

Nonmutual Love

Being in love with someone who does not love you is one of the most painful and universal of human experiences. Almost all of us at some point in our life will love someone or at least be strongly attracted to someone who either will not or cannot return our feelings. Even those who have not experienced this know about it vicariously. Psychologist Bernard Murstein says that it is "an American preoccupation."[3] Most of us can testify to this based on nothing more than watching television or listening to the radio. Popular music is so dominated by songs of unrequited love that heartbreak confronts anyone who turns on a radio. The experience of unrequited love is so central to our culture that those who have not faced it may be treated as though they are in some way inadequate or emotionally stunted. When Rachel, of the popular television show *Friends*, revealed

---

most of them did not yet have much advice to give about appropriate Christian ways to handle such experiences. Many of the illustrations throughout this book are drawn from these taped interviews. In all cases, I have changed names and any identifying details to protect the anonymity both of those who shared their stories and of those about whom they spoke.

3. Bernard I. Murstein, "A Taxonomy of Love," in *The Psychology of Love*, ed. Robert Sternberg and Michael L. Barnes (New Haven: Yale University Press, 1988), 13.

that she had never been dumped, the other characters reacted with disbelief and smug superiority. An important part of her character development during the course of the series was the experience of being rejected romantically. In our culture, heartbreak is treated as a rite of passage into adulthood, a common experience that connects adults to one another.

Many of us also will be loved by those whose feelings we either cannot or will not return, an experience that can be awkward at best and violent at worst. Rejecting someone's offer of love is not easy, and rejecting someone in a way that is both gracious and truthful is downright difficult. Sometimes this may mean learning to say no firmly and clearly to a stranger or distant acquaintance who wants to initiate a romantic relationship. Sometimes this may mean learning to say no tenderly and gently to a best friend in a way that allows the friendship to survive. It may be necessary to say no over and over again, since those who are romantically attracted to us and are rejected often hope for a change of heart. Learning how to speak the truth in love is a challenge for all Christians, and it is never more challenging than when the truth is a rejection of romance.

When we are in the midst of the experience of romance, it is difficult to think clearly. The experience of love colors all other experiences, whether or not our love is returned. We may be less quick to speak of unrequited love, less free to share the experience with acquaintances and relatives, than of love that is returned (although in our tell-all society such reticence is not as automatic as it once was). Likewise, we may be reluctant to talk about the experience of being pursued by someone who does not interest us, either because it is difficult to talk about such experiences without sounding as if we are bragging about a conquest or because the role of the rejector is not typically a sympathetic role. However, even if we do not always talk about such experiences, they dominate our thinking and color our lives.

For many people, unrequited love is a bigger part of life than relationships. Many of us have more experiences of unrequited love than we do of mutual love. When I think about my own life as a single adult, I find that there have been relatively brief periods of time when I have been in a stable, mutually loving, dating relationship. For much of the rest of my adult life, I was either interested in someone who did not return my interest or I was being pursued by someone in whom I was not interested. Once in a while, I was dealing with both experiences simultaneously. In the last few years, I have made a more deliberate decision not to marry, since I have come to believe that God wants me to remain single. This has meant that I have had fewer such experiences, but even now the challenges of nonmutual love recur from time to time. As I talk to other single adults in their thirties and forties, this pattern seems to be quite typical: unrequited love is a large part of our existence, a much larger part than mutual relationships.

For many singles, experiences of nonmutual romance are the most difficult part of being single. One of the people interviewed for this book, a never-married woman in her forties, said, "I think that one of the most difficult things about being single for this long is not the being single, like everybody thinks; it's how many times you live through this pain," that is, the pain either of being rejected or of having to reject someone. Sometimes the rejection happens before there is any relationship to speak of, and we need to deal with the loss of a dream. Sometimes rejection means the end of a long relationship for which we once had high hopes.

Even though these experiences are common, most of us receive little guidance about how to deal with them. Parents, teachers, and youth leaders give advice and direction about the morality of dating. But what is the morality of unrequited love? The self-help section of any neighborhood bookstore is full of advice about how to handle relationships. But there are few if any books about coping with the heartache of loving someone who is indifferent to that love. The rejected person is left with many pressing questions. Do I have an obligation to get over such love? Does faith in God guarantee that when I fall in love with the "right" person, he or she will return my feelings? Is there a God-honoring way to love someone who does not love me back?

Even less discussed is the awkward situation of being pursued by someone to whom we are not attracted. Popular culture teaches us to be on the side of the pursuer. After all, "All the world loves a lover." When we say no to someone who claims to love us, we are therefore taking on a role for which we will receive little or no support. Popular culture encourages romantic pursuers to persist in the face of all obstacles. Therefore, even if we find a way to say no to someone who pursues us, that person may well continue the pursuit in hopes that we will change our mind. Stories like these are common, and I heard many such stories in the interviews conducted for this book. One young man wrote about pursuing a young woman who "would not be wooed." He tried everything.

> Not poetry. Not music. Not vulnerability. My usual tactics had absolutely no effect on her. I was completely lovesick. I burned with passion for her. The more she pushed me away, the more I longed for her. I continued to pursue her, thinking, "She'll come around some time or another." I even drove hundreds of miles to see her.

The startling lesson this young man learned was that his tactics were not foolproof. Only after a long period of persistence did he finally give up, saying, "I couldn't take it any more. Months later I asked her why she wouldn't give me a chance. She said I was too proud." He gave up after a few months, but it is not uncommon to find people who have pursued the one they love for years, continuing to hope that their love will be returned.

Again, questions abound. What is the kindest and most virtuous way to say no to someone who is pursuing me? Is there any sense in which I am obligated to return love when it is offered to me, even if it is offered by someone I find unattractive? Is a lack of physical desire an appropriate reason for a Christian not to explore a potential relationship?

A less obvious question is whether such nonmutual love relationships have any potential value, apart from serving as a rehearsal for a future mutual relationship. The currently popular self-help book *He's Just Not That into You* tells us that they do not.

> No matter how powerful and real your feelings may be for someone, if that person cannot fully and *honestly* return them and therefore actively love you back, these feelings mean nothing. Sure, they may feel powerful, deep, mythic in scope and proportion. You may "never ever have felt this way before." But who cares? If the person you "love" (notice the snotty quotation marks

around that) cannot freely spend his days thinking about you and being with you, *it's not real love.*[4]

This is the most straightforward statement of this idea I have seen, and culture in general supports it. When we find ourselves in love with someone who does not return our feelings, friends and family are likely to be united in urging us to move on, to stop wasting time on this fruitless relationship, and instead to work at finding a meaningful (i.e., mutual) relationship. But is it true that only mutual relationships are meaningful? Given the amount of time and energy many of us invest in nonmutual love relationships, it is disturbing to think that such experiences have no value. Is it true that love is not real if it is not returned? Given the Christian conviction that God's love is powerful precisely because it is not dependent on our response, it seems that we need to challenge this idea, making room in our understanding of romance for a love that has value even though it is not returned.

Although falling in love may not be a choice directly controlled by our will, there are things under our control, choices we can make, that will make us more or less likely to fall in love and will shape the intensity and duration of such love when we tumble into it. Given that our moral obligation extends only to those things that are within our power of choice, what are some of the possible choices when we find ourselves experiencing unrequited love?

It is possible to treat such love as a weakness or even as a sickness and to seek a cure from it. It is possible to treat such love as a source of entitlement, which grants us claim and authority over the one we love and allows us to become bitter and angry when our love is rejected. It is possible to play the romantic hero and enjoy the suffering of a broken heart. It may even be possible for persistent love to kindle love in the other; we may teach someone to love us by our consistent love for him or her. The more difficult possibility is that we may be called to love without the expectation of love returned, to love hopelessly but still

4. Greg Behrendt and Liz Tuccillo, *He's Just Not That into You: The No-Excuses Truth to Understanding Guys* (New York: Simon & Schuster, 2004), 119.

consistently. It may be possible to mine spiritual riches from the experience of loving from a distance and without response.

A Question of Character

Before I was a college professor, I was a pastor. I served a small Presbyterian church in a small town for six and a half years. During that time, I encountered a temptation common to many pastors, the temptation to avoid confronting parishioners with their actual sins and to preach instead about sins we all agreed were horrible but none of us was particularly tempted to try. It was much easier to preach against paganism or the occult than to preach against materialism or gossip. A sharp sermon against the occult would gain the approval of the congregation without any risk of causing offense. This tendency to preach only what is already accepted by everyone present is typically called preaching to the choir.

This same phenomenon of preaching to the choir can be seen in the way most contemporary evangelical Christians approach questions of sexual ethics. We are quick to talk about the need for sexual abstinence outside marriage. We are quick to talk about the dangers of homosexual practice. We are quick to talk about the evil of adultery. But by confining our discussion of sexual ethics to such areas, we allow ourselves to overlook ethical questions that are actually more pressing in our own romantic lives. Frederica Mathewes-Green observes:

> A narrow-focus fight against homosexuality, couched in Bible proof-texts, misses the point. We need to gain a more comprehensive understanding of the beauty of chastity, and we can begin by admitting that it is something we only dimly understand.[5]

She recommends that we begin a search for understanding by listening to the voices of Christians who have gone before us, people who celebrated "joy and serenity, and the invigorating challenge of self-control," who were "looking . . . toward some-

---

5. Frederica Mathewes-Green, *Gender: Men, Women, Sex, and Feminism*, vol. 1, *Selected Writings* (Ben Lomond, CA: Conciliar Press, 2002), 166.

thing they greatly desired: chastity, a shining object of joy."[6] Instead of assuming that our predecessors in faith were ignorant and repressed when it came to sexual matters, we should learn from the wisdom of the great cloud of witnesses that has preceded us.

Let me be clear. I am an unabashed proponent of sexual abstinence outside marriage. I believe that homosexual behavior is outside God's will. I recognize the seriousness of adultery. However, I am also aware—both from my own life and from my experience counseling others—that these issues are not the most pressing for many Christians and that an unbalanced emphasis on such issues may lead to an unhealthy sense of complacency in those who are not tempted in such ways. If you are a person whose romantic experiences have been largely unrequited, abstinence is not your cutting-edge ethical issue. The church's traditional rhetoric about abstinence easily leads people who are not in romantic relationships to conclude that they are immune to ethical concerns in the area of sexual behavior. In fact, however, such people may have some serious ethical questions with which to wrestle. For instance:

- Is it sinful to enjoy an imaginary romantic life? What if I do not imagine having sex; I just imagine being in a great dating relationship. Is there anything wrong with that?
- Is it worse to fantasize about a real person I actually know than it is to fantasize about a made-up person?
- Is there one person God has destined for me? If so, do I have a responsibility to go out and find that person? Or should I assume that God will bring that person to me without my having to do anything about it?
- If I give up on getting married, does that mean I do not have enough faith?
- What are the appropriate reasons for turning down romantic advances from someone? Is it appropriate to reject a person because I am afraid? Because I do not feel I have time for a serious relationship? Because that person does not measure up to a list of qualifications I have developed?

6. Ibid., 165.

Because I am not attracted to that person's appearance? Do I even need a reason?

- How do I say no to someone without being hurtful and unkind?
- If I am in love with or at least attracted to someone, should I tell that person how I feel, even though I am sure I will be rejected?
- If I have been rejected, am I obligated to get over my attraction to the person who rejected me? Is it neurotic to keep loving someone who has turned me down, or is that a way of expressing Christian faithfulness?
- How should I understand the New Testament's apparent preference for singleness?
- To what extent do I have control over when and with whom I fall in love? Is there any way to train myself to be attracted to virtue and godliness rather than to physical beauty or financial success?
- Does God ever cause me to fall in love with someone? If yes, would that make romantic love normative in any way?
- If someone does not love me back, does it follow that God did not cause my love for that person?

None of these questions is addressed by normal discussions of sexual ethics, although some of them may be addressed by those in the church who teach and write about singleness. Even such people, however, rarely address the most private of these questions, those that deal not with external activity but with internal thoughts, feelings, and preoccupations, that is, with the inner life of the imagination and the memory. Such questions are easily ignored by the church. If a woman in the church has a baby out of wedlock, everyone knows about it. If she is desperately and hopelessly pining for the man in the pew in front of her, it is likely that no one will know.

But God cares about our private, inner life at least as much as he cares about our external, public life. He cares not only about what we do but also about who we are. Private, inner life—the life that no one but God can see—is where character is most clear. To develop character so that we become godly people—virtuous people, honorable people—we need to consider not just our public behavior but also our inner life, asking God to search our inmost heart and bring our whole self under his control.

> Search me, O God, and know my heart;
> test me and know my thoughts.
> See if there is any wicked way in me,
> and lead me in the way everlasting.
>
> Psalm 139:23–24

Part 1

Theology of Romance

I know most of you have been where I am tonight: the crash site
of unrequited love. You've asked yourself, how did I get here? . . .
What are these elusive and ephemeral things that ignite passion
in the human heart?

Chris Stevens, "Only You," episode 3.02,
Northern Exposure

Do not stir up or awaken love until it is ready!

Song of Solomon 8:4

1

God's Nature

My God, thou art all love.
Not one poore minute 'scapes thy breast,
But brings a favour from above;
And in this love, more than in bed, I rest.

George Herbert, "Evensong"

Whoever does not love does not know God, for God is love.

1 John 4:8

One of the striking things about the interviews I conducted is how often the Christian people interviewed admitted to questioning God's love and goodness during times of heartbreak. One particularly vivid example is the account of a twenty-one-year-old man who wrote:

The most awful experience I've had emotionally in the last four years or so was breaking up with my girlfriend. Last spring, after watching our friendship grow and blossom, I could tell she wanted to "take the relationship to the next level," and I conceded. Once I said that I was committed to "raising the relationship to the next level," we worked at keeping our friendship strong and honest and fun. Over the summer, I began to realize that I liked her, but I wasn't close to loving her. At the same time, she realized that she truly loved me. For her, our relationship was a source of joy. She told many people about "us." Unfortunately, I felt weighed down with the burden to

23

meet a certain standard of feeling. I tried to create love, tried to force it. I prayed for God to let me love her deeply, but nothing more happened. I just loved her with *philos*, a sisterly love, not with an intimate *eros*-type love.

The night I told her I didn't love her, I just dropped the bomb while we were driving to her house. She kept saying, "I don't understand." Then she started crying hard and pulled off to the side of the road. I tried to be tactful, but that means nothing when you're being real and honest. She said, "Do you know what this means? It means that I'm just like every other girl to you! It means you can't feel what I'm feeling." . . . I kept saying to myself, "What is wrong with me? Why can't I love?" . . . I was praying angrily at God and cursing myself for the pain I'd caused. The last thing I ever wanted to do was hurt her. Plus, she was handling it all so maturely. She cried and said, "I feel bad for you. I just wish that you could feel what I do. I wish you could feel it because it's so good, and yet, it's not right." We drove back pretty silently, and I wanted to throw up. I cried myself to sleep. It was the worst to hurt a sister in Christ and to feel that I'd just dumped the woman in Proverbs. I couldn't believe I couldn't love her, but in the end I learned that love can't be forced.

It is not surprising that this young man felt guilty and was angry with himself, but why was he angry with God?

The same pattern can be observed among those who are rejected: they are often upset not only with their rejector but also with God. Questioning the goodness of the person who has rejected you seems reasonable enough (if a bit narcissistic), but Christians bring God into this experience, assuming that God is somehow behind it. Since the experience is often intensely painful, this assumption of God's agency can be a problem. Yet if this is indeed an experience of love, God must be relevant to it. God must even be the source of it. Therefore, before we think theologically about romantic love, we need to think about the source of all love, God himself.

God Is Love

The first epistle of John includes this startling assertion: "God is love" (4:8, 16). Not God is *loving*, but God *is* love. The context makes clear that John means there is nothing in God or about God at odds with love, since love is the test by which we may figure out whether we are "in God." Further, John explicitly contrasts love with punishment, saying that love leaves no room for punishment and therefore no room for fear. This, then, is our first lesson about Christian love: it is incompatible with vindictiveness or revenge, and it is incompatible with being afraid. Love that is rooted in God has compassion and courage as its fruit.

In our everyday faith, most of us intuitively see the teaching that God is love as one of the most basic, trustworthy, clear, uncontroversial teachings of Scripture. This is obvious from the fact that we teach God's love to children before we teach them anything else. The three year olds in nursery sing, "Jesus loves me, this I know, for the Bible tells me so" and "Jesus loves the little children, all the children of the world." We do not teach children to sing, "God is so just." We teach them to sing, "God is so good; he loves me so." God's love and goodness are clear to us.

In 1 John we also read, "God is light and in him there is no darkness at all" (1:5). The claims that God is light and that God is love are in some ways obviously similar, but at the same time they are different sorts of statements. When we say that God is light, we are being metaphorical. We do not mean that God is a giant lightbulb or a direct source of literal illumination. John uses the metaphor of light to express that God is a source of truthful, reliable knowledge about ourselves, the world, and himself. John also uses the metaphor (in much the same way that Jesus uses it in the Gospel of John [3:19–21]) to talk about holy living. However, the claim that God is love is not a metaphor in this same way. Love is not an image for something else. Love really is the heart of God's nature.

How are we to understand this? Love may be understood as either a feeling or an action, and it is difficult to see how God can be either. But this is one of the ways in which God is different from us. We think about doing this or that but get around to doing only a small fraction of the many things we could do in a lifetime. God is not like that. God is completely actual, that is, completely in act. Everything God *could* be, he is. He cannot improve or grow because he is already infinitely love. His care for us and all his creation does not wax and wane. Rather, his orientation toward us is always love. He is not deciding whether to perform certain loving acts. Rather, he is love in action. His love is fully in play, fully engaged. Even in heaven, our love will not be like God's love, for we are too small to hold the depth and width and breadth and height of such love. If we are united with Christ, however, we may become channels of God's active love, even though that love is bigger than we are. At its best, a Christian form of romantic love is such a channel. The one who loves is participating in the divine nature (2 Pet. 1:4), and the one who is loved is blessed.

Another puzzling problem with thinking of God as love is that love requires an object. To love, you have to love *something*. As the Blues Brothers sing, "Everybody needs somebody to love," and it is true: for a person to be loving, there has to be somebody toward whom the love is directed. Linus, from the comic strip *Peanuts,* says, "I love mankind; it's people I can't stand." We find that funny because it makes no sense. When we love, we give of ourselves to someone else. We cannot give of ourselves in general. Love must always be particular.

Some people have therefore concluded that we human beings are important and even necessary to God, since without us he would have no one to love. How could he be love if we were not around? But most Christians throughout history have firmly rejected the idea that God needs us in any way. Because God is a Trinity—one being, three persons—God can be love without needing anyone else. The Father loves the Son, the Son loves the Father, the Son and the Father join together to love the Spirit, who loves them both in return. The three persons of the Trinity are joined in a dynamic community of self-giving love that requires no one else. God does not need us to be love.

One consequence of God's triune nature is that the act of creation is a free gift of grace to us. God does not need us but created us anyway out of the overflow of love from within the Trinity. God did not start showing us grace with the coming of Jesus or with his death on the cross. Our very existence is a gift of grace. Indeed, we can go further and say that everything we receive from God is grace, because everything that comes from God is a loving gift. Human love that is rooted in God's nature is similarly openhanded, though as humans we are needy in ways that God is not, needing to be loved as well as to love.

Since God is love, the most central, basic, fundamental truth we know about God's nature is that he is always in the act of loving. This is true within God's own nature, in the love between the Father, Son, and Holy Spirit, but it is also true in God's dealings with us. In his book *The Spirit of Love,* the theologian William Law says that God "can give nothing but Blessing, Goodness, and Happiness from himself because he has in himself nothing else to give. It is much more possible for the Sun to give forth Darkness than for God to do, or be, or give forth anything but Blessing and Goodness."[1] Since God is love, everything God does is loving.

I was visiting some friends whose son is eighteen months old. He was drinking juice out of a sippy cup when he dropped the cup, and it rolled across the floor into some dirt. Before he could retrieve it, his mother grabbed it and took it over to the sink to clean it off. He howled. He was sure his mother had taken away his juice. Of course, she had done no such thing. He would have his juice back in a moment, but not until the cup had been cleaned. She was being a loving mother, but her son did not see her actions as loving.

This is a good picture of how we often relate to God. If we believe that God is love, we need to trust that even at those times when we want to cry with rage and frustration because something precious to us seems to have been taken away, God is treating us with love. Even at those times when we feel as though God is punishing us or depriving us of something or treating us unfairly in some way, we must have faith in God's constant love for us, just as children learn to trust their parents.

We must confess that everything God gives us is good. If God is the cause behind our breakups, if God is the reason we are single, then the breakups are good, and singleness is good. If God caused our love for someone who does not love us, then that love is good. This confidence must be the context of all discussion about this subject. Of course, it is not obvious that God is always causally involved in our romantic life in this

1. William Law, *The Spirit of Love* (Grand Rapids: Christian Classics Ethereal Library, 2000), http://www.ccel.org/l/law/love (accessed January 7, 2003).

way. If, however, we credit God with such involvement (and we began this chapter by noting that Christians often do), then we must believe that the outcome is good.

If it appears for a time that God does not love us, we need to ask whether we are somehow blocking his love. Think of God's love as being like the rays of the sun. The sun is constantly sending light and heat to the earth. When we do not have light and heat, it is because something has changed here on earth, not because something has changed in the sun. Maybe the earth is turned so that we are away from the sun, as it is at night. Maybe there are clouds blocking the sun, as is true for most of the winter in Michigan, where I live. Maybe we are hiding from the sun in the shade of a tree or umbrella. Maybe we have closed our eyes. In the same way, our circumstances or decisions may keep us from experiencing God's love fully, even though it is always constantly and unchangingly pouring down on us. Our sin keeps us from experiencing God's love. Fear, cynicism, despair, hopelessness, anger, jealousy, hatred all serve as barriers separating us from God's love. In his book *The Last Battle*, C. S. Lewis tells about some dwarfs who are brought into Aslan's country but are incapable of seeing its beauty. Aslan provides them with a feast, but they taste none of its goodness, convinced that they have been given straw and dirty water. They are prisoners of their own cynicism, their own fear, their own distrust, and their own sin. They are loved, but they are incapable of receiving that love.[2]

Because God is love, you can *know* that he loves you. The children's songs are right. "Jesus loves me, this I know." You need not doubt that you are loved completely by the very one who most deserves your love. No matter what painful romantic rejection you may experience, you can be confident that God will never reject your love for him. God will always love you, unchangingly and constantly, even though he knows you better than anyone else does. You do not need to hide your problems from him to keep him loving you. You do not need to earn his love in any way. You do not need to make yourself into a different kind of person. He loves you. That is a more secure truth than any other. It is more certain than the law of gravity. It is more

2. C. S. Lewis, *The Last Battle* (New York: Macmillan, 1970), 143–48.

certain than the fact that the sun will rise tomorrow. There will be a day when the sun will no longer rise and set, but even then God will love you.

Sometimes it is difficult to believe in God's love when we are being denied what we want most. One woman spoke of how her parents had always discouraged her from thinking about marriage because they wanted her to focus on her career. Therefore, she had always been somewhat ashamed of her desire to get married. She realizes now that she had understood God as siding with her parents in this, impatient with her desire to be married and treating that desire as a sign of her weakness.

> I think in the past I thought God was kind of the enemy of this desire, that he was against me in this, kind of like my parents were, like this is wrong for you to want this. . . . It was like discipleship meant one thing and wanting a relationship meant something else. In the last few years, I started seeing God less as my enemy and more as walking alongside me. . . . I don't think marriage is anti-God, you know? And if it's such a longing in my life, I don't think he'd be just fighting against me on that my whole life. . . . I've struggled a lot with my being unlovable to God, which tied in with that whole thing that God doesn't want this for me because I want it. It's seeing him as kind of a judging Father, the judging parent who is trying to keep me from things that I might actually enjoy or like in my life.

Because God is love, you can be sure that he is not denying you something because he is impatient or because he is your enemy. God is not capricious or sadistic. God wants you to flourish and be happy, to live in eternal joy. The joy that you can imagine and desire is pale beside the fullness of joy that God has in store for you, and everything that God sends you is designed to bring you to that goal. Everything God sends you is for your good.

God also loves the person who has rejected you more than you ever could, and God also loves the person you have rejected. This same woman observes:

> I think as I've accepted God's grace more, I start seeing how much everybody needs grace. And that includes the men that I've been interested in. So when I think back to this guy I most

recently dated, I know he loves God too. . . . So even when I can get really angry at him and frustrated and think, this was your fault, he thinks the same thing about me. We're two sinful human beings. We're trying to make a relationship work, and God loves both of us.

We cannot out love God. If God sends punishment, it is punishment motivated by love. If there is injustice and unfairness, it will always be a gracious injustice and a loving unfairness, giving us more than we deserve, not less. For some people, the experience of God's love will not be pleasant. The Orthodox Church says that the fire of hell and the fire of God's glory are one and the same fire. Here is what Orthodox theologian Thomas Hopko says:

> For those who love the Lord, His Presence will be infinite joy, paradise and eternal life. For those who hate the Lord, the same Presence will be infinite torture, hell and eternal death. . . . The "fire" that will consume sinners at the coming of the Kingdom of God is the same "fire" that will shine with splendor in the saints. It is the "fire" of God's love; the "fire" of God Himself who is Love. "For our God is a consuming fire" (Hebrews 12:29) who "dwells in unapproachable light" (1 Timothy 6:16). For those who love God and who love all creation in Him, the "consuming fire" of God will be radiant bliss and unspeakable delight. For those who do not love God, and who do not love at all, this same "consuming fire" will be the cause of their "weeping" and their "gnashing of teeth."[3]

God does not change; we do. Our inability to love and our rebellion against his will may make his love a torment to us, much in the same way that a parent's steadfast love may become a torment to a rebellious child. A graphic illustration of the pain that love can cause is found in J. K. Rowling's book *Harry Potter and the Sorcerer's Stone*. Harry is told that the sacrificial love of his mother has marked him, entering his very skin, and that this love now protects him from the powers of evil, since evil

3. Thomas Hopko, "Heaven and Hell," in *The Orthodox Faith* (Brooklyn, OH: Orthodox Christian Publications Center, 1981), http://www.oca.org/pages/orth_chri/Orthodox-Faith/Spirituality/Heaven-and-Hell.html (accessed January 7, 2003).

cannot stand to be touched by love. For a person "full of hatred, greed, and ambition . . . [it] was agony to touch a person marked by something so good."[4] Since God is love, there are some who cannot bear his touch.

Because God is love, his love for us is more important than anyone else's. In fact, his love is both the source and the goal of all other loves. The only reason the love of parents, the love of a spouse, the love of children, and the love of friends are precious is because they in some way resemble God's love. All human love derives from God and is meant to direct us back to God. This means, among other things, that romantic love can never ultimately be an end in itself. If you are living in a growing awareness of God's love and with a growing love for God, then you are oriented toward your proper end and your life is proceeding as it should, even if you are not married or in a romantic relationship. If you are deeply in love with someone who is also in love with you, but you have not placed that love in the context of God's love, then you are not oriented toward your proper end and your life is deeply disordered, no matter how happy you may appear or feel. The ultimate meaning of life derives from God's love for us, and that love is sufficient to make life meaningful.

Because God is love, we are able to love one another in ways we could not without help from the Holy Spirit. As a pastor, I long ago decided that I would perform weddings only for people who were able honestly to make this statement to each other: "However much our love for one another deepens, I promise to love God even more than I love you. I ask you to love God even more than you love me, that our growing love for him will draw us closer to one another." Many couples are unwilling to make such a promise. One man told me candidly that he hoped his future wife would always love him more than anyone, even more than she loved God. But this is a disordered way of thinking about love, and it is ultimately counterproductive, since God is the source of all love. A person who loves God most and who is constantly open to receiving God's love will be able to love his or her spouse far more deeply and faithfully than someone who is not in a loving relationship with God. It is only in the power of

4. J. K. Rowling, *Harry Potter and the Sorcerer's Stone* (New York: Scholastic Press, 1998), 299.

God's love that we can dare to make promises to love each other. One young woman understood this particularly well, saying, "I don't want to find someone to marry because I have a hole. I want to have so much love from God that I can just overflow it onto this other person."

It is mysterious to me how anyone could ever dare to be married, to promise to love someone else in sickness and in health until death parts them, except in reliance on the grace and love of God. How can people dare to make such promises based only on their own power? How can people trust such promises when they are made without a reliance on God's grace? The climbing divorce rate in our culture illustrates how ill equipped we are to keep such promises without assistance.

We are invited into the relationship of love enjoyed within the Trinity when the Holy Spirit unites us to the ascended Christ, who has brought our human nature into the throne room of God. Through our participation in the love uniting the three persons of the Trinity, we are able to love others, for the love of God fills us and spills over into our relationships. Even when we reject someone else's romantic advances, there is another sort of love we are able to show that person in God. Even when we are deeply hurt, we are able to resist the bitterness and anger that lead to hatred, maintaining some love for the person who hurt us.

God's Role in Our Experiences of Romance

But does all of this really apply to the experience of romantic love? Surely, the love that God empowers us to offer one another is something higher and nobler than mere romance? Or perhaps in your mind romantic love is actually the higher and nobler love, far more exalted than the dutiful, passionless sort of love you imagine has its origin in God. If we take seriously the fact that God is love and that all love has its source in him, we need to relate all forms of love—whether the love between friends, the love of parents for children and children for parents, the love of country and of neighbor, and even romantic love—to God and to see all forms of love as God's good gifts. If romantic love really is love, then its origin is God. If that is unimaginable to us, then perhaps we are not really thinking of love at all but of some other sort of desire or longing.

Our culture generally elevates the romantic experience of falling in love above religious commitment, teaching us that this emotional experience is both beyond our control and beyond all reproach. Love is a self-justifying experience, not accountable to moral judgment. As Sheryl Crow sings, "If it makes you happy, it can't be that bad."[5] Love is seen as a morally basic or foundational experience, one from which other decisions may follow. As the saying goes, "All's fair in love and war." Those who put their religious commitments above their romantic commitments—by refusing to date people of different religious backgrounds, for instance—are generally dismissed as bigoted or narrow-minded.

It would seem on the face of it that Christians should reject this understanding of romantic experience as morally foundational. For Christians, God's will is morally basic, and our experiences need to conform to that will. However, some Christians still experience romantic attraction as normative because they believe that God causes those feelings. In a recent survey of students at the Christian college where I teach, more than 80 percent said that feelings of romantic love for another person come from God at least some of the time.[6]

When we fall in love, we often do not feel as though we made a choice or did anything. Rather, we feel as though something was done *to* us, as if something happened beyond our control. We were shown something we had not seen before. Sometimes love may be experienced as a revelation even more than as an emotional state. If that experience is then interpreted as being from God, it takes on a high level of moral authority. In this way, Christians and non-Christians often unite in seeing romantic love as self-justifying. Because of this, many Christians expect God to give them explicit guidance about their romantic lives.

---

5. Sheryl Crow, "If It Makes You Happy," *Sheryl Crow* (Santa Monica, CA: A&M Records, 1996).

6. The survey was administered in the spring of 2001 by students in a social research class at Calvin College. Although I consulted with the students about the survey, it was separate from my own research.

This belief that there is a divine plan for our romantic life, a partner for whom we are destined, is not unique to Christians. Plato's *Symposium*, written four hundred years before the birth of Christ, includes several speeches about the nature of love. One of the speakers, Aristophanes, is a comedian and a poet. He gives an account of the creation of human beings, saying that humans were originally created two-sided, with each human having two faces, four arms, and four legs, but that Zeus divided these beings down the middle. Romantic attraction is thus attributed to the desire of human beings to find their other halves and to be made into whole persons. Aristophanes asserts that human beings do not just desire to have sex with someone. Rather, people desire a deep intimacy with one particular person.

> And so, when a person meets the half that is his very own . . . the two are struck from their senses by love, by a sense of belonging to one another, and by desire, and they don't want to be separated from one another, not even for a moment.
>
> These are the people who finish out their lives together and still cannot say what it is they want from one another. No one would think it is the intimacy of sex—that mere sex is the reason each lover takes so great and deep a joy in being with the other. It's obvious that the soul of every lover longs for something else . . . to come together and melt together with the one he loves, so that one person emerged from two. . . . "Love" is the name for our pursuit of wholeness, for our desire to be complete.[7]

Romantic love is thus essentially selfish according to Aristophanes, because it is a search for the completion of the self. This view of romance as the search for the one soulmate for whom a person is destined is still articulated and embraced within our culture. When Jerry MaGuire says to the woman he loves, "You complete me," most viewers react affirmatively, finding this sentiment romantic and appropriate.[8]

However, Aristophanes's speech is not the conclusion of Plato's *Symposium*. Socrates presents a different understanding. He

7. Plato, *Symposium*, trans. Alexander Nehamas and Paul Woodruff (Indianapolis: Hackett Publishing, 1989), 28–29, sec. 192–93.
8. *Jerry MaGuire* (Columbia/Tristar, 1996).

suggests that romantic attraction is one rung on a ladder of loves. Our first experiences of love, the first rung of the ladder, are based on sense perceptions: certain people appeal to us as attractive. But then we move to a higher level of love, when we experience attraction to another person's character, nature, or soul. Eventually, that love also points beyond itself, teaching us to love the goodness and beauty of the world and to love the wisdom that understands the world as good and beautiful. Finally, we learn to love the source of all goodness and beauty, God himself. Romantic love is not an end in itself for Socrates, nor is it about the gratification of desire. Rather, in encountering beauty itself and goodness itself, human beings come to understand both virtue and truth, become capable of living virtuously, and possibly also become immortal.[9]

Both these perspectives can also be found in the Christian tradition. There are those who, like Aristophanes, see romantic love as a completion of the self, the joining with the particular partner God has designed for each person to bring wholeness to otherwise incomplete lives. We will call this the soulmate perspective, and it was dominant among those I interviewed. I suspect that it is the dominant perspective among Western Christians today. There are also those who, like Socrates, see romantic love as one of many possible pointers toward an encounter with God, who is himself love and beauty, goodness and truth. This perspective was dominant among Christians for much of history because historically most Christians believed that every good gift received in this life is from God, meant to direct attention back to God (James 1:17). The person who did the most to apply this Christian idea to romantic love is the poet Dante, so we will call this the Dantean perspective. As should be clear from the previous section, my sympathies lie with Dante rather than with Jerry MaGuire.

One woman whom I will call Karen expressed the Dantean perspective especially well. For nearly two years, she has been in love with a man who does not love her back. When asked

9. Socrates is quoting Diotima throughout, so sometimes this section of *Symposium* is known as the speech of Diotima rather than the speech of Socrates. Plato, *Symposium*, 57–60, sec. 210–12.

how her faith interacts with this experience of romance, she replied:

> I think a lot of it is figuring out that my desires are really desires for God. I think when you desire someone enough that they could become an idol to you it makes you realize how much you need God and how much you really desire God. I mean, if I desire *him* this much, well, I need to desire God infinitely more than that. I have a scale now to measure my desire. And I *see* how romantic love fits into loving God. I never saw that before because romantic love was always just stupid to me; it just makes people do dumb things, and it makes people act stupid. But now I see it more as just this passionate desire for someone to love me back, and maybe you don't need them to love you back, but you passionately desire it.

The very strength of this woman's love—a love that is not returned—helps her to understand more clearly what her love for God should be like. It also helps her to come to terms with the incompleteness of life as we experience it. Deep and passionate longing for something more ought to characterize the life of every Christian. Karen is allowing her unfulfilled romantic desires to enhance this quality of restlessness in her life.

Christians who take the Dantean perspective, who do not believe there is only one person designed by God for them, may still believe that God sometimes causes them to fall in love. Generations of Christians have interpreted their romantic experiences in this way, understanding God as the cause of the experience. This is especially true when people feel as though they did not choose to fall in love; rather, it is something that happened to them. It is also especially true when the romantic experience proves to be spiritually valuable, enhancing one's relationship with God, shaking one out of complacency, and arousing wonder and sacred restlessness.

But if God caused us to recognize the attractiveness and wonder of this other person, shouldn't we expect him also to reveal our attractiveness and wonder to that person? Why would God cause only one person to fall in love? When we experience our own love as a revelation given to us by God, it seems reasonable to expect that God will eventually make the other person love us back. After all, what kind of matchmaking friend would try to get you interested in and excited about someone who is unavailable? If God is intervening in our lives to make us fall in love, why wouldn't he make sure we are loved back? Karen says, "I do blame God somewhat sometimes, because I don't understand why I would have this desire, or even worse, why I have a love that I can't even express to the guy I'm in love with because he's not even around."

Another woman tells of her deep attraction for a good friend, a man who frequently dated other girls but who seemed to keep her on a friendship level. When it appeared that he was starting to be interested in her in a new way, she began to ask God to make a romance happen.

> We emailed, talked on the telephone, but still no conversation about our friendship or moving into a relationship. We were not physically involved, not holding hands or kissing or anything like that. But in my heart I just wanted something to work out. I would pray, and I asked God to prepare both of our hearts.

But the man she was interested in did not return her feelings, despite her prayers. Did she have insufficient faith? Had she misread her own heart? Should rejection lead her to conclude that God did not really send her this experience of love after all?

A young man tells of his deep love for a woman who was one of his closest friends. As they grew closer, he became convinced that they would become romantically involved. More than that, he says, "Frankly I thought we would get married some day." When he finally shared his feelings, she told him that she was still in love with someone else.

> I was crushed, I didn't understand, I felt that God had lied to me. I kept struggling though and eventually, through some miracle, came to understand that sometimes we don't know God's will as much as we think.

Why would her rejection have led him to believe that *God* had lied to him? Somehow, his experience of loving her had felt like a message from God. It had felt like a promise, a revelation of God's will for his life.

Charles Williams, a Christian author who is best known for his imaginative fiction, sees a clear connection between romantic experience and knowledge of God. He presents romantic love as an experience by which we have a vision of the beauty of God. This vision is mediated to us through imagination, which is a tool to see the hidden glory of the beloved, a glory that reflects the presence of God. Romantic love, assisted by imagination, is an experience of revelation, a direct apprehension of God's glory.

Williams suggests that everyone could potentially show us this vision of God. After all, each human being is made in God's image. But it is a divine mercy that each one does not. In our fallen state, we are easily confused and led astray by this vision of glory. We would never be able to deal with seeing every person in this way. "If the gazing fixedly on one divine aspect is apt to intoxicate the soul and send it reelingly astray, what chaos would follow if all men and women were so beheld, what sin, what despair! . . . While we are what we are, the Divine Mercy clouds its creation."[10] So much glory would crush us.

If Williams is right about this connection between romantic love and knowing God, then Christians should indeed consider the possibility that the experience of falling in love contains a message from God to which we should listen. Williams's understanding does not suggest a guarantee that our love will be returned, nor does he think that the experience of revelatory romantic love necessarily includes permission to act on one's feelings. He thinks of romance as a mode of insight into the glory of God's world.

But even if he is right about some romantic experiences, surely *all* romantic experiences are not God initiated. The influence of sin is pervasive, and it makes all natural responses to the world and to one another suspect. Because of sin, we cannot trust our romantic inclinations to be reliable guides to God's will, even if that was God's original design for romantic experience. Romantic inclinations are reliable only to the extent that we have been changed by the sanctifying power of the Holy Spirit and have submitted to the will of Jesus Christ for our life.

10. Charles Williams, *The Figure of Beatrice: A Study in Dante* (Cambridge: D. S. Brewer, 1943), 48.

How can we know whether a particular experience of romance has been sent to us by God? We will consider this more deeply in the next chapter, when we look at God's creational design for romantic attraction, but for now consider this. One way to know whether God has sent the experience of falling in love is by considering the fruits of that love. If you are made aware of the wonder and glory of another person as one who is an image bearer of God, then the experience of romance has borne good fruit. If you are thrown back on God's love and care to sustain you through the experience of rejection, then the experience of romance has borne good fruit. But if you are led farther away from God or into disobedience to his will, then justifying your actions by claiming that God made you fall in love verges on blasphemy.

Furthermore, if we are honest, we need to admit that we played a role in most of our romantic experiences. We fall in love when we are ready for romance, when we leave ourselves open to the feelings. Even though we may convince ourselves that it just happened to us, at least part of the experience was really chosen. Before you see romantic inclinations as a message from God, you need to ask, Have I gone looking for this? Have I manufactured a romance out of something that is actually quite a bit less? Is this romance occurring in my imagination rather than in a true relationship with another person?

Whether or not romantic feelings are sent to us by God, it is surely appropriate for us to pray to God about our romantic frustrations, hurts, and decisions, just as we pray to God about all the details of our life. We may seek God's guidance without believing that God has only one possible path in mind for us. Many of the people I interviewed spoke of receiving comfort in the midst of heartbreak as a result of their prayers. Prayer may help us to find peace in the midst of painful situations and may keep us from giving in to bitterness and anger.

A rather different experience with prayer is seen in the following story told by a twenty-year-old man. He tells of meeting a young woman whom he found attractive in part because of her high moral standards, standards he was not living up to at all. It is fairly common for people to be drawn to a kind of virtue alien to their own experience, particularly if, as was the case with this young woman, the person living out a more virtuous life refrains from being judgmental.

> At first she said that she didn't want anything to happen between the two of us, but then a couple weeks later we found ourselves spending a lot of time together. We both decided to give it a shot. We went to dinner together several times and just had fun together. But then everything got strange when we prayed together. We didn't pray that we could stay together, but rather that we would be able to do whatever would bring us closer to God on an individual level. That got both of us thinking, but it made her realize that she didn't want to take a romantic relationship anywhere with me.

In the rest of his account, he tries to explain why he is now better off, but the explanation rings a bit hollow. He thinks this woman has retreated into a safer relationship, that she is "sheltering herself," whereas he sees himself "heading in a direction that I love." What seems more likely is that her prayer was effective, that God showed her the dangers of dating a man in hopes of improving him. She wisely broke off this relationship before it had harmed her and returned to her high school boyfriend, a young man who shares her values. When we ask for God's will to be done in our life, we need to be willing to accept the results, even if they do not fit our dreams.

In addition to praying for guidance, Christians should pray for the well-being of all those they love, whether friends, family members, or the objects of romantic love, as well as those they find difficult and exasperating, whether coworkers, family members, or those pursuing them romantically. We are much more likely to behave in a virtuous manner toward someone for whom we have been praying because we have been allowing God to shape our understanding of that person. If we pray regularly for the person we love, we are much less likely to use that person as the object of our own lustful fantasies. We are less likely to attempt to manipulate that person by playing on his or her pity for us. We are less likely to become bitter and resentful if we are rejected. God does not tell us to pray because he needs to be informed of our needs but rather because in prayer we submit our will to God's will. Sincere prayer changes us by giving us "the mind of Christ" (1 Cor. 2:16) and by helping us to see others from that point of view (2 Cor. 5:16).

We also need to understand what purpose the experience of romantic love has in God's plan for us, a purpose we may discover by looking at both our created design and our destiny in the new creation. This is the focus of the next two chapters.

2

God's Plan for Creation

The voice that breathed o'er Eden,
That earliest wedding day,
The primal marriage blessing,
It hath not passed away. . . .

Be present, awful Father,
To give away this bride,
As Eve thou gav'st to Adam
Out of his own pierced side.

H. J. Gauntlett, "The Voice That
Breathed o'er Eden"[1]

Therefore a man leaves his father and his mother and clings to
his wife, and they become one flesh.

Genesis 2:24

In the Bible, we read the story of the creation of human beings. First, God creates Adam, the sinless man who has God's
own spirit breathed into him. Yet God describes Adam as
"alone" in a way that is "not good" (Gen. 2:18). Perfect and
sinless communion with God is not enough for him. "There
was not found a helper as his partner," says the book of Genesis
(2:20). The word *helper* is generally a divine word in Genesis,

---

1. H. J. Gauntlett, "The Voice That Breathed o'er Eden," *The English Hymnal*
(Oxford: Oxford University Press, 1933), #348, stanzas 1 and 4.

just as it is in most of the Hebrew Bible. It is the Lord God who is our help. Adam does have a helper in God, who made him and continues to nurture and care for him, but God is not Adam's partner. God is Adam's Creator, the one to whom he owes everything and who owes him nothing. There is no interdependence or mutual need in their relationship. Even though Adam is made in God's image with God's own breath in him (Gen. 1:26–27), even though there is an unbreakable ontological connection between Adam and his Creator, there is also an unbridgeable ontological gap—unbridgeable, at least, from Adam's side.

God is wholly other, utterly unlike us. We are finite; he is infinite. We are temporal; he is eternal. We are changeable; he is immutable. We are needy; he is giving. We are vulnerable; he is invulnerable. These differences are not a result of sin. This is what it means to be a creature in relationship with an all-powerful Creator. Therefore, even though God is Adam's helper, God is also out of reach for Adam. He needs that divine helping presence in his own form in order for it to be comprehensible. He needs a helper who is finite, temporal, changeable, needy, and vulnerable—just as he is. When God creates Eve and presents her to Adam, he greets her with this song: "This at last is bone of my bones and flesh of my flesh" (Gen. 2:23). Here is a helper who is also a partner (Gen. 2:18), divine help and presence in a fitting form that corresponds to Adam's own nature—what the King James Version calls a "meet" form, in describing Eve as a "helpmeet."

This is the first sign in the Bible that the incarnation of God in human form is necessary for us. We need to encounter God's essence in a comprehensible form in order to understand God and have a genuine relationship with him. It is the incarnation of God in Christ that finally bridges the gap in a definitive way, for in Christ, God himself became bone of our bones and flesh of our flesh. When we participate in Christ through the work of the Holy Spirit, we regain the ability to be fitting helpers for one another, an ability that was warped and distorted when Eve spoke the serpent's lies rather than God's truth to Adam.

When a husband and a wife relate to each other as fitting helpers, reflecting God's will and channeling God's grace, their marriage takes its proper place in the order of creation. Think of a set of concentric circles in which marriage is the smallest, central circle. The next circle is the broader community of God's people—Israel in the Old Testament, the church in the New Testament. This community is supposed to reflect the same qualities as marriage in that the members become one with one another, bear one another's burdens, and speak God's truth to one another so that their differences (whether the differences of male and female, of tribal loyalties, or of Jew and Greek) are transcended. The third circle is the relationship between God and his people. In both Old and New Testaments, this relationship is explicitly likened to a marriage. In the Old Testament, God often calls Israel his bride (for instance, see Jer. 2:2), and in the New Testament, the church is the bride of Christ (Rev. 21:2). The fourth and final circle is the loving community of the Trinity, which grounds all other community in human experience. From the very beginning, marriage was meant as a training ground for participation in these higher and broader circles of community, through which we come into an ever more immediate relationship with God.

Marriage in the Creation Order

God's created design for us—a design restored in Christ—is that we will be helpers or partners for one another, especially in the relationship of marriage. This is the insight offered by Charles Williams's romantic theology: part of our human design includes the ability to glimpse ultimate reality and beauty—indeed, to glimpse God's very image—in the particular form of those we most love.

It seems clear that this incarnational relationship of marriage, within which husband and wife reflect God's presence and extend God's help to each other, is the context for romantic attraction within the creation order. The creation story gives us no reason to dismiss the experience of falling in love as part of our fallenness. Although the Bible does not use the language of romance for Adam and Eve, we are told that he sings at the sight of her, that he clings to her, and that this relationship of turning toward and holding on to one another is God's good design (Gen. 2:23–24). Max Stackhouse points out that Christians have seen

45

the Bible as legitimating "the ecstatic joy of sexuality—one that bonded the couple together in mutual pleasure and drew each out of self-control into a committed vulnerability to the other. This delight was itself a proper end of marriage, 'a foretaste of the joys of heaven' as it was said, often with reference to the Song of Solomon."[2] Stackhouse summarizes God's creational design as fidelity, fecundity, and family.

Furthermore, scientists are increasingly confident that the experience of romantic attraction, which we call "falling in love," is transcultural and universal. At one point in the history of social science, it was widely believed that this experience was a social construct invented in the Western world during the High Middle Ages, but in more recent years, anthropologists have exposed this idea as nonsense. Cultures may differ as to how much they value the experience of falling in love, if they value it at all, or how tied the experience of romance may be to marriage, but in every culture throughout history and throughout the world, people fall in love with one another. This is part of how God made us.[3]

God also made us for fidelity and commitment in our romantic relationships, intending these relationships to be covenantal, something that is also recognized across cultures, though there are differences as to how commitments are formalized and how binding they are. Stackhouse observes:

> Everyone knows something of these normative standards and qualities, for what is revealed in scripture and in Christ accords with how God formed all humans at their deepest levels. The religious themes thus are not something imposed on people or distinctive to one cultural-linguistic group but are revealing of how life is really constituted. That is why many believe that all

2. Max Stackhouse, *Covenant and Commitments* (Louisville: Westminster John Knox, 1997), 24.

3. Social scientists used to claim that romantic love was an invention of modern Western culture, but current anthropological studies have debunked this claim. Almost every culture that anthropologists have studied reveals the influence of romantic love. See R. F. Baumeister, S. R. Wotman, and A. M. Stillwell, "Unrequited Love: On Heartbreak, Anger, Guilt, Scriptlessness, and Humiliation," *Journal of Personality and Social Psychology* 64 (1993): 377–94. For a list of the publications put out by the Baumeister/Tice lab, go to http://www.psy .fsu.edu/~dewall/labpublications.htm.

morally honest people know that something is wrong with relationships that are driven only by instinct or emotion or that do not sustain fidelity or hope. That is why people feel violated by the infidelity of those they love, lament infertility, resent social policies that weaken families, and seek to legitimate alternative lifestyles by trying to show how much they approximate normative patterns.[4]

Just as the universality of religion points to the reality of God's existence, so the universality of concern about romantic commitment points to God's design. Just as the specifics of religious traditions are contradictory and therefore poor guides to God's actual nature, so the specifics of romantic practice are not reliable guides to how God designed us to behave.

God designed romantic attraction to strengthen and impel us toward the intimate communion of marriage. Social scientists who look at romantic attraction generally reach a similar conclusion. To produce the strong families that make for a strong social system, "it is necessary to motivate people because the roles of husband-father and wife-mother often involve more burden than gain to the individuals. The interests of society may be opposed to their own."[5] Being in love is most obviously an experience that facilitates commitment to a mate, entering into a marriage, and having children—all behaviors that contribute to the ongoing survival and flourishing of humanity. Whereas the deep, affectionate intimacy of long-married couples takes years to develop, the passionate experience of falling in love can occur more quickly and can bind a couple together during the early stages of their committed relationship, giving their knowledge time to grow. By the time the original sexual excitement drops to a simmer, the network of relational commitments is in place, and the marriage is strong enough to flourish without depending as deeply on sexual attraction. Romantic love is a good gift from God designed to support an even better gift: covenantal and committed marriages.

4. Stackhouse, *Covenant and Commitments*, 20.
5. Bernard I. Murstein, "A Taxonomy of Love," in *The Psychology of Love*, ed. Robert Sternberg and Michael L. Barnes (New Haven: Yale University Press, 1988), 17. Murstein is relying on the research of sociologist S. M. Greenfield.

Why we fall in love with some people and not others is a more complicated question for the social scientist, but here too there are reasonable answers. In her book *The Survival of the Prettiest*, Nancy Etcoff cites examples of studies suggesting that we tend to experience sexual attraction for (and therefore fall in love with) people whose immune systems are most different from our own, a phenomenon that then results in healthy babies. Many of the physical characteristics that draw us to one another are the characteristics that signal health and fertility. Social biologists often explain such attraction in terms of evolution and natural selection. Whether or not you believe that God used evolution as a tool in creation, you may still see evidence of God's good design in such patterns. Consider the experiment in which women were asked to smell the sweaty T-shirts of several men and to identify which T-shirts were repulsive and which were appealing. Women were attracted to the sweat of men whose immune systems were most different from their own. We are wonderfully made![6]

Clearly, such elements of our design are meant to contribute to the blessing of having children. God blesses Adam and Eve in the garden when he says, "Be fruitful and multiply, and fill the earth" (Gen. 1:28). Many people have read this as a command, suggesting an obligation to have as many children as possible and to fill the earth with as many people as possible. Some have also thought of the "filling" in terms of human culture, not only human babies. Ray Van Leeuwen points out, however, that the form of this verse is not a command. If a human being were expressing the wish of this verse, she would say to Adam and Eve, "May God make you fruitful and allow you to multiply and fill the earth." Since God himself is speaking, he does not invoke himself; he simply says, "May this be so."[7] God is not commanding Adam and Eve to have as many children as possible. He is promising to bless their union, making their marriage a source of blessing both for themselves and for the rest of the earth.

6. Nancy Etcoff, *The Survival of the Prettiest: The Science of Beauty* (New York: Doubleday, 1999), 240–41.

7. Raymond C. Van Leeuwen, "'Be Fruitful and Multiply': Is This a Command or a Blessing?" *Christianity Today*, November 12, 2001, 58.

In speaking about the creation order, we need to be clear that this is something other than our present experience of nature or what is natural. The effects of the fall have been far reaching, including the natural order. Although our biology may be a clue to God's design for us, it is not an infallible clue, for our biological and chemical nature is fallen, influenced by sin, just as our spiritual nature is fallen. We must be cautious about drawing conclusions about God's will from the natural order of sexual experience. Stackhouse explains:

> What we examine when we study what is "natural" is what is distorted, incomplete, or contingent, even if it bears traces of God's grace in its capacity to be reformed toward order, purpose, and reliable relationship. . . . Hence to argue that some moral aspect of life is "natural" on the grounds of its frequency or "innateness" or because people feel it is intrinsic to their way of thinking, feeling, or being may not be to state that it is the way God intended it to be in creation. It may be, in fact, to state that what is experienced as natural may be in need of alteration, remediation, and redemption.[8]

Human beings were not designed to die, and yet death comes to each of us. We were not designed for disease, yet most people face sickness at some point in their life. Childbirth was not meant to be painful and dangerous, yet that is what it has become. We must be careful, therefore, about reaching conclusions concerning God's design for us based on what science tells us about the present state of our bodies. These are theological questions, not medical questions.

For instance, scientists suggest that monogamy is unnatural for human beings and that infidelity is "in our genes."[9] This does not mean that infidelity is a part of God's creation order. Scripture clearly tells us otherwise. Scientists suggest that homosexuality may be genetic, but again, this does not mean that God designed people to have various sexual orientations. God designed a man and a woman for each other, and Scripture is clear that other patterns of sexual encounter are a result of sin.

8. Stackhouse, *Covenant and Commitments*, 39.

9. Robert Wright, *The Moral Animal: Why We Are the Way We Are: The New Science of Evolutionary Psychology* (New York: Vintage Books, 1995), 56–57.

The fact that we experience a strong desire for sexual intimacy does not mean that God blesses all sexual intimacy. Sometimes Christians are called to resist biology. On the other hand, the creation order is not just a story about our origins. Christians believe that God's design is still built into the fiber of our existence and that one of the works of Christ is to restore harmony between us and that order.

Because of this distinction between creation and nature, some theologians in the past have seen the experience of romantic attraction as being a result of the fall. In this case, however, there is biblical warrant for believing that God created us with the capacity for romantic love. Not only is Adam said to "cleave" to his wife, but an entire book of the Old Testament, the Song of Solomon, is devoted to exploring the experience of romantic attraction. God uses the language of romance to describe his relationship with Israel, and the love between a husband and a wife is said to be a type of the love between Christ and the church. Romantic love, sexual attraction, and passionate attachment are good elements of God's good creation.

Unrequited Love in the Creation Order?

Given the creational emphasis on marriage, it is unclear whether the phenomenon of unrequited love could have occurred in the world without the existence of sin. It would seem that, within God's good creation order, we are not meant to be romantically attracted to all men or all women; rather, we are meant to be attracted to one person, typically to our husband or wife. Romantic attraction is meant to be particular. Therefore, is nonmutual attraction compatible with God's good creation order? If we lived in a world without sin, would every desire to marry be met with a similar desire?

I suspect not. Such complete mutuality would seem to require believing that God has created human beings as matched sets, that for each person in the world there is a perfect mate made for him or her by God. This is the soulmate perspective on romance discussed in the previous chapter and accepted by many Christians. How could this be, however, given that Jesus Christ, the perfect human, never married? Or given Paul's teach-

ing about the legitimacy of—or God's preference for—singleness? Clearly, not *all* human beings have a mate intended for
them, even though all human beings do experience romantic
attraction.

The study of students at my college showed that more than half
of them believe that God has chosen one specific individual for
them to marry. Such a perspective would seem to be compatible
with a deterministic understanding of God's providence, a belief
that God has already mapped out every facet of each person's
life. However, not all the students who believe God has a mate
for them accept such determinism. Less than one-third of the
same students believe, for instance, that God has determined one
particular career for them to follow. This suggests that their belief
that God has a partner in mind for them does not arise out of a
belief in deterministic providence but out of a belief about the
nature of marriage. Only in this area of life does God give such
explicit and complete direction.

Conversations with these students revealed that many do believe God creates people as matched sets, that they are meant
to find their "other half" or their soulmate, the one God has
made them for and made for them. It is interesting, however,
that younger students seem to hold this belief more firmly. One
young woman offers a clue as to why this might be so.

> I see it all the time with my friends that whoever they're dating, it's
> just like "Oh!" you know, you're just so into that person, you think
> they're so great, and "they could be the one." But then they break
> up, and then they meet someone else, and they're like, "Oh, I don't
> know what I was thinking with so-and-so." Okay, you were thinking
> that you were going to get married and that they were the one, and
> now you're not and you think that this new person is. I see that all
> the time, and so I don't believe in it.

Once you have been sure that you have met "the one" and then
changed your mind, your confidence in your ability to pick your
predestined soulmate out of a crowd will probably be much less
robust. The more often this happens, the less likely you are to
believe that there is only one person out there for you.

Yet this old idea of a soulmate is still widely present in popular
culture. In his novel *On Love*, Alain de Botton refers to this idea

51

as "romantic fatalism" and notes that it tends to arise even in the absence of any religious conviction.

> It was perhaps because I came to feel we were so right for one another [she did not just finish my sentences, she completed my life] that I was unable to contemplate the idea that meeting Chloe had been simply a coincidence. . . . Not normally superstitious, Chloe and I seized upon a host of details, however trivial, as confirmation of what intuitively we already felt: *that we had been destined for one another.*[10]

The narrator of de Botton's novel makes it clear that he has no religious basis for his fatalism. He finds that the experience of love itself requires such an attitude. Otherwise, a lover is admitting the possibility of loving someone else or at least the possibility of not loving this person, a possibility that is at odds with the sense of inevitability often accompanying romantic love. This is not unique to those who believe that God controls their lives in general terms. Many people of little or no religious conviction still believe in "fate" or "destiny" where romance is concerned. The movie *Serendipity* is based on this idea, with the heroine insisting that she will agree to marry the hero only if she can have proof that they are "fated" to be together.[11] *Sleepless in Seattle* advances this same idea of destiny as part of romantic love.[12] Many other movies and novels also express this idea.

I remember once discussing this idea of "the one" with a woman whose children were all young adults, none yet married. She said to me that she had definite hopes for her children regarding their marital choices. She hoped they would marry Christian people. She hoped they would marry people who helped them to serve God with all their talents. She hoped they would be happy in their marriages. But she did not have a particular person picked out for any of her children. It seemed likely to her, she said, that God's design for our romantic lives was similarly open within limits, allowing us freedom of choice in this area as well as in others.

10. Alain de Botton, *On Love* (New York: Grove Press, 1993), 7. The brackets and the italics in the quotation are de Botton's.
11. *Serendipity* (Miramax, 2001).
12. *Sleepless in Seattle* (Columbia/Tristar, 1993).

If God's creational design offered us only one possible life partner, we would expect to experience romantic attraction for only one person in the course of our lifetime, but that is not the way we are made. In fact, we experience varying levels of romantic attraction for many people throughout our life, and part of the dignity of our humanity consists of responding to such attraction appropriately. This is part of our freedom as people made with the ability to make choices, to give in to some impulses, and to resist others. The possibility of unrequited love, a romantic attraction that is not returned, is indeed part of the creation order and is therefore not in itself sinful or the result of sin. This may be difficult to accept since our experiences of unrequited love are tainted by anger, jealousy, possessiveness, unkindness, and other sin. Unrequited love is almost always a painful experience for us, making it difficult to think that this experience could exist in a sinless world.

In his book *The Four Loves*, C. S. Lewis notes that erotic love has an inherent touch of buffoonery, uniting as it does some of our highest aspirations with some of our most basic physical impulses.

> For I can hardly help regarding it as one of God's jokes that a passion so soaring, so apparently transcendent, as Eros, should thus be linked in incongruous symbiosis with a bodily appetite which, like any other appetite, tactlessly reveals its connections with such mundane factors as weather, health, diet, circulation, and digestion.[13]

He continues by saying that when we are in love, "at times we seem to be flying," but then our physical desires give us "the sudden twitch that reminds us we are really captive balloons."[14] Could it be that in the creation order unrequited love was a furthering of this divine joke? In a sinless, perfect world, such attraction could not be a source of lasting pain. Could it have been a source of humor? It is difficult for us to imagine unrequited love that is *not* a source of pain, but can we bring

13. C. S. Lewis, *The Four Loves* (New York: Harvest Books, 1971), 142.
14. Ibid.

our current romantic experiences in line with such a creational possibility?

Romantic love is not the only sort of experience that feels like a revelation from God. Many of us have similar experiences when we encounter something especially beautiful, either in the arts or in the natural world. Perhaps you are listening to a symphony by Beethoven or sitting in a theater holding your breath as an actor expresses emotions you have never been able to articulate. Perhaps you are watching a sunset over Lake Michigan, standing at the rim of the Grand Canyon, or lying on your back looking up at the sky over the Great Plains. Suddenly, you are overwhelmed with an awareness of the beauty and preciousness of the world. You seem to have had a glimpse of something beyond your everyday experience. Time does not seem to be moving at its normal speed. Many people count such experiences as their most significant religious moments, experiences that deepen their awareness of God's goodness and presence.

Although such experiences are in one sense intensely satisfying, in another sense a *lack* of satisfaction is one of their primary characteristics. Joy or delight in the presence of beauty is not final. It is an experience of longing that perpetuates itself. C. S. Lewis observes:

> The experience is one of intense longing. . . . Though the sense of want is acute and even painful, yet the mere wanting is felt to be somehow a delight. Other desires are felt as pleasures only if satisfaction is expected in the near future: hunger is pleasant only while we know (or believe) that we are soon going to eat. But this desire, even when there is no hope of possible satisfaction, continues to be prized, and even to be preferred to anything else in the world, by those who have once felt it. This hunger is better than any other fullness; this poverty better than all other wealth.[15]

One of the primary consequences of such experience is the stirring up of dissatisfaction and further desire so that the experience of longing becomes an essential piece of the experience itself. Jacques Maritain calls this quality "a certain sacred weakness,

15. C. S. Lewis, afterword to *The Pilgrim's Regress*, 3rd ed. (Grand Rapids: Eerdmans, 1992), 202.

and *that kind* of imperfection through which infinity wounds the finite."[16] Guy Sircello suggests that when we truly enjoy something, the experience of enjoyment produces a mixture of satisfaction and heightened desire. Even as our desire for the enjoyable experience is being met, the experience perpetuates our desire.[17] Experiences of the beauty of the world do not produce satiety. Rather, they make us aware of want, need, and desire, stirring up our "restless hearts" to dissatisfaction with any rest apart from a final rest in God.

This longing is a gift from God, protecting us from immersion in our present concerns and leading us closer to him. The seventeenth-century Anglican theologian Thomas Traherne explains that we are made to love what we do not know, to be people longing for something beyond our experience.

> I have found that things unknown have a secret influence on the soul, and like the centre of the earth unseen violently attract it. We love we know not what, and therefore everything allures us. As iron at a distance is drawn by the loadstone, there being some invisible communications between them, so is there in us a world of Love to somewhat, though we know not what in the world that should be. There are invisible ways of conveyance by which some great thing doth touch our souls, and by which we tend to it. Do you not feel yourself drawn by the expectation and desire of some Great Thing?[18]

Just as the forces of gravity and magnetism work on objects, even when those forces are not known, directly perceived, or understood, so too in our experiences of love we are drawn by longing for some "Great Thing," which Traherne believes is communion with God himself.

This longing is part of God's design for us. George Herbert expresses this idea in his poem "The Pulley." Herbert explains

---

16. Jacques Maritain, *Creative Intuition in Art and Poetry*, A. W. Mellon Lectures in the Fine Arts (Cleveland: Meridian Books, 1955), 128, italics in original.

17. Guy Sircello, *Love and Beauty* (Princeton: Princeton University Press, 1989). See especially chap. 4.

18. Thomas Traherne, "The First Century," meditation 2, in *Centuries, Poems, and Thanksgivings*, vol. 1 (Oxford: Oxford University Press, 1958), 3.

that when God created people, he poured all possible blessings on them: beauty, wisdom, honor, and pleasure. The only blessing he withheld was the blessing of rest.

> For if I should (said he)
> Bestow this jewel also on my creature,
> He would adore my gifts instead of me,
> And rest in Nature, not the God of Nature:
> So both should losers be.

> Yet let him keep the rest,
> But keep them with repining restlessness:
> Let him be rich and weary, that at least,
> If goodness lead him not, yet weariness
> May toss him to my breast.[19]

Clearly, Herbert is inspired here by Augustine's idea of the restless heart. It is part of the design of creation that people should not be able to rest in nature. Our experiences in the world are meant to drive us beyond such experiences to find the transcendent and wholly other God.

We destroy such experiences when we try to satisfy this longing, to fill this lack, by our own initiative and with our own resources. We may try to manufacture the experience, to manipulate ourselves into this altered state by repeating the same track on a CD or going to the same spot on the lakeshore where we were overwhelmed before. We may try to possess and control the experience in other ways: by bringing home a piece of rock from the Grand Canyon or buying a video of a theatrical performance. These experiences are essentially *iconic*, that is, they direct attention away from themselves toward something beyond themselves and beyond our experience. When we refuse to look where they are pointing and instead try to recapture the experience itself, we lose the very insight the experience originally offered.

Charles Williams's account of romantic love fits this same category. When we fall in love in this way, it is as if something from beyond this world has broken through, as if the veil

---

19. George Herbert, "The Pulley," in *The Temple and a Priest to the Temple*, ed. Edward Thomas (London: J. M. Dent, 1902), 167 (spelling modernized).

of ordinary experience has been pulled back and something extraordinary has been revealed. Such an experience should result in an increase of our longing for God and for the new creation—the world beyond this one. It should result in an increase of our awareness of God's presence around us. It should result in a heightened awareness of the ways in which human beings reflect God's glory. It should result in gratitude to God that such a person exists in the world. If, however, it results in a need to possess and control, then we are distorting the experience.

Karen, whom we heard about in the last chapter, reflected on such a moment, a moment when she felt that God had shown her a new dimension of a man who had been her casual friend for some time. He was someone she had thought of in a sisterly way, but one day, as she got out of the car he was driving, she looked at him through the car window and saw something she had not seen before.

> I just remember looking at him, and he was different. It was just like he was all of a sudden a person, not that I desired, but I could conceive of desiring, as a person, not just as a little boy or a little brother.

She saw him as a person in his own right, independent of herself. For this woman, this moment of insight was the beginning of a long period of deepening love, a love she now believes was sent to her by God, even though it is still not returned. She describes her love as unexpected, something she did not intend and does not control.

But precisely because her love was not a choice for her, she wonders why God does not send the same sort of revelation to the man she loves. Why shouldn't he be shown the glory in her, just as she was shown his glory?

> I can't say that it's completely hopeless, that he would never look at me and see what I saw, because I didn't do it; that's why I think it wasn't a choice. I didn't do it. I looked at him, and there it was. I don't know how my brain works, but I didn't feel like it was a choice for me. Maybe it's been a choice that I continue seeing him as a friend, but part of me feels like that's not a choice. Part of

me feels like I'd go crazy if I didn't see him, if I could not express in some way at least friendship.

When asked if God made her fall in love, if God was the instigator of this new way of seeing, she answered:

> I think so. I couldn't have shown it to myself. I would never have been able to pick out someone that good by myself, someone who obviously didn't attract me in the beginning. I mean now I find him incredibly attractive, but he didn't attract me at first; nothing about his personality flattered mine. He does not flatter me in any way. He doesn't seem to fall for my things that I do to make guys notice me, doesn't reward me by paying attention to me. He doesn't really fall for that. So I don't think I could have picked him on my own.

She is less sure about how much choice she is exercising in continuing to love him. Maybe she is choosing to continue, but maybe not. She speaks of having asked God to help her get over this love, and yet it has only grown stronger. This experience of unrequited love seems disordered to her, a sign that things are not the way they are supposed to be. "It's hard for me to understand why this situation should not be a result of sin, since it just seems hard. But I can see that it's not." She can see this because of all she is learning about God's love for her in finally loving someone else this much.

How do we reconcile the sense of inevitability that comes with such love and a conviction that human beings have free will and are responsible for their actions? The philosopher Harry Frankfurt says that falling in love is similar to being convinced to believe something that has been incontrovertibly demonstrated by a logical proof, both in that the experience does not feel as though it is chosen and in that the experience does not feel as though it restricts our sense of freedom.

> When we discover that we have no choice but to accede to irresistible requirements of logic, or to submit to captivating necessities of love, the feeling with which we do so is by no means one of dispirited passivity or confinement. In both cases—whether we are following reason or following our hearts—we are typically conscious of an invigorating release and expansion of ourselves.

But how can it be that we find ourselves to have been strength-ened, and to have been made less confined or limited, by being deprived of choice?[20]

Frankfurt's explanation is that the elimination of uncertainty allows us to be "wholehearted" people, putting an end to the ambivalence that typically plagues our lives and allowing us to throw ourselves into the pursuit of something or someone unambiguously wonderful and true. He says that "the necessity with which love binds the will puts an end to indecisiveness concerning what to care about."[21] To be really free, we need to have purpose and direction, which we can find only through love. "Love is the originating source of terminal value. If we loved nothing, then nothing would possess for us any defini-tive and inherent worth."[22] Real freedom, then, is not found in being autonomous selves but in having a worthy direction and purpose that we can embrace completely and wholeheartedly, without ambivalence.

> It may seem, then, that the way in which the necessities of reason and of love liberate us is by freeing us from ourselves. That *is*, in a sense, what they do. The idea is nothing new. The possibility that a person may be liberated through submitting to constraints that are beyond his immediate voluntary control is among the most ancient and persistent themes of our moral and religious traditions. "In His will," Dante wrote, "is our peace."[23]

As Dante points out, in a sinless world, this is how we would love God—with the same inevitability and lack of voluntary control that we experience when we fall head over heels in love with another person. This is the sort of love we anticipate in the next life, a love that will make sin inconceivable to us because our desires will be so completely united to God's desires.

In a sinless creation, we would be able to experience unre-quited love as an awareness of the glory of another human being

20. Harry G. Frankfurt, *The Reasons of Love* (Princeton: Princeton University Press, 2004), 64–65.
21. Ibid., 65.
22. Ibid., 55.
23. Ibid., 66. The Dante citation is from *Paradiso*, 3.85.

that helps us to understand God's nature more clearly, makes us long for God more consistently, and inspires us to be grateful to God. The very fact that love is not returned, that there is a lack of satisfaction, would help the experience point beyond itself to God. In our present fallen world, we may still experience unrequited love in this way, though jealousy, possessiveness, and hurt feelings may get in the way. Karen experiences her unrequited love in this way, largely, I think, because she is regularly in prayer for the man she is in love with. She is not praying that God will give him to her but that God will bless and keep him. The creation order tells us how romantic love ought to function in life, which then helps us to understand what we should pray for. We need to pray for the ability to love without jealousy, without possessiveness, and without allowing our personal hurt to influence us unduly. This is not to say that we should become people without feeling. Rather, our pain should not lead us into bitterness, anger, resentment, or hatred.

Ultimately, however, our goal as Christians is to be people of the new creation. We are on a journey forward to the New Jerusalem, not backward to Eden, and we need to bring our romantic lives into harmony with the future God has in store for us. That future is the theme of the next chapter.

3

God's Plan for the New Creation

Mary bore the Head of this Body after the flesh,
the Church bears the members of that Body after the Spirit.
In both virginity hinders not fruitfulness:
in both fruitfulness takes not away virginity.

Augustine, *De Virginitate*, 2

For thus says the Lord:
To the eunuchs who keep my sabbaths,
    who choose the things that please me
    and hold fast my covenant,
I will give, in my house and within my walls,
    a monument and a name
    better than sons and daughters;
I will give them an everlasting name
    that shall not be cut off.

Isaiah 56:4–5

As Christians, we not only evaluate our lives and culture in light of the creation order but also look forward to the eschatological order, the new creation as it will exist in its fullness when Christ returns. The coming of Christ inaugurated a new covenant. As his followers, we are now oriented toward the culmination of that covenant in the kingdom he has already introduced, which will be fulfilled when he comes again. Already now our life is oriented toward the goal of life in the new heaven and the new earth, and already now we should be trying to conform ourselves to the patterns of that new life.

The Bible gives us glimpses into what life will be like when the kingdom of God is fully realized, and one of the most striking things about those glimpses is that they are not identical with the glimpses we are given of the creation order. At creation, God placed human beings in a garden. In the new creation, we will be placed in a city. The vision of the New Jerusalem is a vision of a new society, complete with social institutions.

The achievements of human culture are therefore honored in the new creation. The life toward which we are moving is not simply a return to the beginning, a wiping out of everything that has been done or everything that has happened since creation. Everything that human beings have done or made or achieved will go through the fire of God's judgment. Everything that survives that fire will be brought into the new creation in its purified form. Therefore, Paul tells us that some people will enter heaven empty-handed because nothing they did will survive the fire. But others have been laying up treasure in heaven, and they will bring that treasure into the kingdom of God (1 Cor. 3:11–15).

A clear illustration of this promise is found in *The Last Battle,* the last of C. S. Lewis's Chronicles of Narnia. Lewis allows us to watch the end of the world of Narnia, but then we are shown the new Narnia, the new earth promised after the destruction of that world, in which all the beauties of the old Narnia are present, though in some way more *real,* more fully themselves than was possible in the old Narnia. As one character puts it, "This is the land I have been looking for all my life, though I never knew it till now. The reason why we loved the old Narnia is that it sometimes looked a little like this."[1]

When there is disagreement between the creation order and the new creation order, Christians must be governed by the new creation, for we are new covenant people. In the same way, a young person making decisions about a course of study must be governed more by her potential and the life she will have someday as an adult than by her history as an infant or a toddler. Knowledge of

---

1. C. S. Lewis, *The Last Battle* (New York: Macmillan, 1970), 171.

where we have come from is helpful, but knowledge of where we are going is essential. The question we must consider is whether the role of romance in the new creation order is in any way different from the role of romance in the original creation order.

In the original creation order, human society was centered on marriage, and romance was a support for marriage. Throughout the Old Testament, God led the people of Israel in the development of a society that placed marriage and family ties at its center. Israel's organization into tribes was essentially an organization based on such biological ties. For a righteous citizen of Israel, marriage was a duty owed to the community. So was raising children, for this was the way in which the community was built up. The laws of the Old Testament served to protect the family and to ensure the continuation of family lines. There is a great deal of discussion in the Old Testament about the importance of marrying within the community, and whenever Israelites intermarried with their unbelieving neighbors, trouble ensued. However, there is little discussion about *whether* a godly person ought to marry. Marriage was the assumed duty of all adults.

Already in the Old Testament, however, the sexual and romantic part of life was less important for the Israelites than it was for many surrounding nations. Other nations worshiped gods who engaged in sexual activity, who created through sexual acts, and whose reason to exist was to bring about fruitfulness. But the God of Israel transcends such things. Israel worshiped the God who made heaven and earth out of nothing. Sexuality was not seen as ultimate or central.[2] Also, as shown in the last chapter, already in the Old Testament, marriage pointed beyond itself in some way to the community of Israel as a whole and to God's relationship with that community, a relationship that is compared to that of a bridegroom and a bride.

Jesus' Teachings on Marriage and Singleness

Christians recognize the coming of Jesus Christ as the turning point of history and his second coming as the culmination

2. Max Stackhouse, *Covenant and Commitments* (Louisville: Westminster John Knox, 1997), 19.

of history. Everything in the world is measured in relationship to those two events. Jesus was the fulfillment of all the promises that preceded him in Scripture, but he also inaugurated a new way of life. The people of Israel, a biologically defined nation, were replaced by the church, a called-out people in whom the barriers of tribe and race are transcended. The kingdom of God broke into history with the coming of Jesus, and that kingdom will be fulfilled when Jesus comes again. From now on our orientation must be toward the future, the promise of the New Jerusalem. The changes that Jesus introduced are far reaching, and one area that was changed forever is marriage.

Reformed theologian Max Thurian summarizes the discontinuity between the old and the new covenant on this subject. He points out that in the Old Testament the primary purpose of marriage was to have children who would carry on the tradition of Israel. In the New Testament, however, marriage is understood primarily in terms of the relationship between a husband and a wife, a relationship that reflects the union of Christ and the church. This shift occurs because under the new covenant we become members of the community of faith through baptism, signifying our adoption in Christ, rather than through being born into the nation of Israel.

> So under the New Covenant marriage takes on a new spiritual meaning. It is no longer indispensable to the propagation of the people of God; it is one of the alternatives for Christian obedience, together with celibacy, which allows a spiritual procreation because it is willed by Christ "for the kingdom of heaven's sake."[3]

The coming of Jesus changed the meaning of marriage and raised the possibility of celibacy, that is, intentional abstinent singleness. On the one hand, marriage is no longer necessary, having become one of two possible ways of obedient life, the other being celibacy. On the other hand, marriage is now sanctified (or resanctified) as a model of the relationship between Christ, the bridegroom, and his bride, the church.

3. Max Thurian, *Marriage and Celibacy*, trans. Norma Emerton (London: SCM Press, 1959), 40–41.

The change is immediately obvious in that Jesus himself does not marry. Jesus is not only the fullness of God in human form but also the one who shows us the fullness of humanity. Yet he never marries. Although some of his disciples are apparently married, they are told that following Christ requires them to renounce their families in some way. Jesus actually speaks about *hating* one's father and mother. This seems to be a provocative and extreme way of asserting the priority of God's claim on our life. When one potential disciple says that he will follow Jesus later, after his parents have died, Jesus says, "No one who puts a hand to the plow and looks back is fit for the kingdom of God" (Luke 9:62). Our primary loyalties shift when we come into contact with Jesus. Whereas in the Old Testament the family was one's primary loyalty, Jesus redefines this, saying, "Whoever does the will of my Father in heaven is my brother and sister and mother" (Matt. 12:50). Jesus is our family now, and the community of faith is our primary social commitment. "Whoever loves father or mother more than me is not worthy of me; and whoever loves son and daughter more than me is not worthy of me; and whoever does not take up the cross and follow me is not worthy of me. Those who find their life will lose it, and those who lose their life for my sake will find it" (Matt. 10:37–39). Jesus insists that his followers live sacrificial lives that will make little sense in the eyes of the world.

When Jesus has a discussion with the Pharisees about divorce and remarriage, he says that remarriage after divorce is adultery, unless the divorce was a result of adultery, or "unchastity." The disciples exclaim that, given such demands, it might be better not to marry at all. Jesus replies:

> Not everyone can accept this teaching, but only those to whom it is given. For there are eunuchs who have been so from birth, and there are eunuchs who have been made eunuchs by others, and there are eunuchs who have made themselves eunuchs for the sake of the kingdom of heaven. Let anyone accept this who can.
>
> Matthew 19:11–12

Jesus neither refutes the disciples' conclusion (though that is probably what they were expecting) nor endorses it. He does not say that marriage is now without value; indeed, the immediate context is a conversation in which he has insisted on the indissoluble nature of marriage, and he has appealed to the story of creation to explain that nature. The comments to the disciples make clear, however, that there is also value in giving up marriage, or "becoming a eunuch," for the sake of the kingdom of God.

This would have been a startling word to the disciples. As John Paul II points out in commenting on this text, "Christ spoke to men to whom the tradition of the old covenant had not handed down the ideal of celibacy or of virginity. Marriage was so common that only physical impotence could constitute an exception."[4] He then goes on to point to the story of Jephthah's daughter in the book of Judges (Judg. 11:3–40). When she discovers she is about to die, she asks permission to go into the hills and mourn for the fact that she is going to die a virgin. Going without sex, which John Paul II refers to as "continence," is a sad and dishonorable state in the Old Testament world. It is especially associated with eunuchs, whom the disciples would have thought of as pitiable and defective. What must the disciples have thought when Jesus referred to being a eunuch for the kingdom of heaven as a positive thing! John Paul says that it is as if Jesus were saying:

> I know that what I am going to say to you now will cause great difficulty in your conscience, in your way of understanding the significance of the body. In fact, I shall speak to you of continence. Undoubtedly, you will associate this with the state of physical deficiency, whether congenital or brought about by human cause. But I wish to tell you that continence can also be voluntary and chosen . . . for the kingdom of heaven.[5]

The idea that being a eunuch, someone who turns away from both marriage and sexual activity, might not be a disgrace but actually a free choice that glorifies God marks a clear discontinuity with the Old Testament tradition.

4. John Paul II, *The Theology of the Body: Human Love in the Divine Plan* (Boston: Pauline Books & Media, 1997), 265.
   5. Ibid., 266.

In another passage, Jesus says that in the resurrection life there will be no marriage at all. In response to a question posed by the Sadducees about a woman who married seven men, asking whose wife she would be in the resurrection, he says:

> Those who belong to this age marry and are given in marriage; but those who are considered worthy of a place in that age and in the resurrection from the dead neither marry nor are given in marriage. Indeed they cannot die any more, because they are like angels and are children of God, being children of the resurrection.

> Luke 20:34–36

Not only is continent singleness introduced as a legitimate option in the New Testament, but Jesus also tells us that the trajectory of human history is moving toward a time when marriage will be obsolete. As already mentioned, when the creation order and the new creation order are not the same, we must be governed by the new creation order. Here there is a clear difference. Marriage is the norm in Eden, but it will be obsolete in the New Jerusalem. Therefore, our communities of faith should be on a trajectory in which they reflect Eden less and less, the New Jerusalem more and more.

Notice that this trajectory is not toward greater sexual freedom but toward greater sexual discipline. Whereas in the Old Testament the law restricted sexual expression to the bounds of marriage, the New Testament contains the possibility that people will abstain from sexual expression altogether. This is in keeping with other changes in the law that Jesus introduces. For instance, Jesus says, "You have heard that it was said to those of ancient times, 'You shall not murder'; and 'whoever murders shall be liable to judgment.' But I say to you that if you are angry with a brother or sister, you will be liable to judgment; and if you insult a brother or sister, you will be liable to the council; and if you say, 'You fool,' you will be liable to the hell of fire" (Matt. 5:21–22). The new law of love raises the bar on our behavior. Jesus does not set the law aside; rather, he expands it, requiring his disciples to internalize God's will.

The reason Jesus gives for there being no marriage in heaven is somewhat confusing. He says that in heaven we will be "like angels." Contemporary readers often take this to mean that we will be either disembodied or free of all passion, but this is not what the disciples and the Pharisees would have understood by this expression. The theologian Edward Schillebeeckx explains:

> For [those] of ancient and biblical times, angels were mighty, concentrated personalities, Powers, who stood always in God's presence, prepared to do his bidding swiftly. That is what is suggested in the idea of the unmarried condition as being "equal to angels"—something very different indeed from our modern attenuated notion of sweet angelic natures for which a body is unsuitable or unnecessary. . . . [A] celibacy "equal to angels" called up the idea of force, the power and might of beings with a free, concentrated centre for their lives, ready for the service of God and [other people].[6]

This concentrated power will be realized completely only when we become children of the resurrection, but it should already be manifesting itself in our lives now.

Schillebeeckx thinks that the call to celibacy is a call to this same sort of concentrated power and that Jesus' use of the word *eunuch* is a clue to this, for a eunuch is someone who has no choice about whether to marry. In the same way, says Schillebeeckx, Jesus is observing that marriage is simply not an option for his disciples.

> The unpleasant-sounding word "eunuch" . . . presupposes the *fact* of the celibacy of Jesus' apostles: there are those who "for the sake of the kingdom of God are incapable of founding a family." Jesus points out that his disciples who have discovered the hidden riches of the kingdom of God could not existentially do other than "leave everything" . . . and "follow him." The gift of the coming kingdom held them so in its spell that they left everything joyfully and without counting the cost; it was not even possible now for them to go back to their married lives (Lk 14:26; 18:29). They could no longer devote themselves to goods and possessions (Mk 10:21; Mt 19:21; Lk 18:22). They could no

6. Edward Schillebeeckx, *Celibacy*, trans. C. A. L. Jarrott (New York: Sheed & Ward, 1968), 55–56.

longer concern themselves with their own livelihood (Mk 8:34; Mt 16:24; Lk 9:23). It was a matter of existentially not being able to do otherwise; in this sense they are truly "eunuchs." There are such people, says Jesus. Clearly this applies to the apostles. . . . In any case, in the group of the disciples of Jesus there are those who have experienced this as a sovereign demand of God's inviting grace: "we have left everything and followed you" (Mt 19:27). For them it was the inner logic of their enthusiastic discovery of the kingdom of God: "for the sake of the kingdom of heaven."[7]

For the disciples, celibacy appears to be an obvious consequence of such an "enthusiastic discovery" of the new kingdom that is coming. This understanding of the text would not support a *law* of celibacy but would see celibacy as a natural response to Jesus' call. In the same way, this text does not support a law of poverty, but it certainly suggests that giving up belongings is a natural response to Jesus' call.

Another reason there is no marriage in heaven is that the creational purpose for marriage has now been fulfilled. In the creation order, Adam and Eve were to embody the presence of God for each other. In Jesus Christ, however, God himself took human form and came to live among us. God himself became bone of our bones, flesh of our flesh—fulfilling the song that Adam sang to Eve when God first presented them to each other. The truth to which marriage is meant to point is now available to us directly. As members of the church, we await our marriage to Christ, the bridegroom. In heaven, being married to any other member of the body would be a distraction from the ultimate relationship with Christ, toward which earthly marriage is meant to direct our attention. Ultimately, we belong body and soul to Jesus Christ; therefore, we are not free to belong to anyone else. Thus, even those Christians who choose to marry recognize in their wedding vows that their marriage is for this life only. Popular movies and love songs notwithstanding, Christians know that marriage ends with the death of one of the partners; it is not forever.

It also seems likely that in the new creation we will find our capacity for enjoying one another, for seeing the glory in one

7. Ibid., 23.

another and delighting in it, expanded. In this life, our capacity for love is small, and to love deeply and truly, we need the confines of committed relationships. But in the next life, our capacity for love will be much greater and will grow throughout eternity. We simply do not know how this love will be expressed, though it will certainly be something that will make our current experiences of sexual intimacy seem pale and uninteresting.

A student once asked me if I was bothered by the possibility of dying without having had sex, of "missing my chance," as it were. It is my conviction that the joy of heaven will more than make up for any pleasure we forego here and that no one in heaven will waste any time pining for pleasures passed over in this life. Greg Johnson says, "I've never spoken to someone . . . who regretted postponing sex until marriage. No one ever regrets sexual purity. But I've met lots of people who regret their sexual sin."[8] I believe this is true even if it turns out that you have not simply postponed sex until marriage but have given it up completely. Millions of people throughout history have made this choice out of love for the kingdom of God.

Whenever I speak to groups of Christians about the biblical trajectory toward singleness, I encounter resistance. Inevitably, someone will say to me, "But if everyone followed this teaching, no one would have any children." No doubt, some of you have been thinking the same thing. This just does not seem to be a practical or realistic way for Jesus to set up his church.

First, it is my experience that those parts of Scripture that I find most unpleasant and difficult are precisely the parts that I need to hear. Whether or not you agree with my interpretation of these texts, if you are a Christian, you must come to terms with what Jesus says about marriage and singleness. Second, throughout the history of the world, God has typically interacted with his creatures in ways that do not make complete sense to us. Paul tells us that "God's foolishness is wiser than human wisdom, and God's weakness is stronger than human strength" (1 Cor. 1:25). We should not be surprised if Jesus decides to establish his church in ways that seem inefficient and needlessly risky. Third, if all Christians everywhere were to take this teaching

8. Greg Johnson, *The World according to God* (Downers Grove, IL: InterVarsity, 2002), 137.

seriously, stop getting married, and stop having children, perhaps the church would start to grow through evangelism rather than through procreation. In this case, the church would be a blessing to the nations, just as we are supposed to be, with most of our nurturing energy going outside our own community. Finally, if we actually converted everyone in the world, and everyone in the world then embraced continent singleness so that no children were being born (a rather unlikely scenario), wouldn't that mean it was time for Jesus to come again? All Christians are supposed to be longing for his second coming and doing everything possible to bring it about.

I do not believe that all Christians need to be single, but all Christians must come to terms with Jesus' teaching that marriage is not ultimate. Taking this teaching seriously will change how we think about the possibility of marriage in our own life and how we treat people around us—particularly within the church—who are unmarried.

Paul's Teaching on Marriage and Singleness

The pattern of moving marriage away from the community's center and lifting up the possibility of singleness continues with the founding of the church, the new Israel. This community is not centered on marriage and biological families but rather takes on many of the former characteristics of the family itself. The early believers had all things in common and lived a common life, which, in the Old Testament, would have been characteristic of biologically defined family groups (Acts 2:42–47). In the New Testament, biology is transcended. People who have no family connection in a conventional sense are bound together as brothers and sisters, even to the extent that the barrier between Jew and Gentile is overcome, so that all members of the church are called "members of the household of God" (Eph. 2:19).

In the new covenant, marriage is no longer an unambiguously good thing for all Christians. The new community of the church is not meant to be replenished primarily by childbirth but by evangelism, and Paul is the primary exemplar of this. Those whom he brings to Christ are his children, and his singleness allows him to have far more children than he could ever have had biologically.

Paul is the paradigmatic leader of the new Christian community; indeed, he tells the church at Corinth to be "imitators" of him, just as he himself imitates Christ (1 Cor. 11:1). Not only is he unmarried, but he tells the Christians at Corinth that it would be better if all Christians remained unmarried so as to be better prepared for Christ's return.

> Now concerning the matters about which you wrote: "It is well for a man not to touch a woman." But because of cases of sexual immorality, each man should have his own wife and each woman her own husband. . . . This I say by way of concession, not of command. I wish that all were as I myself am. But each has a particular gift from God, one having one kind and another a different kind.
>
> To the unmarried and the widows I say that is well for them to remain unmarried as I am. But if they are not practicing self-control, they should marry. For it is better to marry than to be aflame with passion.
>
> 1 Corinthians 7:1–2, 6–9

In this passage, Paul first rejects the idea that sex, even within marriage, is an evil to be avoided. The categorical rejection of a man ever touching a woman under any circumstances appears to have been suggested in a letter that Paul had received from some members of the church at Corinth, but Paul does not affirm such a categorical rejection.[9] Marriage is a good thing, a blessing from God, and within marriage husbands and wives ought to enjoy sexual intimacy. In fact, this is a rather startling passage in that Paul gives the same conjugal rights to a wife as to a husband. A wife's body now belongs to her husband, and a husband's body now belongs to his wife. So he says, "Do not deprive one another except perhaps by agreement for a set time,

9. Calvin Roetzel hypothesizes that the letter from the Corinthians had said something like this: "Given the urgency of the times, we believe married believers should refrain from sexual intercourse. . . . Since we are members of the kingdom, should not those of us who are married act as if they were not, and should not believers divorce any unbelieving partners?" (*The Letters of Paul: Conversations in Context,* 4th ed. [Louisville: Westminster John Knox, 1998], 87).

to devote yourselves to prayer, and then come together again, so that Satan may not tempt you because of your lack of self-control" (1 Cor. 7:5).

Although Paul is an advocate for celibacy, his advocacy is not based on disdain for the body, a desire for personal autonomy, or an unwillingness to sacrifice his own tastes and preferences for the good of another person. Jean-Jacques von Allmen comments on this passage, saying, "Celibacy . . . cannot be justified by the desire to be alone, by egoism and scorn of the opposite sex, nor above all on the basis of a metaphysical dualism which would see in the insistence and demands of the body so many obstacles to purity of Christian life and walking in Christ."[10] The body is good, and marriage can be a good expression of God's created design for our bodies.

At the same time, Paul is also clear that not being married is good, and he seems to recognize only one good reason to marry: marriage makes it easier to deal with overwhelming sexual temptation. In his commentary on 1 Corinthians, John Calvin summarizes Paul's teaching:

> Now the point of the whole argument is this—celibacy is better than marriage because there is more freedom in celibacy, so that men can serve God more easily; yet no compulsion must be imposed, so that it may be permissible to anyone to marry when he thinks fit; and finally, marriage is a remedy ordained by God to help our weakness, and is to be used by anyone who does not possess the gift of continence.[11]

Calvin's primary concern is with his second point, that celibacy should not be compelled. Whereas the Roman Catholic Church requires celibacy of its priests, Calvin believes that each pastor should be free to decide whether to marry. Yet Calvin, unlike many of his followers, still acknowledges that the passage expresses a preference for celibacy and that marriage is for those who cannot be continent, that is, cannot give up sexual activity.

10. Jean-Jacques von Allmen, *Pauline Teaching on Marriage*, trans. Anonymous (London: Faith Press, 1963), 16.
11. Cited in Thurian, *Marriage and Celibacy*, 21.

It is astonishing how often Christians appeal to their lack of self-control as justification for their efforts to get married. In 1 Corinthians, Paul describes the body as "a temple of the Holy Spirit" and argues that sexual sin is thus in some ways worse than other sins, because it is a sin against the body itself, against God's temple (1 Cor. 6:18–20). In his letter to the Galatians, Paul lists self-control as one of the fruits of the Spirit (Gal. 5:22–23). In other words, self-control is not an exceptional gift given to only a few people. It is supposed to be evidence of the Holy Spirit's presence, made manifest in the life of every believer. Yet Christians routinely claim that they could not possibly be expected to manifest self-control in their sexual lives and that no one should be surprised by this.

The church at Corinth was in many ways unlike the church in North America today. There were no second-generation Christians in Corinth who had grown up in the church and were now providing leadership and guidance. In his letters to the Corinthians, Paul found it necessary to explain things such as how to administer the Lord's Supper. Since this was a new church made up entirely of new believers, no one knew how this was done. Many of the Corinthians had been converted, not out of Judaism but out of paganism, and the paganism of Corinth—as was true throughout the Roman Empire—often encouraged sexual promiscuity and licentiousness. It is clear from an earlier passage in the first letter to the Corinthians that the members of this church were unperturbed by sexual behavior that would bother many secular Americans. Given this context, Paul was probably dealing with people with deeply ingrained habits of promiscuity. He recognizes that such people may not be able to step directly into a life of celibacy, that their self-control may not yet be sufficiently developed to deal with this level of temptation. So he counsels marriage as a concession, and he does it without blaming those who will choose to marry. They have not been given the gift of the Holy Spirit's long work in their lives producing the fruit of sanctification.

People enter the contemporary church whose situations are much like that of the Corinthians. They are new believers with no history of Christian faith or moral instruction. They have been living self-indulgent, sexually promiscuous lives prior to their conversion, and they look at celibacy as something foreign and unnatural. Our society, like the society of the ancient Roman Empire, is highly sexualized, and celibacy is profoundly counter-cultural.

But surely this does not, or should not, describe the majority of the members of most Christian churches today. It certainly does not describe the majority of my students. Most of them have been raised in Christian homes. The Holy Spirit has been doing his work of sanctification in their lives since they were very young. One would hope that they are not starting from ground zero in developing the fruit of self-control. Many, perhaps most, are committed to sexual abstinence before marriage, so they are already living chaste lives as single people. It would therefore be odd to assume that the large majority of these students would feel the need to take advantage of Paul's concession that "it is better to marry than to be aflame with passion."

Being "aflame with passion" is different from feeling sexual desire. All healthy adult human beings feel sexual desire, including Paul and, yes, even Jesus. Some people feel more sexual desire than others, and yet there is ample evidence from the experience of Christians—both men and women, young and old, throughout history and throughout the world today—that it is quite possible for all sorts of people to live meaningful, productive lives without having sex. All people, of whatever age or situation in life, want things that they do not have and must learn to deal with dissatisfaction. Being aflame with passion must mean a sexual desire that is beyond self-control, something along the lines of a sexual addiction. For my Christian brothers and sisters who are indeed suffering from such complete lack of self-control, I have great sympathy—as Paul clearly did. But is this really commonplace among Christians in our society? If it were, that would be a sign of a deep problem, a sign that the Holy Spirit's sanctifying work is being resisted throughout the church in the area of sexual morality. If this were the case (and I hope it is not), we should stop talking about sexual desire (which would be only a symptom) and start talking about what it means to be a Christian who is open to the work of the Holy Spirit and undergoing the process of sanctification.

The reason Paul gives for remaining unmarried is that there is an "impending crisis" that will make it easier to serve the Lord if single.

I mean, brothers and sisters, the appointed time has grown short; from now on, let even those who have wives be as though they had none, and those who mourn as though they were not mourning, and those who rejoice as though they were not rejoicing, and those who buy as though they had no possessions, and those who deal with the world as though they had no dealings with it. For the present form of this world is passing away.

1 Corinthians 7:29–31

He goes on to say that unmarried people are "anxious about the affairs of the Lord, how to please the Lord," whereas married people are "anxious about the affairs of the world" and about how to please their spouses. Singleness brings with it a greater freedom for the service of God, especially in times of trial.

Many people respond to this passage by observing that Paul was clearly mistaken. He expected the world to end any day, and yet here we are, nearly two thousand years later, and Christ has not yet returned. If he was wrong about this, and if it was his reason for counseling singleness, then it follows that we do not need to listen to Paul on this issue. From a secular perspective, this is certainly a reasonable response, but my faith does not allow me to say that Paul is simply in error in 1 Corinthians or that this teaching is misguided and may be discounted for that reason. A little reflection convinces me that Paul was not in error. We are people living in expectation of Christ's return. That was true during Paul's ministry, and it is true today. We should each live with the constant awareness that "the present form of this world is passing away" and that the ascended Christ could return at any moment. We should each be longing for that day. True, after two thousand years, it is less natural to maintain this attitude of expectancy, but we are to maintain it nonetheless.

This does not mean, however, that Christians should never marry. There is a transcultural, general principle that we can extract from Paul's teaching in 1 Corinthians 7. His rule seems to be the same whether discussing the problem of out-of-control sexual desire or the question of being ready for Christ's return: we should opt for the state of life that is most conducive to being faithful to Christ. In our culture, single people do *not* always have more time to devote to Christian service than married people. In our culture, marriage is *not* always a distraction from the things of the Lord. It may in fact be a partnership in Christian service. Our culture allows people to marry based on individual choice after an extensive time of courtship, and therefore people can know one another quite well before making this commitment. The past two thousand years have allowed us to develop a pattern of Christian marriage that could not have been known to the Corinthian Christians, many of whom were already married when they converted and whose marriages were therefore not necessarily sources of support for their faith. The transcultural principle Paul is applying is simply this: Christians should be free to marry if marriage will make them better Christians.

It does seem, however, that singleness must be the default choice for a Christian, given the clear preference for singleness expressed in this text and in Jesus' teachings. In other words, the burden of proof is on the decision to marry, not the decision to remain single. Christians should assume that they will be single unless and until they have a godly reason to marry. Christians should never marry out of insecurity, fear, a desire to escape the parental home, a need for affirmation, or a search for financial stability. Christians should marry only those who enhance their ability to live Christlike lives, those able to be true partners in Christian service, those who give them a vision of the image of God and the glory of Christ.

By extension, this should be true of all romantic relationships: the burden of proof is on the decision to enter into such a relationship, not the decision to hold back. One woman told me that her church taught that a single woman had no right to "deny fellowship" to any brother in Christ (by which they meant any single man who was a member of that same congregation) who asked her out. The woman who told this story said that she went on several awkward dates with men in whom she was not remotely interested because she was told it was her Christian duty to be open to relationships with Christian men. There was apparently no such burden placed on the male members of the church; they were not required to accept all invitations issued by single female church members.

Even within Christian communities where this expectation is not spelled out so explicitly, it is often operative. Many of my students, especially the young women, seem to believe that they are obligated to accept a date from anyone who asks them unless they have a reason to say no. Saying yes just seems more available, more vulnerable, more giving—more Christian.

But if singleness is our default, then this thinking needs to change. You need a reason to say yes, not a reason to say no. The reason should be commensurate with what is being asked of you. If you are considering going on a first date with someone, it is not necessary that you have the same depth of reason you would have if you were deciding to marry the person in question. But you need never feel obliged to have a reason for saying no.

For most of us, this is very difficult. We feel as though we need to come up with excuses, as if we need to present convincing reasons for saying no to an invitation, even if it is an invitation to do something that does not interest us. But constructing an excuse simply invites a debate with the other person about the legitimacy of our reasons for saying no. By presenting excuses and reasons, we are assenting to the false idea that anyone who asks us to do something has a claim on full and complete knowledge about our lives, that such a person may not be denied unless we can justify our denial. But this is simply untrue. Not everyone we know has this level of claim on us.

I know a man whose job includes answering phones for a very busy executive whom lots of people want to see. This man has learned how to say no to people, very politely but without giving excuses or constructing reasons. What I find interesting is that this ability has spilled over into his personal life. When he is invited to do something that he either cannot do or does not want to do, he rarely explains. He simply smiles and says something like, "I'm sorry I can't come, but thank you for the invitation." With a closer acquaintance, he may perhaps acknowledge that he "has other plans," but he feels no need to explain what those plans are to any but his closest friends and family members. More of us need to cultivate this ability to say no without concocting excuses, especially when such excuses are less than honest. Saying no without excuse is part of what it means to speak the truth in love to one another.

Called to Community

The call to singleness is not a call to autonomy. We are not moving toward a new creation in which individuals are lost in the contemplation of God without any reference to the rest of their community. Rather, we are moving toward a community richer and more varied than any we are able to experience in this fallen world.

When I talk to people about singleness, they often comment on the freedom and flexibility I probably have as a single person and the fun that I am able to enjoy as a result. A responsible single adult living alone may actually have less time than many married people, since he or she has no partner with whom to share the many chores of maintaining a home and organizing daily life. It is true that some singles may have fewer relational demands, but this is not always the case, since many single people live with family members or friends who have relational expectations that require the same sort of time as those of a spouse. Singles may be freer to opt for a life of Christian poverty, a life of mission that includes the risk of violence, or a life in an intentional Christian community of some sort because they are less likely to have dependents for whom they need to provide. This is clearly what Paul has in mind when he says that single people are "anxious about the affairs of the Lord, how to please the Lord," whereas married people are "anxious about the affairs of the world," how to please their families, and therefore their "interests are divided" (1 Cor. 7:32–34).

Singles *may* be freer in this way. In reality, however, many single people in America today play into the impression that the single life is less responsible and more fun than marriage, so that singleness is used as an excuse for selfishness and narcissism. In his memoir *Blue Like Jazz,* Donald Miller confesses that he was tempted to experience singleness in just this way.

> Life was a story about me because I was in every scene. In fact, I was the only one in every scene. I was everywhere I went. If somebody walked into my scene, it would frustrate me because they were disrupting the general theme of the play, namely my comfort or glory. Other people were flat characters in my movie, lifeless characters. Sometimes I would have scenes with them,

dialogue, and they would speak their lines, and I would speak mine. But the movie, the grand movie stretching from Adam to the Antichrist, was about me. I wouldn't have told you that at the time, but that is the way I lived. . . .

The most difficult lie I have ever contended with is this: Life is a story about me. . . . No drug is so powerful as the drug of self. No rut in the mind is so deep as the one that says I am the world, the world belongs to me, all people are characters in my play. There is no addiction so powerful as self-addiction.[12]

Miller found that the cure for this self-addiction was to live in an intentional Christian community. This was a hard cure, but he was convinced that God had led him into community to deal with his self-centeredness.

While the creational insistence on marriage is transcended in the new creation, the call to community is not transcended. Throughout most of Christian history, the call to singleness has been lived out either in intentional Christian communities (such as monasteries or communal houses) or within an extended family community. Being called to singleness is not the same thing as being called to be a hermit or a solitary. These are legitimate spiritual disciplines, but they ought not to be seen as the norm for all single people. Most unmarried people are called to solitude for limited periods of time, not as a way of life, for Christians are meant to be part of the community of the church. Even during times of solitude, this community connection functions through the power of intercessory prayer and through sharing in the sacraments.

Ironically, even as the church has been elevating the nuclear family, we have been cooperating with our culture in weakening the connections of the extended family and other forms of community. In our culture, young people are expected to move away from their parents to cultivate independence. This is not true in most of the world, but it is certainly true in the United States, to such an extent that a young man or woman in his or her twenties who still lives at home is looked down on, suspected of being mentally unbalanced or at least hopelessly immature.

12. Donald Miller, *Blue Like Jazz* (Nashville: Thomas Nelson, 2003), 181–82.

Young singles in our culture typically create new "families" made up of peers in place of the traditional extended family, which includes people of all generations. This means that many young singles restrict their social interaction to people like themselves, people who share their interests, who are their age, and who are also single.

But Christian singleness is not meant to be an excuse to avoid spending time with people unlike ourselves. Christian singles are called to a community that is bigger than the community of married people, not smaller. Paul's singleness allowed him to travel the known world and to find himself at home with communities of Christians in many places, young and old, rich and poor, male and female, slave and free. He did not use his singleness as an excuse to reduce his friendships to people his own age, people with his educational background, or people who happened to live in the same city he did. Instead, he said, "I have become all things to all people, that I might by all means save some" (1 Cor. 9:22). Our experience of the body of Christ is incomplete if we have fellowship only with people who are like ourselves.

Stan Grenz points out that marriage is a small instance of the sort of "unity in diversity" that reflects God's nature, but the church is the primary instance of such unity.[13] In the Letter to the Ephesians, Paul says that "through the church the wisdom of God in its rich variety might now be made known" (3:10), a variety that is reflected when "the dividing wall, that is, the hostility between us," is broken down through Jesus Christ, who is our peace (2:14). Our experience of the church is meant to be an experience of diversity and variety joined together under the lordship of Jesus. If your only experience of the church is of a group of people just like you—your age, your marital status, your income bracket, your race, your nationality—you have not yet experienced the rich variety of God as it is expressed in the body of Christ.

In his book *Shantung Compound,* Langdon Gilkey shares the story of the two and a half years he spent in an internment camp in China during the Japanese occupation. The Japanese collected

---

13. Stan Grenz, *The Social God and the Relational Self: A Trinitarian Theology of the Imago Dei* (Louisville: Westminster John Knox, 2001), 302.

all the foreigners living in one area of China—two thousand people—and detained them together in a camp. The subtitle of the book is *The Story of Men and Women under Pressure,* for Gilkey's focus is on the social interactions of the detainees and what their behavior can teach us about human nature. For our purposes, what is most interesting is that the Catholic priests were, from Gilkey's perspective, the most useful and widely loved members of the new community, whereas the married Protestant missionaries were much less valuable.

Most of the missionaries were detained with their families, and their care for their families trumped their sense of obligation to the rest of the community. No one had enough space to live with much privacy, but some families who had arrived earlier than others had two small rooms for their family of four or five people, whereas the later arrivals had only one. Gilkey was in charge of housing assignments, but when he tried to get some of the missionaries who had two rooms to rearrange themselves to make the space allocation more fair, he met complete resistance. No family was willing to sacrifice anything for the good of the community, and several parents appealed to their moral duty to look out for the good of their families as a defense for such selfishness.[14]

Gilkey offers his own explanation of the unjust behavior that emerged in the internment camp:

> Injustice to other [people] . . . is the social consequence of an inward idolatry, the worship of one's own self or group. The moral problems of selfishness, the intellectual problems of prejudice, and the social problems of dishonesty, inordinate privilege, and aggression are all together the result of the deeper religious problem of finding in some partial creature the ultimate security and meaning which only the Creator can give.[15]

In the case of the missionary families, the primary object of idolatry was the family, but the broader Protestant community could also serve this role. Gilkey says that the Protestant mis-

---

14. Langdon Gilkey, *Shantung Compound: The Story of Men and Women under Pressure* (New York: Harper & Row, 1966), 85–88.
15. Ibid., 232.

sionaries also had a tendency to keep to themselves, "to their own flock of saved souls, evidently because they feared to be contaminated in some way by this sinful world which they inwardly abhorred." This meant that their influence on the camp was less than that of the Catholic priests, who "*mixed.* They made friends with anyone in camp, helped out, played cards, smoked, and joked with them. They were a means of grace to the whole community."[16] The priests were especially effective because they had both the strength of a community and the freedom of singleness.

God's will for the church is that we might more and more embody the new creation, which is already now breaking in on this world. We must reflect the new creation understanding of singleness as a good gift and the new creation understanding of Christian community as something bigger than the family and bigger than people who are just like us. To hold on to the patterns of the old covenant in the face of Jesus' new work is to pour the new wine of the gospel into old wineskins, and Jesus promises that when we try to do that, the old wineskins will burst. As we look at the disintegration of families in our society and the dysfunctional understanding of human sexuality, we can clearly see that this has happened. This leads us to the next topic: sin and our romantic lives.

16. Ibid., 172.

4

Sin and Our Romantic Lives

He was a good person. . . . He just went over the deep end. He probably just loved her too much.

> Woman talking about the man who just killed himself, her sister, and the sister's three children by setting the car they were in on fire[1]

So I find it to be a law that when I want to do what is good, evil lies close at hand. For I delight in the law of God in my inmost self, but I see in my members another law at war with the law of my mind, making me captive to the law of sin that dwells in my members.

> Romans 7:21–23

One Christian truth that can be proven empirically is that things in this world have gone awry. As Cornelius Plantinga observes, this world is "not the way it's supposed to be."[2] This is painfully evident in our romantic lives, and much of this book—not just this chapter—considers the influence of sin on our experiences of romance. The creational pattern of one man and one woman, brought together to live a fruitful and blessed life, has been undermined. The new creational pattern of chaste singleness is

1. "Rocky Relationship Ends in Fiery Horror and Death of a Family," *Grand Rapids Press*, July 16, 2004, A5.
2. Cornelius Plantinga, *Not the Way It's Supposed to Be* (Grand Rapids: Eerdmans, 1995).

not yet embraced. God designed our sexuality to work in concert with our marital commitment, but that connection has been severed. As C. S. Lewis puts it:

> The monstrosity of sexual intercourse outside marriage is that those who indulge in it are trying to isolate one kind of union (the sexual) from all the other kinds of union which were intended to go along with it and make up the total union.
>
> The Christian attitude does not mean that there is anything wrong about sexual pleasure, any more than about the pleasure of eating. It means that you must not isolate that pleasure and try to get it by itself, any more than you ought to try to get the pleasures of taste without swallowing and digesting, by chewing things and spitting them out again.[3]

Yet everything in our society conspires to isolate the pleasure of sexuality from commitment and intimacy, with the result that sex must become increasingly degenerate to catch our attention. William May observes:

> When the sex act separates from its natural human emotion of affection, it loses its tie with the concrete lives of the two persons performing the act; it becomes *boring*. Inevitably, one must reinvest one's interest in the variety of ways and techniques with which the act is performed—one on one, then two on one, then in all possible permutations and combinations, culminating in the orgy. When affection isn't there, it won't do to have bodies perform the act in the age-old ways. Sad variety alone compensates.[4]

We are not the first society to face this problem, but entertainment technology allows the culture of degenerate sexuality to spread more easily and more widely than ever before. A person wanting to avoid such degeneracy must use constant vigilance.

3. C. S. Lewis, *Mere Christianity* (New York: Macmillan, 1956), 81. Lewis seems to think his example of dysfunctional eating is an obvious absurdity, but in our own era, some people do exactly this.

4. William May, "Four Mischievous Theories of Sex: Demonic, Divine, Casual, and Nuisance," in *Passionate Attachments: Thinking about Love*, ed. Willard Gaylin and Ethel Person (New York: Free Press, 1988), 30.

The beginnings of this problem are seen in the curse God pronounces on Adam and Eve as they leave Eden. The man is told that from now on his life will be dominated by the struggle to eke a living out of the soil, which will no longer cooperate with him. The woman is told, "Your desire shall be for your husband" (Gen. 3:16). A friend of mine once told me that the picture this passage raises in her mind is of a man running endlessly after his job and a woman running endlessly after the man in a futile circle, both depressing and comic. The curse already points to the fact that men and women have different romantic experiences, at least in a fallen world. Mary Stewart Van Leeuwen explains the results of the fall on men and women by saying that, for men, the good calling to have dominion over the earth is twisted into a desire for domination. For women, the goodness of humanity's social nature is twisted into "social enmeshment," such that women are tempted to focus on their personal relationships to the point of neglecting their calling to represent God in the world.[5] God's good design for a relationship that allows a man and a woman to see his glory reflected in each other is distorted by the fall, becoming something that no longer reflects his loving nature. Instead of being God's helping presence to one another, men and women use one another as a means toward meeting their own needs, born of desperation and insecurity. In proper romantic love, there is, paradoxically, both a heightening of the individual's value and a loss of individual distinctiveness in a union with another.[6] In the disorder that results from the fall, one partner is typically concerned primarily with individualization and the other with self-surrender, destroying the harmony God intended.

This dynamic is beautifully illustrated in Henrik Ibsen's play *A Doll's House*. Nora has done something illegal to pay for medical treatments for her husband, Torvald, and now that she is about to be detected, she hopes he will rescue her by taking the blame. Instead, Torvald tells Nora that, as much as he loves her, he cannot compromise his honor—by which

5. Mary Stewart Van Leeuwen, *Gender and Grace* (Downers Grove, IL: InterVarsity, 1990), 44–46.
6. Robert C. Solomon, *About Love* (New York: Simon & Schuster, 1988), 47.

he means his prestige at work. Nora replies that thousands of women have compromised their honor for the ones they love. There is fault on both sides. Torvald is wrong to justify his obsession with work, prestige, success, and the opinions of others by an appeal to honor. Nora is wrong to sacrifice her true honor and integrity in a deceptive way to win her man. Their flaws are complementary, not in that they offset one another but in that they feed off one another. In the end, they destroy their marriage.[7]

Romance after Eden

Despite all our attempts at equalizing the relationship between men and women, as a result of the fall, women in general are more overtly and desperately needy than men when it comes to romance and more often willing to demean and abase themselves to please a man. Lisa Sowle Cahill observes:

> It is ironically appropriate that the more passive sinner, the man, who took and ate, is now condemned to the exertion of laboring to wrest human sustenance from a resistant environment; the more active sinner, the woman, who debated with the serpent and led her husband, is condemned not only to subordination to the man, but also to helpless submission to the inexorable pain of childbirth. But what is the sum effect of the judgment? It is to condemn equally pride as active self-assertion and pride as passive complacency.[8]

Both self-assertion and complacency are forms of pride, but so is the self-absorbed self-abasement that women often fall into as a result of sin.

There is a moment in Shakespeare's *Midsummer Night's Dream* when Helena is chasing Demetrius through the forest, telling him of her love. He is baffled by her persistence, saying, "Do I entice you? . . . Or rather do I not in plainest truth / Tell you

---

7. Henrik Ibsen, *A Doll's House*, in *The Works of Henrik Ibsen*, trans. unknown (New York: Walter J. Black, 1928).

8. Lisa Sowle Cahill, *Between the Sexes* (Philadelphia: Fortress, 1985), 55.

I do not nor I cannot love you?" But Helena is not dissuaded, replying:

> And even for that do I love you the more.
> I am your spaniel, and, Demetrius,
> The more you beat me I will fawn on you.
> Use me but as your spaniel: spurn me, strike me,
> Neglect me, lose me; only give me leave,
> Unworthy as I am, to follow you.
> What worser place can I beg in your love—
> And yet a place of high respect with me—
> Than to be used as you use your dog?[9]

In response to this self-abasing speech, Demetirus says that Helena is now making him sick. Perhaps Shakespeare's first audiences would have found her speech amusing, but it makes me intensely uncomfortable. There are too many women who are in fact willing to be beaten and spurned and treated as no better than a spaniel by the men they think they love. This rings too true to be funny.

One man whom I will call Scott was pursued by a woman who went to great lengths to impress him. No matter how he ignored her, she continued to pursue him aggressively. The situation was complicated by the fact that their families were friends and vacationed together.

> We would see each other at the timeshare, starting when I was thirteen. Each time I went to the timeshare she would constantly follow me around everywhere and would not leave me alone. Her parents would give her money to buy gifts for me like a T-shirt, or soda, or food, etc., and she would do it without me even being around or asking her to do so. One time she paid for us to go parasailing together, which I was really against but figured to take her up on the offer because I would have perhaps never had the experience otherwise due to the cost of the activity. I was not romantically attracted to this girl because she was so annoying. Everything from her voice to her bodily actions and physical movements toward me annoyed me. When we were not

9. William Shakespeare, *A Midsummer Night's Dream,* in *The Complete Works,* ed. Stanley Wells and Gary Taylor (Oxford: Oxford University Press, 1988), act 2, scene 1, lines 199–210.

on vacation and at our homes the rest of the year she would call on a weekly basis or ask to talk to me if our mothers had been on the phone. I would always try to make excuses in front of my mom silently and claim that I was not around. . . . The problem was that I kept having to talk to her on occasion because she kept sending me gifts, cards, and baked goods all the time. She would bake cookies and signify them as "kisses," something that I had no intention on doing with her.

The relationship probably would have folded under the weight of Scott's indifference and rudeness, except that the parents kept things going. Instead of helping this girl learn patterns of modesty and discretion, her parents funded her extravagant gifts for the boy she wanted. Instead of helping this boy learn how to say no with honesty and kindness, his parents forced him into situations in which he was required to accept gifts and to write or phone his thanks for those gifts. His mother also sent gifts in his name to the young woman, who was sure to misunderstand such gestures and be led to hope for a romantic response.

The pursuit continued into college. Scott was a year ahead of his pursuer in school, but—not surprisingly—she opted to go to the same college he did.

At school we both lived on campus, and I really didn't ever have time to talk to her or visit with her that year as she was hoping. I know this was the case because she would call my room all the time and invite me to do various things. I would not return her calls or go out with her in any way. She got very angered by this and complained to her mom and my mom both through phone conversations and email. It was just crazy because I did not like this girl at all. . . . She was always upset at me, and basically I didn't care. She started messing around and wasting time here at school. . . . Finally she dropped out of school because she couldn't handle life at college any more and especially the "way I treated her."

This situation went on for six years before she finally stopped speaking to him. Though she never told Scott to treat her as if she were his spaniel, her self-abasement went almost that far.

If we take the Bible seriously, we must see that the extreme neediness many women experience is a direct result of sin and therefore must be resisted. All too often the church's rhetoric of self-giving love has been used to reinforce the self-abnegation and humiliation of women who are pursuing a man at any cost.

At the same time, men in general find it difficult to let go of relational freedom and independence by making deep, self-giving commitments. Paul's counter-cultural call to men to lay down their lives for their wives addresses this set of issues. You think you own your wife? Paul asks. The kind of dominion God grants you, the kind illustrated by Jesus, is this: you have the authority to die for your wife, to surrender your self-interest and make her welfare paramount (Eph. 5:25–29).

The last one hundred years have seen a dramatic shift in the way romantic relationships are conducted.[10] At the beginning of the twentieth century, romance was cultivated within the context of the home. A young man would be invited to call on a young woman, and the relationship would develop under the watchful eye of family members. This way of doing things gave women a great deal of power, for the invitation to call was issued by the woman, and the courtship took place on her territory. Early in the twentieth century, however, a new form of courtship emerged: dating. A young man would invite a young woman to go out to a public place. Since in this situation the man was the host, he was expected to pay. The role of the extended family was diminished, as was women's power. Now the initiative belonged to men instead of to women. Further, this form of courtship introduced a new economic dimension into the relationship. Although money has always been a factor in decisions to marry, dating made each social encounter into a mini exchange in which men purchased women's company.

More recently, a new courtship pattern has emerged. Dating has given way to spending time in groups. David Brooks, a journalist and a professor at Yale, writes about his observation

10. This paragraph is based on Beth Bailey, *From Front Porch to Back Seat: Courtship in Twentieth-Century America* (1988), as excerpted in Amy Kass and Leon Kass, *Wing to Wing and Oar to Oar* (Notre Dame: University of Notre Dame Press, 2000), 27–37.

of his students: "Often they will tell you they have no time for serious dating. They are more likely to go out in groups—the group has replaced the couple as the primary social unit. And then, of course, they sometimes hook up for sex."[11] One of the students I interviewed reflected this same discomfort with being paired up, saying:

> Even as I'm dating now I don't like to call it a boyfriend and girlfriend just because I don't like to put that label on it. I like to just kind of do whatever and, you know, whatever comes with that. If it's a girlfriend, boyfriend fine, you can call it that, but I'm not going to.

Allan Bloom noted the same pattern fifteen years ago:

> Students do not date anymore. . . . They live in herds or packs with no more sexual differentiation than any herds have when not in heat. Human beings can, of course, engage in sexual intercourse at any time. But today there are none of the conventions invented by civilization to take the place of heat, to guide mating, and perhaps to channel it. Nobody is sure who is to make the advances, whether there are to be a pursuer and a pursued, what the event is to mean. They have to improvise, for roles are banned, and a man pays a high price for misjudging his partner's attitude. The act takes place but it does not separate the couple from the flock, to which they immediately return as they were before, undifferentiated.[12]

A couple emerges from a group only when things are fairly serious. The group dynamic takes the place of what used to be casual dating. Therefore, when a man and a woman are finally ready to identify themselves as romantically linked, the heady enjoyment of early romance is already past. Bloom observes:

11. David Brooks, "Making It: Love and Success at America's Finest Universities," *American Standard* 8, no. 15 (December 23, 2002), http://www.weekly standard.com/Content/Public/Articles/000/000/002017ickdp.asp (accessed January 7, 2003).
12. Allan Bloom, *The Closing of the American Mind: How Higher Education Has Failed Democracy and Impoverished the Souls of Today's Students* (New York: Simon & Schuster, 1987), 123–24.

"Relationships," not love affairs, are what they have. Love suggests something wonderful, exciting, positive, and firmly seated
in the passions. A relationship is gray, amorphous, suggestive of
a project, without a given content, and tentative. You work at a
relationship, whereas love takes care of itself. In a relationship the
difficulties come first, and there is a search for common grounds.
Love presents illusions of perfection to the imagination and is
forgetful of all the natural fissures in human connection. About
relationships there is ceaseless anxious talk, the kind one cannot
help overhearing in student hangouts or restaurants frequented
by men and women who are "involved" with one another, the
kind of obsessive prattle so marvelously captured in . . . Woody
Allen films.[13]

Indeed, such "obsessive prattle" is everywhere. My father,
born in 1930, is bemused by the relationship talk on current
sitcoms and in contemporary movies. When a couple begins to
talk about their "relationship," he shakes his head, criticizing
the script for its lack of realism. "Men don't really talk like that,"
he says. But today's young men do.

Ironically, the movement toward equality for women, which
has achieved many good things, has often hurt women when it
comes to romance. In earlier days, women were protected from
their own neediness by social conventions that kept them from
displaying their desire for a man in an overt manner until they
had been courted and received a proposal of marriage. Two of
my favorite authors are Jane Austen and Anthony Trollope, and
a common feature in the novels of both is that a proper woman
does not admit to being in love—ideally, not even to herself—until
a man has declared his love for her.

Clearly, this is not the way it is supposed to be either. Eve
was created to be God's helping presence for Adam, and that
includes being a truthful presence. The restraint, self-denial,
and disguise required by the old code are a far cry from the
creational design for men and women. However, the creation
order also did not require clothing, whereas our current sinful
life does. The creation order did not require modesty, whereas
our current sinful life does. Although the old conventions of
restraint were too extreme, at least they did promote a certain

13. Ibid., 125.

emotional modesty that protected people from the self-destructive tendency to express too much feeling too soon, thereby setting themselves up for rejection and heartbreak.

Austen's novel *Sense and Sensibility* addresses this directly. One of the two heroines of the novel, Marianne, is determined to flout convention and show the world how much she loves Willoughby. She is an advocate of "sensibility" as opposed to "sense," of being guided by emotion and desire as opposed to reason. Her frank, honest, transparent adoration charms Willoughby, and for a while it seems that he loves her too. Ultimately, however, he rejects her, and her excessive sensibility leaves her helpless to deal with the rejection. She has lost her modesty and her dignity. Despair threatens her health. It is not until the end of the novel that Marianne recognizes her own shortcomings, acknowledging that she should have been more like her self-controlled sister Elinor.[14]

In the name of liberation, most Americans today—both men and women—would be in Marianne's camp. We live in a tell-all society, and we tend to assume that our romantic relationships must be founded on complete self-disclosure—not a self-disclosure taking place slowly over a lifetime, or at least over the length of a courtship, but an immediate self-disclosure that holds nothing back from the first date onward. *O, The Oprah Magazine* carried a story by Ann Marsh, a woman who engaged in a marathon search for the right man using personal ads as her tool. She claims to have "dated" one hundred men in six months, though in most cases the dates were more like job interviews, leading her to experience "personal-revelation fatigue."[15] She was unwilling to waste time on relationships that would not yield a long-term commitment, and therefore a lot of information had to be covered quickly and efficiently in the first or second meeting. Though not many women have the stamina to go through one hundred men in only six months, the attitude is common: speed up the process of getting to know one another

14. Jane Austen, *Sense and Sensibility*, vol. 1 in *The Oxford Illustrated Jane Austen* (Oxford: Oxford University Press, 1988).

15. Ann Marsh, "What I Learned from Dating 100 Men," *O, The Oprah Magazine*, February 2003, 146.

as much as possible so that no time is wasted in the hunt for the right man.

One woman tells of such a first encounter, though less structured than one of Marsh's personal-ad dates.

> I met him at church for the first time and thought he seemed pretty nice. A week or so later I saw him at [the school coffee shop], but he had no idea who I was. Of course, I said "hi" to him, and he looked at me with a blank stare, so I continued to find a seat. As he was leaving, he stopped by my table to ask where he knew me from. This was the beginning of our relationship.
>
> We must have sat there for two hours, talking in deep conversation with one another. We talked about our hurts and happiness! We talked about our first impressions of each other. For example, he thought I was kind-hearted and intensely loving, but very timid and fearful. And then I told him of my very first impression of him. Without knowing anything about him hours before, I felt I had been thrown into a pool of emotions that I know now was probably too deep for me to be in with someone I had just met.

She ended up being the rejector in this relationship, saying, "I think all of this was happening so sudden and so soon, it turned me off. Maybe, if it wouldn't have started so deeply emotional from the first moment, the relationship *might* have had a chance." Another woman's story leads to the same conclusion:

> I had given him everything I had (not physically, but definitely emotionally). I was totally empty and heartbroken by his rejection, and this affected me for a long time afterward. Even though I am really emotional and romantic, I have not given myself to any guy with that same intensity since. I was very naïve about love at that point; he taught me about rejection. I think this experience has affected even my friendships. I used to give cards, flowers, and much encouragement to my friends and people I cared about, but after that, I stopped doing these things. I was (and still am) afraid of giving myself to anyone (friendship-wise or romantically) for fear that these emotions will not be returned.

Much like Austen's character Marianne, this young woman was hurt by an excess of sensibility, but unlike Marianne, she has no model of how she ought to have conducted herself. She is drawing back from relationships because she has no idea how to be simultaneously modestly guarded and graciously welcoming.

One of the sad results of sin is that when a man and a woman both practice emotional transparency, the woman is still usually the more vulnerable because of a temptation to become enmeshed. The creation order contained equality between men and women, but we live in an unequal world. Just as we need medicine to fight diseases, so we need codes of conduct to fight our inner ailments. The old conduct codes have not been replaced in our society. We have rejected the old but have not embraced anything new.

There have been a few attempts to create a new code. The book *He's Just Not That into You*—written by two people whose authority for giving romantic advice is based on their work on the TV show *Sex and the City*—has one basic rule: a man's excuses for staying out of a relationship are just polite ways of telling a woman, "I'm just not that into you." Women should therefore adopt a zero-tolerance policy for such excuses, move on, and find someone who will appreciate how wonderful they are.[16] The possibility that a given woman might not be all that wonderful is not considered.

Another controversial contemporary effort to create such a code and to help women be less vulnerable romantically is seen in Ellen Fein and Sherrie Schneider's popular book *The Rules: Time-Tested Secrets for Capturing the Heart of Mr. Right*.[17] This book advocates that women be "honest but mysterious," restrict how available they are to the men who interest them, and conceal their own interest and desire in the early stages of a relationship. Some of the rules seem ludicrously specific and inflexible, such as "Don't accept a Saturday night date after Wednesday." Most of the rules seem manipulative. The premise that it is appropriate to hunt men in this cold-blooded way is troubling. And the authors certainly have no religious motivations for their suggestions. The rule "Don't live with a man" has nothing to do with morality and everything to do with tactics.

16. Greg Behrendt and Liz Tuccillo, *He's Just Not That into You: The No-Excuses Truth to Understanding Guys* (New York: Simon & Schuster, 2004).

17. Ellen Fein and Sherrie Schneider, *The Rules: Time-Tested Secrets for Capturing the Heart of Mr. Right* (New York: Warner Books, 1995).

However, even with all these failings, there is a dimension of this book that makes sense. If you must pursue men, at least do it with some self-restraint, some modesty, some control, and some self-respect. If you cannot believe you are a complete human being without being in a romantic relationship, at least try to pretend you believe it. If you have no interests in life apart from romance, at least feign such interests in order not to look too desperate. My hope would be that the pretense would eventually become real, even if Mr. Right never appears.

In a fallen world, emotional modesty is as important as physical modesty. Just as a modest, Christian woman would never think of stripping off her clothes in front of a man on a first date, so she should never think of unveiling her entire emotional life. A thoughtful, mature, godly Christian woman should have no need for *The Rules*; her own conscience, modesty, and wisdom are a much better guide to right behavior.

The lack of a social code for romance is often hard on men in a different way. For one thing, as Allan Bloom noted above, men are unsure of the rules, since they change from woman to woman. I remember telling a male friend that I was uncomfortable going up to the bar to order a drink and that I would appreciate it if he would do this for me. He was happy to oblige. He said he had not offered for fear of offending me by seeming to suggest that I was incapable of taking care of myself. With another woman, he may in fact have given offense. Many of the small courtesies that once eased life between men and women have become occasions for tension and uncertainty.

In addition, for men, the temptation is to put work and success first. Just as sin has resulted in the tendency for women to abase themselves in pursuit of men, so sin has resulted in the tendency for men to lose themselves in the competition of work, turning God's good call to fill the earth into a need to dominate. Men also need to practice modesty. They need to be willing to sacrifice their own ambition for the sake of those they love. Men may also experience the need to be cared for and a fear of being alone, though it may manifest itself differently in men than in women. As a pastor, I have watched many recently widowed men rush into a second marriage simply because being on their own is too terrifying. For some reason, widowed women are much less likely to do this.

Another result of the current lack of social direction when it comes to romance is that long-standing differences between men and women are being eroded, especially among young people who have not fully internalized adult gender roles. Some male students are every bit as emotionally vulnerable and needy as Marianne Dashwood. Similarly, some female students appear to be tempted toward domination in a way once seen as essentially masculine.

As my father has observed, there are men (though I suspect not as many as movies and sitcoms would lead us to believe) who have taken on the female patterns of enmeshment. Instead of resisting the temptation to dominate by becoming genuine godly helpers, they resist the temptation to dominate by giving in to neediness, becoming just as prone to romantic navel-gazing, just as willing to sacrifice dignity and self-respect in the name of romance as women have traditionally been. Such men need to practice emotional modesty in the same way that many women do: as a protection against inappropriate self-abasement. Then there are women who have taken on the traditionally masculine pattern of domination. Instead of resisting the temptation to become enmeshed by becoming genuinely independent women, made in God's image, reflecting the person of Christ to the world, they resist the temptation to become enmeshed by giving in to domination and control, becoming just as afraid of commitment, just as absorbed in personal advancement and sexual conquest as men have traditionally been. Such women need to practice self-giving love.

Love You Know Is Bad for You

One of the clearest effects of sin in human life is that we love the wrong things. We love things more than we love God. We love bad things more than we love good things. As sinful people, we are drawn to what is perverse, ugly, wrong, and unhealthy. This is just as true in romantic life as anywhere else. In the worst cases, we see how self-destructive a romantic relationship is, and even so, we stay in it. Carla Ulbrich's song "It Reminds Me of You" puts this in vivid terms:

Television's been good to me
24-hour availability
I flip the channels and fill my head
All that talk and nothing is said
It reminds me of you

Credit cards are my best friends
If I only had a nickel for every dollar I spend
But the money's gone when the bills come in
Feels like a typical fair-weather friend
It reminds me of you

Chocolate is my best bet
I'll eat as much as I can get
Have to admit it hasn't failed me yet
For a moment of pleasure and days of regret
It reminds me of you

I like the things that taste too sweet
And shine too much and look too sleek
And seem too easy and move too fast
I always find the snake in the grass
But if I can't have what's good and true
I guess I'll take the substitute
I close my eyes I take the stuff
The problem is, there's never enough.[18]

She compares her relationship with the man to whom she is singing to all her most unhealthy habits. How is it that there can be such similarities between addiction and romance? Why is it that so many of us indulge in romantic relationships that we know full well are bad for us? Here is one account:

> I felt really strongly for Josh. I was sixteen, met him through a friend, and the first night we met we talked for about four or five hours. He was very handsome and quite charming. I couldn't believe a guy as good-looking as him would like a girl like me. I'd heard questionable things about his reputation (i.e., that he was a big-time *player*!), but I chose to deny what I'd heard. I fell head-

18. Carla Ulbrich, "It Reminds Me of You," *Her Fabulous Debut* (Clemson, SC: A Major Record Label, 1999). Used by permission.

over-heels for him. We "saw each other" (his terminology—I just wanted him to be my boyfriend!) for a few weeks, then split up. We remained friends but were on and off again romantically. Six months later he told me he wanted to get back together and was crying, blah, blah, blah. He didn't really follow through on that. I decided a few months later that I was tired of the emotional roller coaster (of getting back together, then being friends, of wanting to "fix" him—he was having family troubles as well as spiritual ones), so I decided not to talk to him for three months. Three months turned into three years. It was just easier not talking to him or seeing him.

This account reveals many problems, but one of the most striking is this young woman's decision to deny the reality of all the ways in which Josh was bad for her in order to enjoy the high of romantic involvement. Ultimately, the only solution was not seeing him at all.

Mark is a man who, by the time he reached his mid-forties, had never had a healthy relationship with a woman. He had been divorced years earlier and had experienced a string of painful relationships in which he was mistreated and abandoned by women for whom he eventually came to have no respect. Finally, Mark did a little self-analysis. Looking over the list of abusive and painful relationships, he realized that all the women with whom he had been involved had similar personality traits, traits to which he was attracted but that invariably led to problems. In contrast, Mark had had many healthy friendships with women throughout his life. Those women also shared similar personality traits, traits that contributed to long-lasting friendship but had never sparked much romantic interest.

Mark decided it was time to change his destructive patterns. He decided he would date only women who fit his typical friendship model, even though his initial response to such women was not one of great romantic attraction. He saw this as a conscious decision to encourage healthy relationships and to discourage destructive ones. He hoped that if he gave attention and time to such healthy relationships, an attraction would grow. As it turned out, his hopes were justified. For the past fifteen years, Mark has been happily married to a woman he considers his best friend and with whom he is very much in love.

Many of us have a type of person who is bad for us but to whom we are attracted. This unhealthy attraction may form a repeating pattern; we get over one destructive infatuation only to fall into another similar one. Even more worrisome is the tendency to justify such unhealthy patterns using spiritual language and categories. We may convince ourselves that we are helping the other person, that we are sacrificing ourselves in appropriately Christian ways, or that we are expressing "a servant's heart."

In truth, such destructive patterns need to be broken. God designed men and women for each other in order to strengthen, not weaken, their ability to serve him. Adam and Eve were initially given to each other to speak God's word to each other and to serve as God's helping presence for each other, not to draw each other away from God. Particularly at the beginning of a romantic relationship, before any commitments have been made, it is important to ask yourself whether the relationship is healthy, whether it has the potential to strengthen you and help you flourish, whether your influence on the other person is for the good—in short, whether it is a relationship that is compatible with God's design for romantic relationships.

Relationships that prompt us to regression and disintegration are not relationships we should encourage. Relationships that are addictive, undermining our freedom and making us behave in ways that violate our values and commitments, should prompt us to seek recovery, just as we would seek recovery from any other addictive experience. Real love should bear good fruit in our lives, not destructive fruit. Real love should equip us to be the best people we can be. Sylvia was a friend of mine in college who was planning to get married. The man to whom she was engaged was not as flashy or as dramatically handsome as the men she had dated in the past, and many of her friends thought she could do better. But Sylvia said, "I am a better person when I am with him than when I am alone." I thought then, and I still think now, that no better sign can exist of an appropriate love relationship.

For a Christian, love for a non-Christian must fall into the category of love that is bad for you. Paul forbids intimate relationships in which we are "unequally yoked," as the King James Version puts it, or "mismatched with unbelievers" (2 Cor. 6:14

NRSV) because it is not possible to serve two masters. When we love someone, we open ourselves to being influenced by that person, and it is not appropriate to be vulnerable, intimate, and involved with someone whose most fundamental values and life orientation are other than our own. Mary tells the story of how she learned this lesson:

> I had always been taught that it was wrong to date non-Christians, and so I never have, but when I was younger I sometimes dated men who were Christian in name only, or maybe they really were believers, but still our values were a long way apart. I remember when I first started going out with Tom, a man I met at church, and I realized his past dating relationships had always been sexually intimate. I was surprised, but he told me that he respected my values and he wouldn't pressure me to sleep with him. I thought that was good enough, until one day I was at a meeting at church about recruiting new Sunday school teachers, and someone suggested that Tom would be a good teacher for the senior highs. My immediate reaction was, "Oh no, that would be a bad idea," because I didn't trust what he'd teach them about sexual morality. Then it suddenly dawned on me that I was dating this man and even thinking about marrying him, and yet I didn't trust him as a teacher of senior high school students! So how could I think about entrusting him with my own children? I started to imagine the kind of instruction that he'd give to our kids if we were ever to get married. I imagined him saying, "Sex outside of marriage is perfectly normal, but it would upset your mother if she knew about it, so humor her by not letting her know." I broke up with him soon after, and from then on it was never enough for me to date a man who was willing to "respect" my beliefs. He has to share them. I find that some men think this is pretty intolerant of me, especially men who think of themselves as good Christians. They think I'm being too judgmental. But I just ask myself, "Would I trust this man to raise my children?" I figure that there's no point in dating someone I wouldn't want to raise my kids.

Mary offers a good diagnostic question to use when thinking about whether you would be "unequally yoked" with someone. Would the two of you be united in the values you want to pass on to your children? Would you trust this person to raise your children alone if something were to happen to you? Even if you have no desire to have children, this is still a good question to ask when trying to figure out how compatible you really are with someone.

This does not mean you should date or marry only people who are clones of yourself. Some differences are nonessential or even enriching, such as different hobbies or tastes in food, different styles of work or ways of learning. Even if I am not crazy about baseball or Tex-Mex cuisine, I would have no objection to having my hypothetical children exposed to these things, and were I to date someone who loved these things, I might begin to appreciate them as well. Even if I find one way of organizing a home most logical, I know that when I live with other people I must adapt to other styles of organization, other ways of approaching household chores, and other ways of thinking about money. The ability to bend to others in these ways makes me a better person. Most married couples have many such differences. But there are differences that matter more, differences that are not enriching but nonnegotiable divisions. The newspaper frequently carries stories of bitter custody battles between parents whose values are incompatible and who are outraged by what their ex-partners are now teaching their children. Such couples probably married in the optimistic hope that love would conquer all their differences only to find that some differences conquer love instead.

This is not a popular way of thinking in our culture, which tends to view the unwillingness to date people with different religious beliefs as a form of bigotry. Some of the people interviewed seemed to share this view, seeing the unwillingness to date someone of a different religious tradition as a weakness on their part. One man, Ben, was even in therapy to deal with this reluctance.

> Coming from my tradition, I had it embedded in my brain that I had to find somebody that was quite compatible on a spiritual level. I remember as a kid, well, it would have been a stretch to date somebody that wasn't a member of my denomination! That was what was expected. Even as old as I am now, it still plays a part in my psyche, as much as I don't like to admit it. In fact I'm in counseling, and part of why I'm in counseling right now is to deal with stuff around romance issues, because I want to figure out exactly what some of my own issues are that may keep me from having the relationships I think that I want.

Ben then tells of dating someone whose religious background was very different from his own and who was dabbling in a variety of New Age religious practices.

> Part of me is listening and understanding; the other part of me is saying, this is weird! I don't think I could be married to somebody that is into this! Why I feel that way is because of the way I was brought up, I'm sure.

One of the problems revealed in this account is culture's assumption that making judgments based on religious commitments is intolerant and wrong, even in one's romantic life. There is also the assumption that it is more virtuous to be open to relationships than to be closed to them. Yet it is perfectly appropriate—indeed, necessary—for a Christian to rule out a romantic relationship with someone who lacks a clear Christian commitment. Ben thought such judgments needed to be corrected through therapy.

In contrast, a young woman tells about being courted by a young man she had dated briefly in the past.

> He said that he would do anything to be with me, in particular that he would change his lifestyle and start attending church. He said that I make him want to be a better person . . . and that I help him get there. Well, as flattering as that was to hear . . . it also made me want to vomit. . . . It was not even that I wasn't romantically attracted to this young man because I was and am even now, but, if I were to be with him he would bring me down spiritually. He would not feed me spiritually or challenge me spiritually, but rather do just the opposite.

She is—very wisely—running away from a love that is bad for her.

Being committed to someone in marriage also rules out loving anyone else. Any other romantic relationship is by definition a love that is bad for you, because it is a love that is at odds with one of your most fundamental commitments. Although our attractions are not usually under our immediate and direct control, it is possible to develop habits of attraction, to train ourselves to turn our attention in some directions and not in others. It is possible for married people to train themselves to reduce their attraction to people other than their spouse. At the very least, a married person is expected to resist the temptation to act on such attraction and to see such attraction as unhealthy.

Similarly, those who are not married need to train themselves to reduce their attraction to people who are already married. One woman has been very disciplined about this.

> I never let myself fall in love with an inappropriate person because they were just always off limits. . . . I just think you set limits. I've lived in several cities and have met a lot of very interesting men, single, married, unhappily married. I would say I've had *many* experiences of unhappily married men gravitating toward me, and I just don't allow it. It's not acceptable to me. It's like, "You know what? You've got some stuff going on, and I am not the answer, so either you need to work it out with your spouse, or you need to get counseling, or you need to go individually to your pastor, or anything but get involved with another woman."

She says she rarely allows herself even to develop friendships with married men, and when she does, she makes a point of being friends with the couple, not just with the man. "I always put the girlfriend or the wife first. Always. 'Cause if she doesn't like me, then I'm not acceptable in that situation." Most college students think that non-romantic friendship between men and women is normal, but as we grow older, it becomes less and less normal, requiring more and more finesse and care. This woman, who is in her forties, has mastered the art of setting appropriate boundaries and does not allow herself to be drawn into friendships with men who might then tempt her to cross those boundaries.

Love that is bad for you is also often harder to let go of and harder to recover from than a healthier sort of love. A healthy love that is not returned is painful, but at least it does not include the mix of guilt, humiliation, and shame that is part of unhealthy love. Unrequited love may be of spiritual value even though it does not result in a mutual relationship, but love that is bad for you draws you away from God rather than pointing you toward him.

In commenting on John Keats's poem "La Belle Dame Sans Merci" (The Beautiful Woman without Mercy), Ed Friedlander, a student of English literature, says:

Keats seems to be telling us about something that may have happened, or may happen someday, to you.

You discover something that you think you really like. You don't really understand it, but you're sure it's the best thing that's ever happened to you. You are thrilled. You focus on it. You give in to the beauty and richness and pleasure, and let it overwhelm you.

Then the pleasure is gone. Far more than a normal letdown, the experience has left you crippled emotionally. At least for a while, you don't talk about regretting the experience. And it remains an important part of who you feel that you are.[19]

He then compares the experience both to drug addiction and to failed romance, experiences that are radically debilitating but that people still find difficult to abandon. Similarly, Gabriel García Márquez suggests that "the symptoms of love [are] the same as those of cholera."[20] Nausea, listlessness, dry mouth, and a rapid pulse all could be signs of love—or signs of illness!

Gilbert and Sullivan's operetta *Iolanthe* concerns a kingdom of female fairies whose laws forbid them to marry mortal men. The penalty for violating this law is execution. However, all the fairies pine after mortal men throughout the musical, much to their queen's dismay. When her subjects petition to be allowed to marry mortal men, the fairy queen exclaims in frustration, "Oh, this is weakness! Subdue it!" to which one of the fairies replies, "We know it is weakness, but the weakness is so strong!"[21] For us as well, often the weakness is so strong. A pattern of unhealthy romantic attraction may be as difficult to break as any other sort of addiction, but it can be broken.

19. Ed Friedlander, "Enjoying 'La Belle Dame Sans Merci,' by John Keats," http://www.pathguy.com/lbdsm.htm (accessed January 7, 2003).

20. Gabriel García Márquez, *Love in the Time of Cholera*, trans. Edith Grossman (New York: Vintage International, 2003), 62.

21. Williams S. Gilbert, *Iolanthe or The Peer and the Peri*, http://math.boise state.edu/gas/iolanthe/libretto.txt (accessed January 7, 2003).

5

Virtuous and Nonvirtuous Romance

Like a dam which helps to turn the power of water into electricity, restraint helps to turn the power of sex into love.

Walter Trobisch, "Love Is a Feeling to Be Learned"[1]

And all of us, with unveiled faces, seeing the glory of the Lord as though reflected in a mirror, are being transformed into the same image from one degree of glory to another.

2 Corinthians 3:18

When we are caught in an unpleasant romantic tangle, we may find ourselves puzzling over what we should do. We may pray for guidance, hoping to be shown what action to take. But sometimes this is the wrong approach. Instead of thinking so much about what we ought to do, we should think more about who we ought to be. This is especially true in a situation in which there is not much to be done. You love someone who does not love you. There is not much to be done. Someone loves you whom you do not love back. There is not much to do about that either.

1. Walter Trobisch, "Love Is a Feeling to Be Learned, " in *The Complete Works of Walter Trobisch: Answers about Love, Sex, Self-Esteem, and Personal Growth* (Downers Grove, IL: InterVarsity, 1987), 128.

Instead of focusing on actions, we should focus on forming our character, on becoming a Christlike person.

Paul tells us that we should have "the mind of Christ" (1 Cor. 2:16) and that in Christ are hidden "all the treasures of wisdom and knowledge" (Col. 2:3). In the midst of the confusion of romance, we need the wisdom that is hidden in Christ. We need to see the world as he sees it, truly and accurately. We need to see things from God's viewpoint, as they really are, without self-deception and without being deceived by others. C. S. Lewis talks about this sort of wisdom and its abandonment when he says:

> For the wise men of old the cardinal problem had been how to conform the soul to reality, and the solution had been knowledge, self-discipline and virtue. For . . . applied science [which Lewis takes to be the dominant ideology of his age] the problem is how to subdue reality to [our] wishes.[2]

We see the world rightly when we pay attention to it, particularly when we pay close, loving attention to it. The sort of love that values another person for being an independent person and understands that person without reference to our own needs is a *prudent* sort of love, that is, a love based on seeing the way things really are.

When we love someone else in this way, we see that person more accurately and truly than we see most other people. The more of the world we can see that way, the more prudent we become, the more in tune with God's view of the world. Josef Pieper says that to be prudent in the Christian sense is "to allow the more deeply experienced truth of the reality of God and of the world to become the measure and standard for one's own desire and action."[3] The other virtues are built on this foundation of prudence, since without a truthful understanding of reality, we cannot act rightly, nor can we order our inner life correctly. As Mark Achtemeier says, "Real liberation," by which he means especially liberation from sin, "cannot be separated from our

2. C. S. Lewis, *The Abolition of Man* (New York: Collier Macmillan, 1962), 88.

3. Josef Pieper, *A Brief Reader on the Virtues of the Human Heart*, trans. Paul C. Duggan (San Francisco: Ignatius, 1991), 20.

apprehension of God's truth and our clinging to it with all our might."[4]

This sort of truthful wisdom is important in painful romantic interactions. It is important to acknowledge when you have been unfair to someone else, when you have made implicit promises by your actions, promises you had no intention of keeping, or when you have led someone to believe you care for him or her when in fact you have no real interest in that person. It is important to acknowledge when you have no real claim on another person, that your love does not justify taking over someone else's life or saying belittling things about a rival. The work of the Holy Spirit makes this sort of truthfulness easier.

The people interviewed for this book identified themselves as Christians. A high percentage of them were willing to take responsibility for having mishandled a romantic situation. A low percentage of them reacted to rejection with bitterness and a sense of entitlement. This was in sharp contrast to the study I was replicating, which was done at a large public university. Few of those students accepted responsibility, and many reacted to rejection with both bitterness and entitlement.[5] The difference between these two groups is a sign of the effectiveness of the Holy Spirit's work.

Many Christians think of ethical behavior in terms of obedience to a sovereign God rather than in terms of a transformed nature. The picture is more often one of doing as we are told without questioning than one of becoming people who learn to love and desire the same things God desires. In the first picture, the motivation for our actions is external—the command of God. In the second picture, the motivation is internal, for our nature has been renewed so that we share God's will and desire what he desires. Surely this should be the goal of Christian living.

Think of how good parents train their children in good behavior. When a two-year-old is sitting in a shopping cart in the grocery store checkout line and pockets candy off the temptingly

---

4. P. Mark Achtemeier, "The Upward Call of God: Submitting Our Sexuality to the Lordship of Christ," *Theology Matters* 2, no. 5 (September–October 1996): 2.

5. Roy F. Baumeister and Sara Wotman, "Unrequited Love: On Heartbreak, Anger, Guilt, Scriptlessness, and Humiliation," *Journal of Social and Clinical Psychology* 9 (1990): 165–95.

available rack, she will put it back because her parents tell her to do so. As she grows older, her parents hope she will come to share the value of honesty, that she will mature to the point at which she will not steal candy even when her parents are not present. They hope she will become not just honest out of obedience but an honest person. So too when we are transformed into the likeness of Christ. As we grow into our role as God's child, we come to share our Father's values. In speaking of this transformation, Paul says, "Thanks be to God that you, having once been slaves of sin, have become obedient from the heart to the form of teaching to which you were entrusted, and that you, having been set free from sin, have become slaves of righteousness" (Rom. 6:17–18). Becoming "obedient from the heart" so that we are "slaves of righteousness" means that we have become people whose very nature is dishonored when we sin.

God wants us to grow in grace and virtue, and through the Spirit's work, he makes such growth possible. This chapter looks at attitudes toward love that need to change if we are going to be prudent and virtuous in the way we handle romance.

"Falling Upward"

Social psychologists have found that people have a tendency to "fall upward," to be drawn to people who are more desirable—physically, economically, and socially—than themselves.[6] This is one reason why romantic love is not always mutual. The idea that there is a hierarchy in romance is not new. In Shakespeare's play *All's Well That Ends Well*, the heroine Helena (no relation to the Helena from *A Midsummer Night's Dream*) laments that she, a mere doctor's daughter, has fallen in love with an aristocrat who is far beyond her reach. "'Twere all one that I should love a bright particular star and think to wed it, he is so above me," she observes. Because of this, she knows that her enjoyment of love will always be from afar.

> In his bright radiance and collateral light
> Must I be comforted, not in his sphere.

6. Ibid., chap. 2.

> The ambition in my love thus plagues itself:
> The hind that would be mated by the lion
> Must die for love.[7]

Before the play is over, Helena does "die" for her love, but—this being Shakespeare—she recovers and finds not only that he has come to love her but also that she has been lifted into her beloved's "sphere" of life, thanks to the good offices of the king. Therefore, their marriage is now permissible.

Such a sense of hierarchy is not found only in stories from a feudal past. Our own society, so democratic in many ways, still maintains a sense of romantic hierarchy. Tal Bachman's popular song "She's So High" sounds like a paraphrase of Helena's speech. He sings, "I know where I belong, and nothing's gonna happen, 'cause she's so high, high above me; she's so lovely." This song recognizes the idealized woman as superior in terms of physical attractiveness but also in terms of wealth and class. It concludes with the question, "What could a guy like me ever really offer?"[8]

Rob Gordon, the melancholy hero of the movie *High Fidelity*, reflects that at least one of his past relationships failed because he was out of his league, pursuing a woman who was beyond him. He was always wondering what she saw in him and waiting for the day when she would leave him for someone more appropriate—which, indeed, she eventually did. "You've got to fight your weight," he observes.[9]

Research shows that men are usually drawn to women who are more physically attractive than they are, whereas women tend to aspire to men who are wealthier or better educated than they are, men who appear to be good potential providers.[10] But attraction theory also supports the idea that people typically marry someone in their own "weight class." Therefore, the trade-

---

7. William Shakespeare, *All's Well That Ends Well*, in *The Complete Works*, ed. Stanley Wells and Gary Taylor (Oxford: Oxford University Press, 1988), act 1, scene 1, lines 87–91.

8. Tal Bachman, "She's So High," *Tal Bachman* (New York: Sony Music Entertainment, 1999).

9. *High Fidelity* (Walt Disney, 2000).

10. Nancy Etcoff, *The Survival of the Prettiest: The Science of Beauty* (New York: Doubleday, 1999), 65–67.

offs look reasonable even to those outside the relationship. One popular psychology textbook puts it this way: "Each partner brings assets to the social marketplace, and the value of the respective assets creates an equitable match."[11]

How should a Christian think about this analysis? Given that falling in love is part of how God made us and therefore an experience that must be able to function in a righteous way within a God-glorifying life, we should question the physical, economic, and social hierarchies that are such a large part of romance in this world. As Christians, we are not supposed to be slaves to the hierarchies of attractiveness, status, and money that fuel the phenomenon of unrequited love. In fact, we have the highest level of obligation to those who are most marginalized. Therefore, the "falling upward" phenomenon should disturb us. What little research there is about the differences between Christians and non-Christians in how they evaluate the desirability of a potential romantic partner suggests that there is little difference when people are looking for someone to date, though there are some differences when they are looking for someone to marry.[12]

One young man told of being rejected because he was not wealthy enough.

> I think that there were many outside factors that prevented her from fully liking me. Money was one of them. She comes from a very wealthy family and attended a local high school known for its snobbishness, so she has a very messed up image of life. I on the other hand came from a more down to earth area. I didn't have the same things like a great car, boats, or any connections to ensure any lucrative future. All of the people she surrounds herself with are very wealthy and have a similar attitude about how to live. I feel that there was a social-class barrier between us, even though I come from a more highly educated background than she did.

He does not seem to disagree with the stratification involved, just with the criteria the woman who rejected him used. He thinks

---

11. David Myers, *Social Psychology* (New York: McGraw-Hill, 1999), 435.

12. NICS study cited in Karen Lee-Thorpe and Cynthia Hicks, *Why Beauty Matters* (Colorado Springs: NavPress, 1997), 69.

his family's education should be counted as more important than her family's wealth. In his account of a time when he rejected someone who liked him, he reveals that he was operating with a hierarchical understanding of romance.

> This past fall there was this girl I had met through my roommate. She was pretty cool and had a similar background to mine. We talked a lot, and then I just lost interest. This sounds really bad, but I just didn't think she was very pretty. I didn't like her hair, and I thought she was gaining too much weight. I just quit returning calls, and we've lost touch. Every now and then she still calls, and I think that I'd like to get in touch with her again because I think that I was a jerk and I've realized that I kind of liked her. Shallowness hasn't gotten me anywhere!

At least he has the grace to realize he was shallow and to feel some guilt about it.

Another student shows no such self-knowledge. In her account of her role of rejector, she tells of being pursued by a man who was "something of a social outcast, very intelligent in math and science, but completely socially inept. I didn't even consider myself to be friends with him, although if someone had asked me, I would have said that 'yes, we were friends,' just to be nice." She does not seem bothered by the fact that social status is so important to her, that she makes decisions about friendships and relationships based on whether the other person is a social outcast or socially accepted. But surely a Christian should be disturbed to find this quality in herself?

Even if we agree to be disturbed, however, it is unclear what we can do to challenge this pattern. Should we attempt to make ourselves be attracted to those who are less physically desirable than we are, those of a lower social standing, those with no earning potential? Should we attempt to observe a new "Christian maturity" hierarchy, pursuing those whose spiritual walk is more advanced than our own? I hear such language from my students, especially the female students, and I wonder how often it is simply a gloss on the old hierarchy. When a girl tells a boy that he is not spiritually mature enough for her, how often does she really mean that he does not seem very responsible or likely to hold down a good job and become a good provider? Christians who use this language are not always being completely honest with themselves. Often it seems that the real reason for the rejection is a difference in ambition, which is then packaged as a difference in spiritual maturity.

Although we may not be able to exert direct control over our romantic attractions, we can consciously ask God to reorder our heart so that we are drawn to qualities and personal attributes that please him, so that we move closer to seeing others with his eyes, seeing inner beauty or attractiveness, not just what is external. In 2 Corinthians 5:16, Paul says that Christians no longer see anyone from a human point of view. We are to share in the viewpoint of Christ.

We often say, "Beauty is in the eye of the beholder." If by that we mean that what attracts us is *subjective*, a quality of our looking rather than a quality of the object we are seeing, then this proverb is untrue, because beauty is an objective quality of the created world, flowing from the beauty of God, who created that world. Within the world, human beings are particularly beautiful because they are made in the image of God. Human beauty includes more than physical attractiveness; it also includes inner beauty, or being the person God designed us to be. Even though this is not an externally measurable quality, it is still not subjective. This is illustrated in the movie *Shallow Hal*, in which the title character, Hal, is hypnotized and receives the ability to see women as they "really" are, to see their inner beauty or inner ugliness.[13] When he sees a woman as stunningly beautiful, he is seeing something that is really in her, not a projection of his own imagination, so it is not subjective. However, not everyone can see what he sees.

There is nothing subjective about the presence of beauty in God's creation, but in real life, we cannot be hypnotized to see it, to look at the inside of the people we meet. We need training. Not everyone has a natural ability to perceive beauty, just as not everyone has a natural ear for pitch. All of us may improve our ability to recognize the beauty around us by spending time in the presence of the one who is beauty, just as we are able to improve our ability to distinguish truth from lies by spending more time in the presence of the one who is truth. In a sermon

13. *Shallow Hal* (Twentieth Century Fox, 2001).

on 1 John 4:9, Augustine said, "How shall we become lovely? By loving him who is every lovely."[14] In his famous sermon "The Weight of Glory," C. S. Lewis reminds us "that the dullest and most uninteresting person you can talk to may one day be a creature which, if you saw it now, you would be strongly tempted to worship, or else a horror and a corruption such as you now meet, if at all, only in a nightmare."[15] As our ability to see the whole, integrated person improves, we will be more accurately aware of those around us who are truly beautiful.

Because I have been using the language of beauty, and because we do not usually describe men as beautiful, it may seem as though I am talking only about how we perceive women. However, if we understand beauty in the broad sense of that which attracts or draws us, then it should be clear that the same requirement to reshape what we find attractive applies when we are considering how to evaluate male attractiveness. We must learn to see and appreciate and be drawn to qualities such as gentleness, wisdom, faithfulness, and truthfulness rather than a muscular body or a high earning potential.

Scientists have discovered that when infants three to six months old are shown pictures of faces of people they do not know, they look longer at conventionally beautiful, symmetrical faces. This is true across cultures, suggesting that we are born with some idea of the ideal face.[16] Our ability to recognize the most obvious and shallow forms of attractiveness is already present before we take our first step. But surely it would be foolish to assume that a mature adult should evaluate other people with the same level of insight shown by a three-month-old baby! Babies also show a preference for music that has no dissonance, whereas most musically sophisticated adults appreciate the dynamics of dissonance and resolution in music. We recognize that when it comes to food our palettes develop increasing sophistication as we grow older, and few adults would

14. Augustine of Hippo, *Homilies on the First Epistle of John: Homily IX,* http://www.ccel.org/fathers/NPNF1-07/augustine/1john/t132.htm (accessed November 4, 2004).

15. C. S. Lewis, "The Weight of Glory," in *The Weight of Glory and Other Addresses,* rev. ed. (New York: Collier, 1980), 18–19.

16. Study by psychologist Judith Langlois, reported in Etcoff, *Survival of the Prettiest,* 31–32.

be content to eat the foods an infant finds palatable. And yet we generally make no effort to develop our romantic "palette." It is possible to train our romantic attractions to some degree, and to that degree we are responsible for our attractions.

On the television show *Home Improvement*, Tim makes the mistake of telling his wife, Jill, that maybe she should have some breast enhancement surgery to restore a more youthful look to her body. His neighbor Wilson assures Tim that since men are "wired" to be attracted to young, fertile women, his desire for Jill to appear young and fertile is simply instinctual; Tim should not be surprised to find such a preference in himself. This makes sense to Tim, who responds by saying that if he just tells Jill it was his instincts talking, that he couldn't help himself, he will be off the hook. But that is not the lesson Wilson is trying to teach. No, Wilson says, "you have to learn to understand your instincts, and then you won't be on the hook in the first place."[17] You must become responsible for your attractions, cultivating an ability to resist your instincts when they lead you astray and maybe even developing new patterns.

The issue of "falling upward" is also relevant when it comes to non-romantic friendships with those of the opposite sex. There is a great spiritual danger to watch out for: that consciously or not we will treat people whom we consider below us or ineligible with an inappropriate flirtatiousness or friendliness out of pity, insensitivity, or convenience because it is comfortable. The boundaries we would observe with someone we consider our equal may seem unnecessary to us, but they probably do not seem unnecessary to this other person.

One man told of entering into such a friendship out of a desire to help a woman who was obviously needy.

> I think I became her friend mostly because I felt bad for her. I just wanted to be a friend that she could talk to and be able to tell things to. Unfortunately, I don't think she saw my reasoning to be good. I started noticing changes in her when she was around me, because all of a sudden conversation became strained. . . .

17. Tim Allen and Diane Ford, "What You See Is What You Get," episode 0723.23, *Home Improvement*, original air date, May 11, 1994, http://www.more power.com (accessed March 11, 2005).

Then came the immensely awkward day. I was sitting one day watching TV when she came in. I knew something really weird was going to happen because you could really just feel it coming. At that point she leaned over, tried to get way too close to me and kiss and hold me. Even though I knew this was coming it was such a scary and odd feeling because this girl just threw herself on the line and now you need to completely destroy her feelings. Anyway, I told her that I didn't have the same feelings for her and that we should stay friends (even though after that we both knew there was no way). This wasn't the right thing to say. She got very upset, started to cry and left. I felt like such a jerk for so long.

In retrospect, this young man knows that he led this woman on, and now she is hurt and he is left feeling guilty, even though his original intentions were kind, not hurtful.

When an available man and an available woman become friends, the odds are good that one will begin to think of other possibilities. If you are in such a friendship and you do not want it to become a romance, then it is your responsibility to make those boundaries clear—not necessarily by saying things explicitly (though that is the safest way to communicate such boundaries) but at least by carefully avoiding behavior that could be misconstrued as flirtatious or inviting. As another young man wrote, "It is really hard for guys and girls to be really good friends without wondering if it is going somewhere."

I have a good friend who is overweight. She is also bright, funny, talented, domestic, educated, cheerful, forthright, and a deeply committed Christian. She would make a marvelous mother and homemaker, and that is what she most desires. In the years I have known her, she has been drawn into several close friendships with men who found her company delightful and led her to believe they were romantically interested in her. I think they did this unintentionally for the most part. Because she is overweight, they simply did not consider her a romantic prospect. Thoughtful Christian men who would never intentionally lead a woman on, who would normally be careful about maintaining proper boundaries and sending clear messages, let down their guard around her because they thought her ineligibility was so obvious. But it was not obvious. Measured by all

117

the other factors in the romantic hierarchy (such as education, intelligence, spiritual maturity), not one of these men was in her league. If their patterns of attraction were less instinctual and more Christlike, they could have seen this. Even though they were not attracted to her, they should have treated her with the care and respect they would show to any other eligible Christian woman.

It is not just overweight people who face this problem. Sometimes differences in age produce this effect. A woman who went to college in her late twenties found that her male classmates, most of whom were seven or eight years younger, were happy to be her friends but thought it was self-evident that they could not date her. She did not think it was self-evident at all. Often people with a physical handicap are treated this way. Many of the people I interviewed mentioned the stress of romance with those who come from a different race or from a different ethnic background. One woman told of her frustration with men of other races who would flirt with her and appear to find her very attractive until she expressed interest, at which point they would draw back abruptly.

> These men find the idea of a dark girl attractive, exotic, etc., but when it came down to it they didn't feel comfortable in a close relationship with me. . . . I get the sense that a fellow is attracted to me, but when I show interest they avoid and grow uncomfortable and ignore me to show me that the attraction could never become a relationship. It's a disturbing thing, and I guarantee you it's been a source of major self-identity crisis. . . . I suppose I should be thankful because "the process of elimination" is sped up in cases like these. I wouldn't want to waste my time on a racist fellow. Perhaps it's too strong to call him racist. He's uncomfortable with non-white—I'll say that much.

Often one person will believe such a difference makes a serious relationship obviously impossible, whereas the other person will believe nothing of the kind. Even though you do not need a reason to say no to a relationship, you still need to treat other people with dignity and care. You may not lead other people on because you assume they are beneath you or that your incompatibility ought to be obvious to them.

We do not need to become blind to more shallow forms of attractiveness. The face of a fashion model possesses a certain level of objective beauty, thanks to its symmetry and regular features and its conformity to God's design for a human face. There is no need to deny that beauty. But if that fashion model is a shallow and godless person, the beauty will also be shallow. In contrast, someone like Mother Teresa possessed a facial beauty that may not have been obvious to every viewer. Still, to those who could see it, her beauty was much deeper and more fully a part of her than the beauty of a fashion model. She appeared lit from within, luminous and radiant. People were drawn to her and wanted to spend time with her. Hers was a beauty that emerged from within, whereas a fashion model's beauty is imposed from without.

Furthermore, a fashion model's beauty is a commodity. It can be purchased, if only you have enough money. This is the beauty of people who buy perfectly tailored and tasteful clothes, who are always clean and manicured, who have had proper dental care from birth, whose diets are nutritious and healthy, who never have to work with their hands, and who have leisure time to spend on fitness programs. Fashion magazines make clear that such beauty is an investment and may be purchased. Buy the right clothing and makeup, go to an upscale stylist, spend hours each day in the gym, submit yourself to reconstructive plastic surgery, and you too can be beautiful. If beauty is a commodity, then we as Christians need to evaluate the legitimacy of purchasing it, just as we would evaluate buying any other wildly expensive luxury item.

The experience of being physically attracted or even in love is never morally basic for a Christian. No matter how deeply in love you are, there are always more basic moral commitments. This is why a married person who falls in love with someone other than his or her spouse is not thereby justified in getting a divorce and pursuing new options. Our biological nature and emotional needs are a starting point for Christian decision making, not an end. Clearly, some parts of the "falling upward" experience are more easily controlled than others. We may find it easier to resist society's emphasis on money than more primal questions of physical attraction. But we are responsible to shape our own romantic tastes to the extent that we can.

Earlier we considered ways in which Christians may be called to resist the normal romantic patterns of the world, training ourselves to experience romantic attraction in holier ways. One remarkable student testified to such a change. In a class discussion, he talked about how, when he was first dating in early high school, he wanted to go out with the most beautiful and most popular girls he could. However, he soon found that such dates were not really much fun. He decided instead that he would try to get to know as many people at his school as he could and to pursue friendships with everyone who seemed interesting, male or female, popular or unpopular, physically attractive or plain. He found that often his friendships with interesting girls developed into dating relationships and that he came to find these young women attractive once he got to know them. By the time he finished his story, every woman in the room was looking at him with awestruck admiration.

However, such retraining is not possible by our own power. We cannot simply grit our teeth and by sheer willpower change the ways in which we experience attraction, freeing ourselves from the demands of the body. When change is beyond our ability, we must trust God to change and free us.

Love and Need

Oftentimes we confuse love with need. "I love you; I need you." We say these two things together, as if they are two sides of the same coin. When we love someone, we feel as if we cannot live without that person's presence. Love desires to be united with its object, and it is natural and right that we want to be with the one we love and that we experience that desire as a deep need. This is a need that is created by love itself. The love comes first, and the need emerges from love.

However, the process often goes the other way. We start with a need, or a set of needs, and then we convince ourselves that we love the one who seems able to meet those needs. We may need attention, or affirmation, or care. Some of us are terrified of being alone. We may have sexual needs, or emotional needs, or financial needs best met by finding someone who will love and care for us. Some of us avoid making decisions for ourselves at all costs. We want a rescuer who will take over the unpleasant duties of our life. We want someone who will be responsible for us, take care of us. Both men and women fall into this trap, although the sorts of things we fear and the ways in which we hope to be cared for may differ. As Erich Fromm puts it, "Immature love says, '*I love you because I need you.*' Mature love says, '*I need you because I love you.*'"[18]

Irving Singer makes a similar distinction between what he calls "appraisal" and "bestowal." He uses the example of different ways to value a house. A realtor appraises the value of a particular house quite objectively, considering the value of surrounding houses and what the market in that area will bear. A buyer appraises the value of that same house individually, in terms of whether it will meet his or her specific needs. Both the realtor and the buyer are *appraising* the value of the house, considering the house in terms of its "ability to satisfy prior interests—the needs, the desires, the wants, or whatever it is that motivates us toward one object and not another."[19] But imagine another buyer whose grandparents had lived in that house, someone who has memories of visiting that house as a child. Such a person has bestowed value on the house that has grown out of the relationship he or she has had with the house over many years. Such a person loves the house and values it in ways that cannot be reduced to the house's objective value.

Many of our day-to-day relationships with other people are based on appraisal. Deciding whom to hire as a lawyer, for instance, involves a process quite similar to buying a house. As Singer puts it, "We are means to each other's satisfactions, and we constantly evaluate one another on the basis of our individual interests. However subtly, we are always setting prices on other people, and on ourselves."[20] Such appraisal may be necessary for much of our life, but it is not love. Yet some people approach finding a husband or a wife in much the same spirit as they approach shopping for a house, while simultaneously expecting

18. Erich Fromm, *The Art of Loving* (New York: HarperCollins, 2000), 38.
19. Irving Singer, *Plato to Luther*, vol. 1 of *The Nature of Love*, 2nd ed. (Chicago: University of Chicago Press, 1984), 5.
20. Ibid., 6.

that when they find the right person, the one who meets all their criteria, they will experience love. They are looking for someone who will fulfill their shopping list of needs, which means that they are engaged in the work of appraisal, something fundamentally opposed to love.

> [When] we . . . bestow value in the manner of love . . . [we] then respond to another as something that cannot be reduced to *any* system of appraisal. The lover takes an interest in the beloved as a *person*, and not merely as a commodity. . . . He bestows importance upon *her* needs and *her* desires, even when they do not further the satisfaction of his own. . . . In relation to the lover, the beloved has become valuable for her own sake.[21]

Singer lists the sorts of actions that reveal a bestowing relationship rather than an appraising one, and they all involve putting the other person above ourselves, caring for the other person as an end in himself or herself rather than as a means to meet our needs. He sees the desire to have children together as a sign of a bestowing relationship in which two people want to join together in loving a third person.

> In general, every emotion or desire contributes to love once it serves as a positive response to an independent being. If a woman is *simply* a means to sexual satisfaction, a man may be said to want her, but not to love her. For his sexual desire to become a part of love, it must function as a way of responding to the character and special properties of this particular woman. Desire wants what it wants for the sake of some private gratification, whereas love demands an interest in that vague complexity we call another person. . . . Love is an attitude with no clear objective. Through it one human being affirms the significance of another, much as a painter highlights a figure by defining it in a sharpened outline. But the beloved is not a painted figure. She is not static: she is fluid, changing, indefinable—*alive*. The lover is attending to a *person*.[22]

Other relationships—such as those between children and parents or creatures and Creator—may legitimately begin with

21. Ibid., 6–7.
22. Ibid., 8.

need, but they must not end there. If we really love our parents, we will eventually value them for themselves, not just for what they give us or do for us. If we really love God, we will eventually praise him for who he is, not just for what we can get from him.[23] Ultimately, with *all* love—not just romantic love—we must see and value another person as a person, not just as one who meets our needs. We must interact with others as independent people who are ends in themselves, not means to the gratification of our needs. One woman told of her experience with a dating service. She ultimately decided it was a bad way to meet people because there was no context, because the person was being used as a means to dating. A dating relationship ought to emerge out of a relationship with a person.

One young man tells of his realization that his relationship with his girlfriend was not a loving one but was based on need.

> We had been dating for two months, and then I went on spring break away from her. On the trip there were two girls that I really got to know well and became friends with. These girls were extremely funny and fun to be around. I think that over that week I saw how much I was more like these girls and not like my girlfriend. Now I didn't cheat on her, nor did I start liking any of these girls, but I just realized that I was with her just to be with someone. Being away from her gave me a chance to look objectively at the two of us to see how different we were. . . . When I told her that I didn't think we should date because we were really different and my feelings for her were not romantic, she just cried and wouldn't talk to me.
>
> A couple days later she wrote me an email trying to counter everything I said and trying to keep our relationship going. I really saw her tendency to not let go of things as well as always try to fix things.

This man did not like being alone and was drawn into a relationship for that reason. He dared to break it off only after his attractiveness to other women had been established. The psy-

---

23. I take it this is the message of Psalm 131: We need to love God, not as a nursing child, who sees his mother as the source of food, but as a *weaned* child, who loves his mother for herself.

chologist L. Casler observes, "A person who does not have the inner resources to stand alone can usually impose himself upon someone who is equally incapacitated."[24] As this story shows, such relationships are not stable and usually end in rejection, with one or both partners being disillusioned. Such relationships are especially difficult to get over, since so much self-respect has been sacrificed to keep the relationship going.

There is a healthy way for need to function in a mutual relationship. John Ciardi beautifully sums it up in his poem "Most Like an Arch This Marriage":

> Most like an arch—an entrance which upholds
> and shores the stone-crush up the air like lace.
> Mass made idea, and idea held in place.
> A lock of time. Inside half-heaven unfolds.
>
> Most like an arch—two weaknesses that lean
> into a strength. Two fallings become firm.
> Two joined abeyances become a term
> naming the fact that teaches fact to mean.
>
> Not quite that? Not much less. World as it is,
> what's strong and separate falters. All I do
> at piling stone on stone apart from you
> is roofless around nothing. Till we kiss
>
> I am no more than upright and unset.
> It is by falling in and in we make
> the all-bearing point, for one another's sake,
> in faultless falling, raised by our own weight.[25]

Ciardi's vision is of love as a safe space where our deep neediness may be exposed and acknowledged, even though the other person cannot meet that neediness. This is a need that is recognized and

24. L. Casler, *Is Marriage Necessary?* (New York: Human Sciences Press, 1974), cited in Bernard I. Murstein, "A Taxonomy of Love," in *The Psychology of Love*, ed. Robert Sternberg and Michael L. Barnes (New Haven: Yale University Press, 1988), 15.

25. John Ciardi, "Most Like an Arch This Marriage," in *Poems of Love and Marriage* (Fayetteville: University of Arkansas Press, 1988), 17. Reprinted with permission of the University of Arkansas Press.

mutual, leading not to grasping but to radical self-giving. The need that grows out of real love is a source of humility, honesty, and finally strength.

In the case of unrequited love, the safe space of mutual commitment is not created, and it may be possible to sustain the illusion that this other person could meet all our needs. The masquerade under which need passes itself off as love sometimes goes on for a long time. It is typical of unrequited lovers to be so focused on *their* needs that they do not even notice how much pain they are causing the person for whom they claim to care. At its most extreme, this focus on need becomes manipulative and nasty. One powerful example is the protagonist of the novel (and opera) *Werther.*[26] Werther's love for a married woman destroys her marriage, even though she does her best to resist him. When, at the close of the novel, he kills himself in despair, he arranges his death in a way that will maximize the pain and guilt felt by the woman he claims to love.

On the other hand, for some people, a deep experience of unrequited love helps to break the false connection between love and the meeting of needs, since loving someone who does not love you back does not meet many of your needs for affirmation or relationship. One man put it this way: "The whole thing that unrequited love is all about is that it helps us get beyond that illusion of what we're supposed to do for someone else through romance." Unrequited love has an advantage over mutual love relationships: it does not give you anything, and so you cannot pretend that any of your needs are being met by it. It is like practicing poverty, but it is an emotional poverty. There is something you can learn through it that you cannot learn elsewhere. Even if you do not end up in a mutual love relationship, it can still have value.

In contrast to appraising someone to meet our needs, "bestowing" love is an appreciation of another person's independent reality. As Rainer Maria Rilke says, "Once the realization is accepted that even between the closest human beings infinite distances continue to exist, a wonderful living side by side can

---

26. J. W. von Goethe, *The Sorrows of Young Werther,* Harvard Classics Shelf of Fiction, vol. 15, part 1 (New York: Collier & Son, 1917), http://www.bartleby.com/315/1 (accessed January 7, 2003).

grow up, if they succeed in loving the distance between them which makes it possible for each to see the other whole and against a wide sky."[27] When we love someone, we delight in that person's existence, and we want to help that person be all that God designed him or her to be, even if that design may not have anything to do with us. That is not the same thing as seeing the other person as the fulfillment of our needs.

Romantic love becomes idolatrous when we expect a relationship to meet all our needs and longings. We are made to long for God, to be restless until we rest in God. When we expect to find satisfaction of our desires in another person, we fool ourselves. Sometimes we fool ourselves very well and for long periods of time, believing that in finding "the one" we have given meaning, purpose, and direction to our life and have solved all our problems. We are created by God to need him, and no one else can ever fill our deep sense of neediness. When we look to someone else to do this for us, we fulfill Jorge Luis Borges's cynical definition of what happens in romantic love: "To fall in love is to create a religion that has a fallible god."[28]

Loving another person in an idolatrous way is bad enough. It is even worse to idolize something as abstract and nearly unreal as the idea of being in love or the idea of being married. One woman wrote, "It is often the case that if we aren't in love with someone specifically we just feel 'in love'; i.e., sometimes I think, 'I know I like someone,' but I forget who it is that I like."

Consider a movie like *Muriel's Wedding,* in which the heroine is not really interested in being married but longs to have a big wedding.[29] Students tell me that this obsession with weddings is common among their female friends, some of whom have been maintaining wedding notebooks for years. One episode of the popular sitcom *Everybody Loves Raymond* included a flashback to the day Raymond proposed to Debra, the woman who is now his wife. Within minutes of their engagement, she had produced such a notebook, full of plans for the big day. She told him she

27. Rainer Maria Rilke, "Letters on Love," in *Rilke on Love and Other Difficulties,* trans. John J. L. Mood (New York: Norton, 1993), 28.

28. Jorge Luis Borges, cited in "Verbatim: Love and Hate," *Science and Spirit* 14, no. 2 (March/April 2003): 3.

29. *Muriel's Wedding* (Miramax, 1995).

had been keeping the notebook for years, even though she had met him only a few months earlier. "You were just the missing piece," she said.[30] Our culture's obsession with weddings is seen in the spate of television programs devoted to planning and executing the big event. This wedding cult suggests a worship of romance that is not even dignified by being centered on a particular person made in God's image. The person you marry then becomes a means to the end of having a wedding rather than being someone you see as an end in himself or herself.

If you are a Christian, you should not go looking for a spouse armed with a checklist of needs and requirements to be met, no matter how much you desire to be married. This is treating other people as objects to be evaluated and shopped for, as potential functionaries to be appraised for their ability to meet particular needs. The dynamic is similar to that of our desire for heaven. If we "love" God in hopes of getting to heaven and avoiding hell, we are seeing a relationship with God in utilitarian terms. We are using God as a means toward a selfish end. If, however, we love God and delight in him, we will come to desire heaven because it is the place where we will spend eternity with him. The difference is subtle but essential. The first path leads to narcissism and frustration. The second path leads to fullness of life.

The same difference applies to the pursuit of marriage as an end in itself rather than as a natural outcome of the love for another person. If you "love" another person in order to be married, you are treating that person as a means to an end. The other person has value only insofar as he or she meets your needs and fits your requirements. To use Singer's language, you have reduced this other person to a commodity. This is a selfish and manipulative way to approach marriage. If this is your starting point, it is unlikely that you will end up with the radical self-giving that Ciardi describes, a self-giving love that—according to Paul—reflects the love of Christ and the church. If, however, you come to love and value someone else for his or her own sake, as an independent person whose

30. Ray Romano and Philip Rosenthal, "The Wedding: Part 1," episode 9724, *Everybody Loves Raymond,* original air date, May 11, 1998, http://www.every bodylovesray.com (accessed March 11, 2005).

very independence is a source of delight and joy, then you will naturally desire to spend your life with that person. The desire for marriage, the "need" to be in the other person's presence, will grow out of the love for the other person. This is Erich Fromm's definition of mature love.

One student notes that her long-term attraction for a man who did not return her feelings grew more out of need than a genuine connection.

> I see this guy, and I think—boom—maybe he's "the one." He's funny, friendly, charming, sensitive, kind, loving, caring. Everything I would ever want in a guy. . . . This attraction stayed for at least a year, year and a half, whereas he didn't feel the same way towards me. I think this was because I was too wrapped up in wanting a boyfriend and wanting to be loved by a guy.

She continued to dwell on her attraction for him out of a need to have a man in her life. He was the closest she could manage at the time, so she hung on.

Sometimes the need that destroys love is not ours but the need of the one who claims to love us. One interviewee said:

> I felt like he lost himself. I didn't know who he was. Whatever I was into, he was into. So I could never figure him out. "Who are you?" I said that to him, and he couldn't understand that. I said, I can't figure out who you are, because I feel like you're glued to me. I feel like you've become a part of who I am. He didn't have a lot of friends, not a big friend network. He seemed to have this pattern: he gets really attached to one person. [In his last relationship] the things that they did were so totally different from my interests and the things we were doing together that I thought, well, where do *you* fit into this? It feels like you're a part of who you're with. And that just didn't feel right. That was part of why I said, I can't do this anymore.

This man's need to be accepted was so extreme that he remade himself to fit each dating relationship. If you like opera, I will like opera. If you like hiking, I will like hiking. This same dynamic is seen in the movie *Runaway Bride*, in which the lead character, who has had a string of boyfriends and has almost married most of them, has always remade her interests and tastes to fit the man she was with.[31]

In the movie *Broadcast News*, the character played by Holly Hunter worries, "I'm beginning to repel the people I want to seduce!" Albert Brooks replies, "Wouldn't this be a great world if insecurity and desperation made us more attractive, if 'needy' were a turn on?"[32] Such desperate neediness is ultimately self-defeating, since it drives people away rather than attracting them.

Cultivating Virtue

Paul tells us that as Christians we should have nothing to do with "fornication, impurity, licentiousness, idolatry, sorcery, enmities, strife, jealousy, anger, quarrels, dissensions, factions, envy, drunkenness, carousing, and things like these," for "those who do such things will not inherit the kingdom of God" (Gal. 5:19–21). An astonishing number of these vices are directly related to romantic relationships. At the head of the list are descriptions of sexual sin—sexual relations outside marriage and the indulging of sexual thoughts and lewd speech. Mark Achtemeier comments on the "puzzling association which the Bible so often makes between sexual sins and idolatry."

> As the creation falls away from God, the communion between male and female which is willed by God, including its sexual manifestations, also falls away from God's intentions for it. . . . As the human race turns from the one true God to follow after idols, so also our sexuality falls away from God's intention for it and becomes unraveled and broken in its manifestations. This is precisely the connection which Paul draws in the very important passage found in Romans 1:18–26. Paul there describes the sinful perversity of human beings whose lives have been given over to false gods.[33]

Loving another person in place of God is one form of idolatry, but so are ways in which we twist our sexual desires away from God's design.

31. *Runaway Bride* (Paramount, 1999).
32. *Broadcast News* (Twentieth Century Fox, 1987).
33. Achtemeier, "Upward Call of God," 3.

"Strife, jealousy, anger, quarrels, dissensions, factions, envy" all describe the sort of behavior that commonly occurs in the wake of romantic rejection. Anger and envy and the harsh words that come from being hurt by rejection may all seem so natural, so normal as to be excusable, but Paul treats these sins as serious barriers to communion with God.

Drunkenness is another sin that may be related to romantic troubles. Drunkenness reduces self-control, and people who have had too much to drink may find themselves doing things they would not do if they were more self-aware. One young woman writes about going camping with a group of college friends, including Steve, a young man to whom she was attracted.

> What I was thinking, knowing they were primarily going so that they could drink, I don't know. . . . I don't drink, and I didn't that night. But I let Steve, who had been drinking but wasn't "drunk," get a little too cuddly—which is not like me at all. I, thinking of course, "oh, maybe he is romantically interested in me after all," let him kiss me. When I finally decided he was going a little too far, I pushed him away. I wasn't sure what I thought at that point. Then he said, "It's nice to have someone to hold, especially a good friend like you." I knew then and there that he wasn't feeling like I was. He told me not to tell anyone about it. I didn't. Later I found out that he had gone back to all the guys and bragged about it. He never apologized or mentioned it to me again. I haven't said more than two words to him since.

This story could have had a much more painful ending. Even though this young woman was not drinking, romance combined with an event organized around drinking is a dangerous mixture. Paul writes to the church at Ephesus, "Do not get drunk with wine, for that is debauchery; but be filled with the Spirit, as you sing psalms and hymns and spiritual songs among yourselves" (Eph. 5:18–19). The lack of self-control that comes from drunkenness is contrasted with the surrender of self to the Holy Spirit's control in worship. The first is self-destruction and waste, whereas the second is what we are made for.

"By contrast, the fruit of the Spirit is love, joy, peace, patience, kindness, generosity, faithfulness, gentleness, and self-control" (Gal. 5:22). These virtues should characterize all our interactions with other people.

Whether we are rejecting someone else's romantic advances or loving someone who has rejected us, we can still show the sort of love that the Holy Spirit inspires. As discussed in the previous section, the quality that all forms of love share is the ability to value another person without reference to our own needs and desires. That ability is something the Holy Spirit gives us when we are equipped to see one another from God's perspective. In our own power, we are self-centered, and we have a tendency to interpret the world in reference to ourselves. If it rains on a day when we have planned to do something fun outdoors, we may react as if the rain purposely came to inconvenience us. If a person we desire does not desire us, we may react as if that person is intentionally trying to hurt us. But the world does not revolve around us. The actions, feelings, hopes, and aspirations of the people around us are rarely formed with us in view. The Holy Spirit helps us to stop seeing everything as related to us. It is only when we step out of the center that we are able to love others truly. Real love casts out fear, and a relationship of union with Christ gives us the joy and peace that come from his presence. A person who is fearless, joyful, and at peace will not make romantic decisions out of loneliness, desperation, or insecurity.

Patience, kindness, generosity, and gentleness are also fruits of the Spirit. In romantic interactions, this means we will not be demanding and that the spirit of entitlement will be banished. We will not give in to exasperation when someone who bores us phones or emails over and over, nor will we avoid honest confrontation just to spare our own feelings. We will consider the feelings of the other person even more than our own, tempering the harshness of what we have to say even while speaking the truth. We will be generous, not in giving extravagant presents but in being truthful, in respecting the other person enough not to raise false hopes, in placing the most generous possible construal on the other person's actions, in attributing the best possible motives even to actions that seem unkind or thoughtless. This does not mean fooling ourselves into believing that someone loves us who really does not. It means trying to understand that unrequited love in a generous way. When someone we love does not love us back, it is tempting to construct an explanation that makes the other person seem inadequate in some way. "He doesn't love me because he's emotionally stunted." "She doesn't love me because she's afraid of commitment." Such self-protective constructions are neither generous nor honest.

Faithfulness is a virtue that may be misunderstood in unrequited romantic relationships. Faithfulness requires us to be true to our promises and to keep our commitments, especially in our relationship with God. Faithfulness requires us to keep God preeminent in our life, for loving anyone more than God is not faithful to him. However, faithfulness does not require us to be unchanging in our romantic feelings. When your offer of love is rejected, faithfulness does not require you to stay in love unendingly. You do not sin if you choose to let go of a love that has been rejected.

Self-control is one of the virtues most obviously relevant to romance. Self-control requires us to control and moderate our behavior. A self-controlled person is not driven by sexual desire, does not give in to anger or bitterness, and is free from being controlled by his or her desires and wishes. Self-control allows us to set our wants aside and to care about the needs of another instead. Mark Achtemeier observes:

> G. K. Chesterton once defined hell as the place where you get what you want. The New Testament is crystal clear that simply being free to indulge our desires without regard to God's truth is not freedom but slavery—slavery to sin, slavery to our impulses. "Their God is the belly" is the way Paul puts it [Phil. 3:19]. In Romans 6:15–22 he puts the matter very starkly: You have a choice between slaveries, he says. We can either be slaves of sin, or we can find our true liberation in becoming slaves of God.[34]

When we give in to our desires without exercising self-control, we allow ourselves to be enslaved by those desires, to our out-of-control impulses, and to the sin that now dominates us.

Not all loss of self-control is a sin, and not all control of the self is a virtue. For a long time during Christian history, theologians believed that sex before the fall had been purely volitional and that the lack of self-control humans now experience in the act

34. Ibid., 2.

of intercourse is a mark of sin. Augustine's theory was that in the Garden of Eden Adam would have been able to give himself an erection, which is necessary in order to have intercourse, simply by an act of the will, without losing his self-control in any way and without having his desires aroused. Augustine thought that sinless sex would be dispassionate sex, because he believed desire that was not fully under control was sinful.

Most theologians today would disagree with this assessment, arguing that part of the joy of sexual experience is the loss of self-control, the vulnerability that comes with surrendering control in the safe context of commitment, trust, and love. However, it is certainly true that outside the safe context of commitment, trust, and love—that is, outside the context of marriage—the loss of self-control that comes with sexual desire is a problem. Because our ability to control our romantic and sexual desires is so imperfect, we must often fight our desires in order to be obedient to God.

We are not slaves to our biology or to our passions. We may and must rise above them. The New Testament often understands virtue specifically as the control of one's passions. Within the Augustinian tradition, virtue is understood as the right ordering of one's desires. A desire for a good thing may still be an inordinate desire, a desire that needs to be held in check. Just as a desire for unlimited chocolate cake does not mean it would be healthy to eat unlimited chocolate cake, so our romantic desires are not reliable indicators of godly behavior. Just as it is possible to resist the cake, so we can—and often must—resist our romantic inclinations.

Simply restraining one's desires is known as being *continent* or practicing *continence*. A continent person still has strong desires but has learned to control those desires, to hold them in check. Christians are called to the even deeper virtue of *temperance*, a state of life in which desires themselves are transformed rather than simply resisted. Temperance is marked not only by self-control but also by modesty and even by an appropriate shame. Temperance recoils from evil rather than being drawn to it. When we become genuinely temperate people, we are no longer at war with our desires; we have come to desire only what God desires for us. However, the only way to get to this state of integration, in which the inner life and the outer life

133

are in harmony, is to start with the disciplined self-control of continence. We learn to be temperate by resisting our desires until, ultimately, those desires change.

It is sad to see mainline churches backing away from this conviction. My denomination, the Presbyterian Church (USA), has made many bad statements about sexuality in recent years. In some circles, it is considered rude at best and cruel at worst to insist that temperance and self-control are virtuous. Many of my friends and colleagues seem to suffer from what I see as "married guilt"—that is, they are uncomfortable insisting that anyone live up to a standard they themselves are not meeting. Because they are married, they feel they have no right to hold unmarried people to high standards of chastity. Certainly, there is something admirable about an unwillingness to rush to judgment. There were times in the church's past when sexual sins were treated as uniquely unforgivable, and it is good to let that heritage of unbending judgment fall away. Many contemporary Christians, however, have gone beyond being forgiving to denying that there is anything to forgive.

The demeaning of self-control is connected to the assertion that human beings are nothing more than bodies, an assertion we will examine in the next chapter. If we no longer believe there is a part of ourselves that transcends the body and should control the body, at least in some circumstances, then the virtue of self-control makes little sense.

In his book *The Abolition of Man*, written in 1947, C. S. Lewis says his age is characterized by people "without chests," people who try to define themselves only as minds and passions while eliminating any reference to the central character, the heart-based self, which classical understandings of human nature suggest should unify the mind and the passions. Lewis says:

> The head rules the belly through the chest—the seat . . . of Magnanimity, of emotion organized by trained habit into stable sentiments. . . . It may even be said that it is by this middle element that man is man: for by his intellect he is mere spirit and by his appetite mere animal.[35]

35. Lewis, *Abolition of Man*, 34.

If this understanding of character was being devalued when Lewis was writing in 1947, how much more is it under attack today. Our age of tolerance and open-mindedness has tried to eliminate the function within us of discrimination and self-control, the place where emotion is "organized by trained habit into stable sentiments." This habitual training of the emotions and the inner life, such that the self finds a coherence and a purpose that allow it to control the actions of both mind and body, is what earlier ages meant by virtue.

Training your emotions in this way does not mean you will never fall in love against your will, but such training prepares you to handle the experience of falling in love when it happens. Keith Clark, a Catholic priest who has mentored many younger priests through questions about their commitment to celibacy, tells them that "falling in love is normal and natural for everyone. It's part of our emotional and physical make-up as sexual beings."[36] He finds that many of the priests with whom he works assume that once they fall in love celibacy is all over for them, that the experience of falling in love is so powerful it cannot be denied. Clark disagrees. He says that falling in love is natural, normal, and good. The experience is likely to produce heightened energy and excitement in life. But this does not mean it is an experience that must be acted upon or cultivated. If you have made other promises, it should *not* be acted upon or cultivated. Clark says that falling in love is confusing because it is "a temptation, not to something bad, but to something good and beautiful."[37] But it can be a temptation nonetheless. Virtue is training in resisting temptations.

Faith and hope are also virtues, but being a person of faith and hope does not mean you believe everything will turn out the way you want it to. It means you believe everything will turn out the way God wants it to. Most conversations about romance skip over the "whether" question—whether you should be seeking a romantic relationship—and jump to the "who" question—who is the right person for you. As already discussed, many Christians

36. Keith Clark, *An Experience of Celibacy: A Creative Reflection on Intimacy, Loneliness, Sexuality, and Commitment* (Notre Dame: Ave Maria Press, 1982), 66.
37. Ibid., 68.

take a step even further away from the "whether" question by assuming that God has one particular mate selected for them and that their task is to find the one person for whom they are destined. Someone who remains unmarried into middle age thus faces the additional worry that perhaps he or she has failed to discern God's will correctly, missing God's signals through inattention or lack of faith.

Even though the old self has not yet completely died away, the new self is in the process of coming to life, and with that new self comes the ability to reflect the image of Christ. We "are being transformed into the same image from one degree of glory to another" (2 Cor. 3:18). This is meant to be a present reality for Christians, not just a future promise. Inner transformation is a sign of God's grace. Jonathan Edwards says:

> Godliness in the heart has as direct a relation to practice as a fountain has to a stream, or as the luminous nature of the sun has to beams sent forth, or as life has to breathing, or the beating of the pulse, or any other vital act; or as a habit or principle of action has to action for it is the very nature and notion of grace, that it is a principle of holy action or practice.[38]

When grace touches our life, it naturally changes our inner nature, making us people who experience godliness within and practice holiness without. When grace is allowed to work, it will make us virtuous people.

---

38. Jonathan Edwards, *The Religious Affections* (1961; repr., Carlisle, PA: Banner of Truth, 2001), 320.

Part 2

Interactions with Culture

Lucy: Someday, Charlie Brown, you're going to meet the girl of your dreams.
Charlie Brown: Really?!
Lucy: Of course, and you're going to ask her to marry you.
Charlie Brown: How nice . . .
Lucy: Whaddya mean "nice"? She's going to turn you down and marry someone else. This is very high on my list of "things you might as well know."

Charles Schulz, *Peanuts*

I wrote to you in my letter not to associate with sexually immoral persons—not at all meaning the immoral of this world, or the greedy and robbers, or idolaters, since you would then need to go out of the world. But now I am writing to you not to associate with anyone who bears the name of brother or sister who is sexually immoral or greedy, or is an idolater, reviler, drunkard, or robber. Do not even eat with such a one.

1 Corinthians 5:9–11

6

Embodiment and Sexual Identity

True love includes awe. This is one of the great secrets of sex and marriage that our age has tragically forgotten: awe at the mystery that sex is. Science has not explained away this mystery, nor has psychology. No true mystery is ever explained away. Sex, death, love, evil, beauty, life, the soul, God—these remain forever infinite mysteries that we never exhaust and should not want to. They are like the ocean, for us to swim in, not like a glass of water for us to drink and drain dry.

Peter Kreeft, "Perfect Fear Casts Out All 'Luv'"[1]

For we know that if the earthly tent we live in is destroyed, we have a building from God, a house not made with hands, eternal in the heavens.

2 Corinthians 5:1

Romantic love is necessarily about a bodily response to another person. It is not *just* a bodily response, but we cannot understand romance unless we understand ourselves as both body and soul. The communion of like minds is a wonderful thing, but if it is unaccompanied by physical attraction, it is a sign of friendship, not romance.

One woman disclosed that, during her growing-up years, she had thought of herself as unattractive, and therefore she had

---

1. Peter Kreeft, "Perfect Fear Casts Out All 'Luv,'" http://www.peterkreeft.com/topics/fear.htm (accessed March 11, 2005).

mentally divided herself into two parts: her physical self, which was a failure, and her intellectual/mental self, which was a success. Her parents unintentionally reinforced this division in their efforts to affirm the things she was good at, assuring her that her academic successes were more valuable than other people's athletic successes, that the life of the mind was more valuable than the life of the body. She taught herself to disdain people who found their identity in physical accomplishment or attractiveness. However, she had one problem. For her, romance was exclusively connected to the physical self, the part of herself that she considered unattractive and unsuccessful. As she put it, she did not see herself as a "unified package," and therefore she did not expect men to be romantically interested in her. In recent years, she has addressed this disconnect in her life quite directly. She is teaching herself to enjoy physical activity and to appreciate her body. "I have kind of decided for various reasons to put this package together. When somebody's attracted to me, he's attracted to the whole person, including who I am physically. . . . I'm starting to feel much more complete as a person." As a result, she has been able to have several meaningful dating relationships.

Putting the package together is a challenge for many of us, especially since contemporary culture sends us confusing messages about the worth of our body. Television, movies, and magazines all bombard us with images of perfect bodies, suggesting an ideal to which almost none of us can come close. Such images suggest that our identity is reducible to our appearance, causing all sorts of trauma about body image. Most of us—both men and women—are self-conscious about our body, aware that we are being judged by how we look and sure that how we look is inadequate.

The image of an ideal body includes being sexually desirable. In fact, media presentations of beautiful bodies suggest that the whole point of having an ideal body is that you will be a magnet for the opposite sex and will then be able to indulge in lots of sexual activity, which is what gives life meaning. According to this view, we are nothing but a body. There is no soul, no spirit, no part of our nature that is not material. This view tends to support the idea that our sexual desires are constitutive of who we are. Since our body is our identity, and since sexual desire is such a strong force in our physical experience, particularly in this over-sexed culture, sexuality quickly moves to center stage in terms of understanding personal identity. This is especially seen in the homosexual movement, in which homosexual orientation is presented as constitutive of one's entire identity. Heterosexuals speak this way as well.

Paradoxically, the same popular culture that sometimes expresses the conviction that the body is all we are, at other times expresses disdain for the body as something to be used. We receive the message that sex can be casual precisely because it does not involve the deepest part of who we are. It is simply and only a natural function, akin to eating and drinking, that should not be invested with too much significance. The assumption driving this way of thinking is that our body can somehow be divorced from who we are, that physical interactions are not essential to our identity. Although this way of thinking may present itself as being positive about sex, it is actually disdainful of the body. Some philosophers advocated ideas like this already in Augustine's day. Their argument was that since the body is unredeemable and will be left behind after death, what you do with it during this life is not all that important. You might as well take some pleasure from it.

In addition, many of us are increasingly disconnected from physical association with one another. Communication technology allows us to develop relationships without ever being in the same room with other people. Some people even date online, as if the physical presence of the other person is irrelevant to a romantic relationship. Advice columnist Carolyn Hax notes, "Humans come with five senses factory-installed to help them interact with their world. How bright is it to try to mate without using any of them?"[2] Yet many people think that connecting through the ether, without any physical connection, allows them to get to know a person more deeply than if they met in person, where the physical presence would distract them from the "reality" of the other person.

As Christians, we have the resources to walk the line between these various misunderstandings of our nature, between a dis-

---

2. Carolyn Hax, *Tell Me about It: Lying, Sulking, Getting Fat . . . and 56 Other Things* Not *to Do While Looking for Love* (New York: Hyperion, 2001), 26.

dain for our body and an absolutizing of our body. Christians have always confessed that the physical world is created by God and therefore good. We also believe that our future resurrected life will be in some way embodied, so there is no Christian basis for disdaining our body or thinking that the body is an evil that we will someday transcend or leave behind. In the incarnation of Jesus, God himself took on a human body. When Jesus ascended into heaven, he retained his full human nature, including his resurrection body. Our human embodiment is something we share with Jesus Christ himself. Yet we also believe that we are not reducible to our body and that our current experience of embodiment is marked by sin and therefore inadequate to express what embodiment will someday mean for us.

Bodies and Souls

The distinction between the order of creation and the order of the new creation—a distinction discussed in chapter 3—is relevant to our experience of being embodied. Paul tells us that we will all be changed in an instant, in the twinkling of an eye, and that our current body is related to our resurrection body much as a seed is related to the plant that emerges from it (1 Cor. 15). In other words, there may be some rather sharp discontinuities. We do not know what those may be. Our only clues come from Jesus' postresurrection appearances, since Jesus is the only person to have been resurrected thus far.[3] It appears that the disciples, people who had known Jesus well for three years and had lived with him on a daily basis, nonetheless had trouble recognizing him. It appears that Jesus was able to move through doors and to appear and disappear suddenly. It also appears that Jesus was still indisputably physical, that he was able to eat and drink, that he could be touched. These are the clues we have to go on when thinking about resurrection bodies and the ways in which they may be different from bodies as we know them now.

3. Lazarus, for instance, was not resurrected; he was resuscitated and eventually died again.

What we can know is that our current body is part of God's good creation and therefore good. Our body is also included in the redemption that Jesus Christ offers, since our body will be resurrected and transformed. Salvation is not just a matter of the spirit; it is also a matter of the body. Yet our current experience of embodiment is not identical with that redeemed embodiment, when we will have what Paul calls a "spiritual body" (1 Cor. 15:44), that is, a body completely dependent on God's spirit for its power.

Our bodily life is of eternal significance. Because Christians value the body as a temple of the Holy Spirit, we cannot believe sex is a casual, impersonal activity. Scripture tells us:

> The body is meant not for fornication but for the Lord, and the Lord for the body. And God raised the Lord and will also raise us by his power. Do you not know that your bodies are members of Christ? Should I therefore take the members of Christ and make them members of a prostitute? Never! Do you not know that whoever is united to a prostitute becomes one body with her? For it is said, "The two shall be one flesh." But anyone united to the Lord becomes one spirit with him. Shun fornication! Every sin that a person commits is outside the body; but the fornicator sins against the body itself. Or do you not know that your body is a temple of the Holy Spirit within you, which you have from God, and that you are not your own? For you were bought with a price; therefore, glorify God in your body.
>
> 1 Corinthians 6:13–20

Nothing in this passage suggests that the body is unimportant; it is precisely because God values our body and claims it that we need to be careful about what we do with it.

It is not only New Testament people who believe that sex is important. Already in the Old Testament, God impressed this lesson on his people.

> The Hebrew tradition emphasized and symbolized the element of deliberateness in sexual life. . . . Human sexual life is properly itself only when it is drawn into the self's deeper identity. Thus, against those who reduce sex to the casual, the tradition says sex is *important*, and should be subjected to discipline like

anything important and consequential in human affairs. . . . The Manichaeans disciplined sexual activity in the sense that they sought to eradicate it altogether; they justified radical denial on the ground that sex is inherently *evil*. The Jew and Christian, on the other hand, justify discipline on the basis of the goodness of sexual power.[4]

William May points out that the Bible speaks of discipline in terms of what is good, not what is bad. It is because children have the potential to learn that we impose the discipline of education. It is because music is worthwhile that we discipline ourselves to study and practice it. So too it is because sexual desire is a good gift from God that we discipline ourselves to control how we express that desire. Greg Johnson makes a similar point. "Were I to throw money around unwisely, paying fifteen dollars for a cup of coffee, no one would tell me I value money too highly. But when a man gives away sexual intimacy to every woman he meets, the world assumes he really loves sex. *Wrong*. He despises sex. He's treating God's good gift like something cheap."[5]

All orthodox Christians throughout history have affirmed the goodness of God's material creation. It continues to be fashionable among theologians and amateur church historians to doubt this and to cast aspersions on the theologians of the past, asserting that the early and medieval church was so corrupted by Greek philosophy that it denied the biblical understanding of human nature as essentially embodied. But this is at best a gross oversimplification. Augustine is a frequent target, yet he deliberately attacked the heretical Manicheans, who thought that the material world and therefore the body is somehow unclean and evil. Augustine asserted that the material world is made by God and is therefore good.

Where Augustine differed from many modern Christians is in his conviction that our sinfulness has changed our experience of embodiment, such that the natural desires of our

4. William May, "Four Mischievous Theories of Sex: Demonic, Divine, Casual, and Nuisance," in *Passionate Attachments: Thinking about Love*, ed. Willard Gaylin and Ethel Person (New York: Free Press, 1988), 37.

5. Greg Johnson, *The World according to God* (Downers Grove, IL: InterVarsity, 2002), 134–35.

body (for food, for comfort, for sexual pleasure) are now out of control, dominating and enslaving us. Augustine found this to be true in his own experience, and most Christians, if they are honest, will confess that it is also true in theirs. We may differ in terms of what bodily impulse is hardest for us to control, with some of us finding it harder to control our appetite for food than our appetite for sex, but we all know from experience that our bodily desires can be disordered.

Christians have also always confessed that the material world is not absolute. God is spirit, and those who worship him must worship in spirit, something that is possible for us because we are spirit beings, even while we are also physical beings. Most often, this spiritual dimension of our existence has been called the soul, but whatever it is called, Christians believe that the material world in which we live is not all there is, that we also participate in a world of spiritual realities.

This idea is found already in the Old Testament. When Adam is created, God breathes his own life into Adam so that human beings are hybrids, animals on the one hand, the image of God on the other. Old Testament people viewed the world as charged with God's glory and believed that the hosts of heaven were constantly interacting with the world of earth. The spirit world was constantly present to and through the physical world.[6]

In the New Testament, belief in a world beyond the material is strengthened by the experience of the resurrection and the new confidence that ensues about the continuation of life even after death. Even when our body dies, something that is truly ourselves lives on. Paul writes:

> Even though our outer nature is wasting away, our inner nature is being renewed day by day. For this slight momentary affliction is preparing us for an eternal weight of glory beyond all measure, because we look not at what can be seen but at what cannot be seen; for what can be seen is temporary, but what cannot be seen is eternal. For we know that if the earthly tent we live in is destroyed, we have a building from God, a house not made with

6. Thanks to my colleague Tom Boogaart of Western Seminary for this idea.

hands, eternal in the heavens. For in this tent we groan, longing to be clothed with our heavenly dwelling.

2 Corinthians 4:16–5:2

The New Testament is full of promises that we need not fear death, because even when we die, we do not pass out of existence. That is not a Greek idea. It is a gospel idea.

Throughout Christian tradition, there have been different ways to understand the relationship between the body and the soul. Augustine believed that, although both the body and the soul are good, the soul is the real center of the self, and the body is like a house for the soul. He found support for this view in Scripture, in passages such as 2 Corinthians 4:16–5:2, quoted above. Many theologians throughout history have understood human nature in just this way, including the Protestant Reformer John Calvin.

Others, however, such as Aquinas, have seen the body and the soul as more organically connected so that the body is an essential component of who we are. Under this view, when the body and the soul are separated at death, something occurs that is radically opposed to our true nature that is set right only in the resurrection of our body and the reunion of body and soul at the last judgment. The Reformed theologian Herman Bavinck is in this camp, saying, "The nature of the union of soul and body is incomprehensible . . . ; it is not moral but substantive; it is so intimate that a single nature, a single I, is the subject of both in all their activities."[7] To emphasize the "single I" that is both soul and body, some Christians prefer not to speak of "having souls" or "having bodies." They think doing so makes it sound as though the soul is the real self and the body is an object owned by the soul; it sounds as if the soul and the body can be easily separated. Yet Christians believe that the body and the soul *will* be separated for a time at death.

A newer, third perspective claims there is no possible division between the physical life and the spiritual life, between the inner nature and the outer nature, between the body and

7. Herman Bavinck, *Gereformeerde Dogmatiek*, vol. 2, 521, cited in Gordon J. Spykman, *Reformational Theology: A New Paradigm for Doing Dogmatics* (Grand Rapids: Eerdmans, 1992), 238.

the soul. According to this view, the unity of body and soul is an *ontological* unity. In other words, humans are really just one thing. The body and the soul *cannot* be separated from each other, not even at death, meaning that our soul dies when our body dies. This creates obvious difficulty for those who believe in a life after death. In more recent decades, the commitment to this unity has grown to the point at which there are now Christians who are unwilling even to say that souls exist, who claim that we are simply bodies. Nancey Murphy, a proponent of this view, labels it "nonreductive physicalism," which she defines this way: "The person is a physical organism whose complex functioning, both in society and in relation to God, gives rise to 'higher' human capacities such as morality and spirituality."[8] She distinguishes this view from "reductive materialism," which holds that "the person is a physical organism, whose emotional, moral, and religious experiences will all ultimately be explained by the physical sciences."[9] As I understand the difference, nonreductive physicalism allows us to believe that God and society are both agents in our personal development and that such agency needs to be taken into account when explaining human behavior. According to reductive materialism, all human behavior could be explained if only we had a clear enough understanding of the human body, including the brain. Both views, however, agree in dismissing any talk of the soul, since humans are only physical beings.

Such materialism is, of course, in harmony with the thinking of the broader culture. But is it in harmony with the Bible? Those Christian thinkers who speak of a human being as an inseparable body/soul or as just a body generally claim that they are returning to a more authentically Hebrew understanding of the human person, that they are casting off the influence of centuries of Greek philosophy on Christian faith. This claim is mistaken on several counts. First, they have misunderstood Old Testament, Hebrew anthropology, exaggerating differences between it and Greek anthropology. Second, they have discounted

8. Nancey Murphy, "Human Nature: Historical, Scientific, and Religious Issues," in *Whatever Happened to the Soul?* ed. Warren Brown, Nancey Murphy, and H. Newton Malony (Minneapolis: Fortress, 1998), 25.
9. Ibid.

the clear teaching about the soul found in the New Testament, especially in the letters of Paul. In fact, this understanding of human nature requires a fairly low view of Scripture, such that things can be dismissed from the New Testament that are believed to be the result of Greek philosophical influences. Since Christians must see all the Bible as authoritative, we cannot dismiss Paul's teaching about the soul, and if the New Testament teaching on this subject differs from the Old, the New Testament must dominate our thinking. Third, these thinkers, though often well meaning and sincere believers, have themselves been influenced by a currently fashionable strain of philosophy and are in fact much farther away from a biblical understanding of the human person than was Augustine.[10] Christianity is not compatible with any form of materialism, reductive or nonreductive.[11]

What does all this have to do with our sexual behavior? A great deal. If we believe, like Augustine, that the body is a house for the soul, then whenever the soul fails to govern the body, we will know that something has gone awry. We will think that it is reasonable for us to practice physical disciplines, such as fasting and sexual abstinence, so that the body will always be held in check. If we believe, like Aquinas, that we are body/soul unities, then we may believe there are times when the body knows best—as, for instance, when we know to run from danger without having to think about it. At the same time, we will not think that our body is everything we are, and we will be able to talk about the right balance between an emphasis on the body and an emphasis on the soul. If we believe, like Nancey Murphy, that we are a body and only a body, it becomes much more natural to see our bodily desires as all good and as central to who we are as a human being.

This is exactly what has happened in much contemporary Christian thought. Already in 1975, James Olthuis affirmed,

10. I cannot trace the entire argument in this chapter, but I refer interested readers to John Cooper's excellent book *Body, Soul, and Life Everlasting: Biblical Anthropology and the Monism-Dualism Debate* (Grand Rapids: Eerdmans, 2000).

11. See Alvin Plantinga's lecture "Against Materialism," summarized at http://www.maclaurin.org.

"When we say that God created male and female, we are affirming that man is through and through a sexual being. Human sexuality is a total thing, not simply one dimension of man. Maleness and femaleness affect everything a man or woman does."[12] If this is true, how is it that the Bible promises us "there is no longer male and female; for all of you are one in Christ Jesus" (Gal. 3:28)? More recently, Letha Scanzoni noted:

> Sexuality encompasses so much more than sexual anatomy or sex-role attitudes. It has to do with our entire *being* as body-spirit creatures. It involves our self-image, our body image, our self-esteem. It has to do with—perhaps more than anything else—our capacity for relationships, our desire for connectedness, our longing to be at one with somebody, our yearning to transcend our separateness.[13]

Increasingly, the emphasis is not on maleness or femaleness but on "sexuality"—especially on sexual desire, which is now understood as central to human identity. The movement in culture at large in which people define themselves in terms of their sexual desires is now being embraced by some people within Christianity as well.

Traditionally, Christians have understood that desire is central to our identity and that an important part of being human is getting our desires properly aligned, understanding that our ultimate desire is for God. But when this broader category of desire is reduced to sexuality, our self-understanding becomes skewed. Philip Turner, in his article "Sex and the Single Life," considers the consequences of the assumption that our sexuality is fundamentally our identity.

> Assumptions like these about "sexuality" are just those that Michel Foucault says accompany modern ideas about the "self." . . . Foucault says that "sexuality" now serves the same purpose as did the word "soul" in the Middle Ages. At that time, "soul" provided its users with a way to unite the various aspects of

---

12. James H. Olthuis, *I Pledge You My Troth: A Christian View of Marriage, Family, Friendship* (San Francisco: Harper & Row, 1975), 7.

13. Letha Dawson Scanzoni, *Sexuality, Choices: Guides for Today's Woman* (Philadelphia: Westminster, 1984), 13.

human identity and, in so doing, gave it significance. It is now the function of the word "sexuality" to do the same thing. Thus "sexuality," "self," and "identity" are closely linked by present usage—sometimes to the point that the notions meld one with another. Denial of one's "sexuality" is akin to denial of "oneself" and so also one's basic "identity." It is, therefore, easy to understand why more and more people believe that it is wrong to deny a sexual relation to oneself or to anyone else simply on the basis of marital status, sexual orientation, or gender identification. To do so is tantamount to denial of one's sexuality and so oneself. A denial of the self's basic needs is in turn both harmful and an infringement of each person's right to pursue a full and whole life.[14]

This is far from a biblical picture of human nature. But given this picture, it is not surprising that so many single people—both Christian and non-Christian—believe they have no worth if they are not involved in a romantic or sexual relationship.

In questioning whether your sexuality should define who you are, I am not talking about whether your sexual orientation can be changed. That is a question well outside my expertise. My point is that even if you think your sexual orientation is a given, part of the way you were born, that is still no reason to understand your sexual desires as *the* definition of who you are. If sexuality is the essence of who we are, then there can be no defense of celibacy.

It is because of this bias toward understanding the self as identical with the body that Christians who are obedient in their sexual lives and who wait to have sexual intercourse until they marry are seen as strange and unnatural. In his book *Sex and the Single Person,* Bob DeMoss tells of being interviewed by a radio host who found his position on abstinence ridiculous. In the course of the interview, DeMoss said, "I'm thirty-six and I'm single and I'm a virgin, and I'm proud to say that. Not everybody is doing it. And that's why I feel personally assaulted when kids say they can't wait." The radio host found this claim astonishing, assuring DeMoss that if he did not do something

14. Philip Turner, "Sex and the Single Life," *Theology Matters* 2, no. 5 (September–October 1996): 9. Reprinted from *First Things* (May 1993).

soon he would explode. She continued to ridicule him for the rest of the program.[15]

Virginity is seen as a stigma by younger people as well. One man wrote of an encounter he had the summer before he started college with an extremely desirable young woman, who suggested that they experiment sexually. His response was panic.

> I was dumbfounded—flabbergasted! First at her bluntness, and then—how would I tell her I am a virgin! I had enough guts to spit it out—but then when I told her I was a virgin, rather than withdrawing she said that that even attracts her more. That night I wasn't sure if she was a girl I would want to date.

When virginity is not met with disdain, it is seen as a challenge. It should not require courage to share the fact that one is a virgin, whether at eighteen or at thirty-six. And yet in our culture it often does.

At the same time, the focus on saving oneself for marriage, or on maintaining virginity, can be used as an excuse to indulge in other sexual behavior. In the Middle Ages, when the church was most supportive of virginity and when much was written about the value of remaining a virgin for Christ, theologians emphasized that virginity was not a matter of biology but a matter of will and desire. They argued that a woman who was raped could still be considered a virgin, but someone who had intentionally experienced orgasm—whether by masturbation or by a sexual encounter that was short of intercourse—should not be considered a virgin.[16] Many today would find that a sobering definition of virginity. Rather than argue about what conditions are necessary for one to claim to be a virgin, it is more helpful to talk about purity, which focuses on inner life and challenges us to keep both our mind and our body clean. We need to recognize that those of us who are virgins and those who are not all need to work on being pure in our desires and in our choices. All of us need to confess, with Frederica Mathewes-Green:

15. Bob DeMoss, *Sex and the Single Person* (Grand Rapids: Zondervan, 1995), 22.

16. Pierre J. Payer, *The Bridling of Desire: Views of Sex in the Later Middle Ages* (Toronto: University of Toronto Press, 1993), 162–65.

A few years back I read a lengthy collection of lives of the saints, and gradually realized that they all, from the first century till mid-way through the twentieth, shared a common view of the body. Distressingly, it was a view I could barely grasp. It was as if they could see a distant mountain peak that was to me just a blur. Elements I could discern included joy and serenity, and the invigorating challenge of self-control. Homosexuality was viewed as a matter-of-fact impediment, one example among many, and not an object of special loathing. Instead, they were looking in the other direction, toward something they greatly desired: chastity, a shining object of joy. I could hear themes of the walled garden and of keeping oneself pure, even at the cost of death.

But my own garden I have not kept. Living in an oversexualized culture, I can barely comprehend purity. It is as if the borders of my garden are trampled and destroyed, and I can only walk the edges and imagine what God meant to be there, and what older brothers and sisters in the faith so readily saw and loved.[17]

Sexual impurity is so pervasive in our culture that it is like a wallpaper we no longer notice. It influences all of us, and to escape that influence would require a radical separation from the world around us.

The Christians of the past who so impressed Frederica Mathewes-Green were perfectly aware of the strength of sexual desire. They did not value chastity because they were ignorant or naïve. It is the one who resists a temptation for months and years who knows how strong that temptation is, not the one who gives in the first time he or she is tempted.[18] Bob DeMoss is in a much better position than the radio host to testify to the strength of sexual desire. Those who resist temptation, not those who give in to it, are qualified to give advice about conquering it.

Chemistry and Attraction

The most common reason that the people I interviewed gave for rejecting a romantic advance was that they were not attracted

17. Frederica Mathewes-Green, *Gender: Men, Women, Sex, and Feminism*, vol. 1, *Selected Writings* (Ben Lomond, CA: Conciliar Press, 2002), 165–66.
18. C. S. Lewis, *Mere Christianity* (New York: Macmillian, 1956), 109–10.

to the person pursuing them. One man told of a friendship relationship with a woman whose way of thinking was compatible with his.

> We really communicate well. Eventually we had a conversation about us. We both expressed our love of each other, but I wasn't attracted to her. So, I told her I wanted to be friends still. We both know if we started dating we could never go back to being friends. It wouldn't be a casual thing. So, I felt that I didn't want to "try it out." . . . I think we would be really good for each other but I don't find myself attracted to her.

Is physical attraction or its lack a legitimate factor in a Christian's decisions about dating or marriage? Most people do not even ask that question. It is simply a given. "I'm sorry; I'm not attracted to you in that way" is a standard line for rejecting romantic advances, and it *is* a standard line precisely because we are all expected to understand it. But is this reliance on physical attraction legitimate for a Christian?

Some Christians have said no. For instance, in the book *An Uncommon Correspondence,* two unmarried Christian women, both professors, both over thirty, correspond about their struggles with dating and marriage. One of the two, Ivy George, is originally from India, and in the course of the book, she decides to travel home to India and allow her family to arrange a marriage for her. They arrange for her to meet a Christian man named Abraham, and the first meeting goes very well. The two of them spend the day talking with each other, and they have a pleasant time, but Ivy George writes to her friend, "Abraham is in many ways quite acceptable (faith, intellect, social awareness, etc.); on the other hand my *heart* has not responded to him, and I am concerned about that. I am just not drawn to him."[19] Later, however, as she is traveling on the train back to her family, she has an experience that causes her to rethink her concern.

> I had a sort of mystical "visitation" experience, shall I say, wherein I was badgered with a list. A list of unconditional prerequisites

19. Ivy George and Margaret Masson, *An Uncommon Correspondence: An East-West Conversation on Friendship, Intimacy, and Love* (New York: Paulist Press, 1998), 125.

in a marriage I desired. . . . A man of faith. A man who loves the world. A man who could love me. A man I could respect. A man who could respect me. A man who was acquainted with grief (this was especially important to me for all sorts of reasons). A man who was humble, and so on. But there was one feature that had become so second nature to me that it had never been subjected to any great examination, it was just assumed—*I had to be turned on by this man.* . . .

I felt that I was being held to account by some strange Spirit, a kind and good Spirit it was. Abraham was brought back to me. Well, as I told you there was no way I could consider Abraham seriously because of the lack of "energy" between us. It was a recipe for disaster to pursue someone who did not hold your attention. Well, Margaret, I felt compelled in this time of nocturnal encounter to define "energy," "being turned on," and I was terribly unnerved as I backed into a corner unable to define it as anything other than lust. The concept of "being turned on" I knew, but the conception itself (the actuality of "chemistry," "being in love," and so on) escaped my grasp. I was humiliated and embarrassed by my cockiness and utter folly. I was unwilling for this revolution at this stage in my life. I needed no more lessons. No, no, no—not him, never. He was without flash and flamboyance. It would be a loveless life!

I was challenged back into the ring. He was a man of quiet faith, was he not? . . . Abraham had inherited all the right sympathies for a meaningful life. Has humility ever resided happily with flamboyance? He wasn't overly impressed with me; is this not what I wanted? . . . I was finding out that I was infected by the irrational bug of romance more viscerally than I had thought.[20]

If physical attraction is nothing other than lust, and if lust is a sin, then its absence should be a cause for rejoicing, not a cause for concern. Ivy George ultimately concluded that it should not be a factor, married Abraham, and is apparently now very happy. But *is* physical attraction nothing other than lust? Must a Christian discount it altogether?

Physical attraction is part of God's creational design for the reinforcement of marriage, and in a sinless world, attraction would be a pretty good guide to whether two people should marry. Has sin so distorted attraction that it is not trustworthy

20. Ibid., 130–31.

in and of itself as a guide to Christian relationships? Yes. Has sin so distorted attraction that now we should marry only in its absence? No. Chemistry between a husband and a wife is a good gift from God, but there is no switch inside us somewhere that we can flip on the day we marry in order to go from no attraction to God-honoring attraction. It seems reasonable to look for at least the beginnings of such attraction before deciding to marry.

One woman said that the "spark" includes physical attraction but is also more than that.

> There is something you see in that other person that you connect with. And to me it's not all physical. For me, it's somebody who has strength and who has ambition and has a sense of confidence about himself. That's what I'm attracted to. The physical part of it is just a part of it for me. The average person looking at a picture of the man I'm attracted to might not see that at all.

The attraction grows out of the relationship, out of the interaction of two personalities. It is not inherently shallow. In fact, it may be the result of giving careful, sustained attention to another person who would be quite unremarkable at first glance.

The Bible celebrates such chemistry, or physical attraction. The Song of Solomon revels in the sexual attraction between a man and a woman, recognizing its power and treating that power as a created good. The easy response to our culture's deeply disordered obsession with sex and sexual desire is to devalue both. This response would say that valuing or not valuing sexual desire is an all-or-nothing affair; we must either say yes to all or no to all. But God is the creator of sex and even of sexual desire. Therefore, responding to culture's disorder by devaluing this gift is not only too simple but also a distortion of the truth. The truth is, not surprisingly, much more complicated. Our task is not just to love what God loves and hate what God hates but also to love appropriately, to give our loves the proper weight, to rank our loves in the proper order. This is much harder to do than the on/off approach to right value.

We need to distinguish between different kinds of physical desire. First, there is a superficial attraction you may feel toward someone about whom you know nothing at all but who is physically good-looking. This is the sort of attraction that is simply a matter of biology. Men and women are wired to be drawn to each other, and there are certain physical characteristics that are attractive in almost every culture—particularly characteristics that indicate health, youth, and fertility. For instance, researchers in America and in England have discovered that, although different eras have different ideas about how thin or heavy a beautiful woman should be, there is a consistent ratio of waist size to hip size among women considered beautiful—the ratio most conducive to bearing a healthy baby safely.[21]

Second, there is the way in which our bodily attraction mirrors and reinforces deeper human attraction so that the physical reality of a person we care about deeply becomes precious and even desirable to us. These are different experiences, and yet sometimes it is difficult to separate them. Furthermore, both superficial attraction and "bestowal" love, in which another person's body is attractive to us because of our relationship, can be experienced in sinful or virtuous ways. The deeper attraction that grows out of a relationship is not inherently virtuous. It is only virtuous if the relationship that gives rise to the attraction is itself virtuous. If the relationship is a rebellious one, then the attraction may be something akin to addiction or obsession, even though it grows out of the relationship rather than being simply physical desire. Superficial attraction is not inherently sinful. It is only sinful if it is an occasion for lust, the process of turning another person into an object for our gratification. We can see that lust is being appealed to by advertising that does not show a full human being but only a particularly sexualized or beautiful part of a human body. When attraction can be cataloged, specified, or limited to particular parts of the body, it is lust.

These various forms of attraction may have similar physical manifestations and yet be very different, just as the feeling in the pit of your stomach may be the same when you are riding a roller coaster and when you are suffering from the flu. Yet the experiences of riding a roller coaster and having the flu are not at all the same. David Myers explains:

21. For the record, the ratio is 0.7. Reported in Nancy Etcoff, *The Survival of the Prettiest: The Science of Beauty* (New York: Doubleday, 1999), 192–94.

An emotion involves both body and mind—both arousal and how we interpret and label the arousal. Imagine yourself with pounding heart and trembling hands: Are you experiencing fear, anxiety, joy? Physiologically, one emotion is quite similar to another. You may therefore experience the arousal as joy if you are in a euphoric situation, anger if your environment is hostile, and passionate love if the situation is romantic.[22]

The most important factor in deciding whether you are experiencing lust or love is not your physical response but the mental construct through which you interpret a relationship.

Chemistry or attraction can grow out of deep Christian love and commitment. If attraction does not emerge after months of deep Christian friendship, that is a good sign that the relationship should not move on to marriage, that the level of commitment and love is not strong enough or is of the wrong sort for marriage. To some extent Ivy George experienced this sort of chemistry. After several months of long-distance letter writing and phone conversations, she found that she was experiencing a growing affection for Abraham and that she would miss him if he were to drop out of her life. That attraction is not always a reliable guide of compatibility early in a relationship, but it may be a useful guide later in a relationship.

Sometimes it does not take months. Someone who was very attractive to you when you first met may become quite the opposite once you get to know him or her better. In the movie *Tin Cup*, the heroine loses her attraction for the man she has been dating once she discovers that the people who have told her "he hates old people, he hates children, and he hates dogs" are right. His lack of virtue makes him unattractive in her eyes.[23]

Cultural Conditioning

Although part of attraction is biological, another part is culturally conditioned. Therefore, what one culture considers adornment would be considered mutilation in another. The part of

22. David Myers, *Social Psychology* (New York: McGraw-Hill, 1999), 454.
23. *Tin Cup* (Warner Studios, 1996).

attractiveness that is connected to adornment, clothing, and the presentation of the self is much harder to pin down scientifically than simple biological attraction and is also much more socially conditioned. One question this raises is the extent to which people communicate true and valuable information about themselves through the ways they choose to dress and decorate their bodies. Is it legitimate to reach conclusions about people based on how they present themselves via things that are, after all, under their control?

Our culture also creates expectations of what is normal when it comes to romantic interaction. Most people who watch movies and television end up watching a lot of sexual behavior. If sitcoms are to be believed, *not* sleeping together by the second date is abnormal behavior. Young people raised on sitcoms are apt to believe this picture of what is normal unless they are presented with an alternative picture that is equally compelling.

Marva Dawn sounds a familiar refrain when she bemoans "the overtness of genital sexuality in our milieu."

> Because our society has lost the meaning of mystery and sexuality, . . . sexual expression has to become more and more explicit to excite. Human nature requires a continuous escalation of stimulation, especially if the scintillation itself is the only meaning that remains.
>
> We see, hear, and feel the effects of this escalating explicitness everywhere—outrageously graphic promotion of sexual violence in rock music and rap, sexy models advertising all kinds of products, jokes about the local prostitution associated with military bases, condom distribution in schools, television sitcoms with many young characters asking for birth control, sleeping together, or pregnant. Overtness about genital sexuality even invades the political sphere. . . . When our senses are so bombarded by explicit sexual behavior, when our social milieu is so saturated with sexual innuendoes, we must be driven to urgent questions about this loss of meaning.[24]

It is interesting that Dawn concludes that overtness has undermined the mystery of sex. Rather than making sex more

24. Marva Dawn, *Sexual Character: Beyond Technique to Intimacy* (Grand Rapids: Eerdmans, 1993), 4–5.

important, this overtness in some ways belittles and trivializes sexual experience.

Lawrence Stone argues that society's obsession with sex makes it difficult to distinguish between love and lust.

> Today, the role of passionate attachments between adults in our society is obscured by a new development, the saturation of the whole culture—through every medium of communication—with sexuality as the predominant and overriding human drive, a doctrine whose theoretical foundations were provided by Freud. In no past society known to me has sex been given so prominent a role in the culture at large, nor has sexual fulfillment been elevated to such preeminence in the list of human aspirations—in a vain attempt to relieve civilization of its discontents. If Thomas Jefferson today was asked to rewrite the Declaration of Independence he would certainly have to add total sexual fulfillment to "Life, Liberty and Human Happiness" as one of the basic natural rights of every member of society. . . . We find it scarcely credible today that in most of Western Europe in the seventeenth century, in a society whose marriage age was postponed into the late twenties, a degree of chastity was practiced that kept the illegitimacy rate—without contraceptives—as low as 2 or 3 percent. . . . Under these conditions, it seems to me almost impossible today to distinguish passionate attachment in the psychological sense—meaning love—from passionate attachment in the physical sense—meaning lust.[25]

Our obsession with sexuality is what makes chastity seem so impossible, but history tells us that it is perfectly possible, that billions of normal human beings have found it quite possible to live without sexual intercourse for years at a time, or sometimes even for a lifetime.

This continues to be true. In *The New Celibacy*, Gabrielle Brown points out that most people are celibate for most of their lives without undue hardship.[26] Many married people are going without sex too, thanks to sickness or busyness, travel or estrangement. But because of the messages we see in the media

25. Lawrence Stone, "Passionate Attachments in the West in Historical Perspective," in *Passionate Attachments*, 19.

26. Gabrielle Brown, *The New Celibacy* (New York: McGraw-Hill, 1980), chap. 1.

all the time, this no longer seems normal. Elizabeth Abbott, author of *A History of Celibacy*, came to have a new appreciation for abstinence while researching her book.

> Celibacy has become the "problem." Now, the fear of *not* having sex is a driving force in all our lives. Young teenagers write to advice columnists, "I'm not having sex. What's wrong with me?" while grownups take pills, go to therapists, attend classes, read books and spend billions of dollars a year, in an effort to amplify their sexual lives and prevent the merest possibility of going a week without having sex.
>
> But amid all the clamor, we've forgotten that a person does not have to feel diminished in abstaining from sex, that having an active sex life is not integral to being a healthy, sane, well-rounded person. When I began discussing my decision to become celibate with my friends, I was surprised at how few scoffed; some burst out with confidences about their own celibacy or their interest in it. In our resolutely sex-obsessed society, a quiescent but important segment of people prefer abstinence.[27]

Abbott's decision to embrace her celibacy was not religiously motivated. Rather, she decided, "If you simply accepted your celibacy, you would be so much more in *control*." It was a way for her to find contentment with her life rather than constantly pining for some other life. She concluded that "life . . . can be a richer place when some lusts are left unrequited."

The overtness of sexuality undermines the protection of innocence. It is difficult to be overcome by desire for something you have never experienced, but in our current culture, most people have a high level of virtual sexual experience even before they have an actual sexual experience, meaning that desire is stirred up prematurely. I am not speaking only about pornography but about popular block-buster movies, most of which have at least one sex scene that leaves little to the imagination. The recurring refrain of the Song of Solomon is a warning against such premature awakening of desire: "Do not stir up or awaken love until it is ready" (Song of Sol. 2:7; 3:5; 8:4).

27. Elizabeth Abbott, "Time Alone," http://www.nerve.com/personalessays/abbott/timealone (accessed August 7, 2000).

As I have grown older, I have become more selective about the sorts of movies I go to, precisely because I do not wish to have highly sexualized language playing in my mind and I do not wish to have highly sexualized images embedded in my brain. Many of the students I work with assure me of their ability to practice Christian "discernment" when they go to the movies or watch television, and they are confident that they are not being influenced by what they see. In fact, they see it as a sign of spiritual maturity that they can go to such movies without being influenced, telling me that whereas some people, such as their younger brothers and sisters, might not yet be spiritually mature enough to handle this, they themselves are. I beg to differ. I never regret having failed to see a movie, but there are many movies I have seen that I wish I could unsee, because those images are now forever a part of me. As I grow spiritually, I become more sensitive to what I am watching and more easily offended by it, not less, because I am more likely to wonder whether God would be pleased with me for viewing what I am viewing.

Here is a radical idea. A Christian who has never been married should not be able to imagine the act of sex with any clarity. What we cannot even imagine, we cannot desire deeply, and our imagination should be pure, just as our body should be pure. However, once you have watched sexual intercourse happen on the screen, it is not difficult to let your imagination run wild. Desire is stirred up and awakened before it should be. Monastic communities speak of the discipline of keeping "custody of the eyes," controlling what you allow yourself to see. This is an idea that is directly applicable to contemporary Christians living in the midst of a highly sexualized culture. Do not preserve just your body until marriage; preserve your mind and your imagination too.

7

Romance and Imagination

I've never met you, yet never doubt, dear;
I can't forget you. I've thought you out, dear.
I know your profile, and I know the way you kiss,
just the thing I miss on a night like this.
If dreams are made of imagination,
I'm not afraid of my own creation.

Lorenz Hart, "Isn't It Romantic?"

From now on, therefore, we regard no one from a human point
of view.

2 Corinthians 5:16

Culture conditions our expectations for romance and how we
interpret our experiences. At the beginning of the movie *High
Fidelity*, Rob muses about the interrelationship of romance and
culture:

What came first? The music or the misery? People worry about
kids playing with guns and watching violent videos; we're scared
that some sort of culture of violence is taking them over. . . .
But nobody worries about kids listening to thousands—literally
thousands—of songs about broken hearts and rejection and
pain and misery and loss. Did I listen to pop music because

I was miserable, or was I miserable because I listened to pop music?[1]

It is difficult to overemphasize the influence culture has on our patterns of attraction. We are encouraged—especially by popular music, which creates an expectation of romance in those who listen to it—to fixate on the unknown but ideal "someone." Love songs create the impression that something impossible is in fact normal, setting the listener up for disappointment. Popular music tells us the way romantic life is "supposed" to be, fueling an image of ideal love.

From the time we are small, we read stories about princes rescuing princesses who then live happily together in marriage. We are exposed to the music of popular culture—music that is almost exclusively concerned with questions of romance. We see movies in which people separated by class, nationality, education, and religion transcend these barriers because of their love for one another and go on to live happily ever after. Little girls are especially vulnerable, from the time they receive their first Barbie doll and start asking for a matching Ken.

Many of us chart our own experiences in the light of music, movies, or stories. One woman noted:

> When I was 5, 6, 7 years of age, I started to hear pop music. I can't say that I was aware of a lot of sexual stuff there, but I got the idea that there is a lot of goo-goo-ga-ga—you know, romance, fireworks—around men and women. And so I thought, "That's going to happen someday."

Another young woman told of the "break-up tape" her roommate made for her after a particularly painful romantic experience. Music is especially powerful in that it can offer a soundtrack for one's life. One man talked about how he would work out his grief over a failed romance while driving, listening to emotional love songs and singing along.

> All of a sudden I realized . . . that I'd stopped playing those tapes. I'd moved beyond that, and I didn't need to throw that tape in

---

1. *High Fidelity* (Walt Disney, 2000).

the tape player as soon as I got in the car and listen, over and over again, to that woman singing those songs. I'd probably not been doing that for a month or more when I suddenly realized I wasn't doing it, and there was this epiphany that I had taken a step forward and moved on.

Sometimes music is used not as a tool for moving on but rather as a tool for remaining in the pathos of the painful experience, for reliving the rejection, for keeping alive a fantasy that should have been allowed to die. One woman told of the pain she experienced during her senior year in high school when the boy she was in love with began to date her best friend. She listened to a particular CD over and over, and now, she says, "I really can't listen to it without feeling like it's the spring of graduation year."

Television and movies play an increasingly large role in our understandings of the world, including our understandings of romance. When asked about the origin of their romantic ideas, many of the people I interviewed talked about television and movies in addition to books and music. In retrospect, many people questioned whether this influence was a good one.

> I think some of my romance ideas—distorted ones—came out of the media, like television and fairy tales and that kind of stuff. . . . I think that television presented romance as interesting while you're dating, but then if you get married it's not as interesting, because there's not this tension about where this is going to go, or if this is going to go anywhere. *Friends* does that too, I think. People are interested in romance, but if you're married, then it's boring, or the romance part of it is not as interesting, because there aren't these questions, and people aren't in a state of angst about how this is going.

This same person remembers that one movie in particular had a large influence.

> I remember there was this TV movie that was on every year that I thought was just the most romantic thing: Rogers and Hammerstein's version of Cinderella. . . . I can sing along with those stupid songs yet. We used to play Cinderella. We would play Cinderella in the basement and sing these songs.

My niece, now six years old, knows all those same Cinderella songs, although she knows them from the newer production of the musical featuring Brandy as Cinderella. The newer production has some multiculturalism absent in the older version, but the dream of a handsome prince is still there, love at first sight is still possible. The prince still sings, "Do I love you because you're beautiful, or are you beautiful because I love you?" Both versions of the movie suggest that beauty is the right reason to love someone and that if someone has become beautiful to you only because you love that person, then you should distrust your love. This children's movie teaches a preference for appraisal love over bestowal love. It teaches children that they should look out for their own needs when they get ready to love someone.[2]

One woman observed that she could tell that certain things in popular culture were bad influences because they left her feeling sad and dissatisfied. She was especially struck by the shallowness of the magazines targeted at teenage girls.

> I stopped reading them because I knew they made me sad. They made me think about my looks and clothes, feeling like all those things were important to have, and I knew that was wrong. I'm so glad that I grew up in the family that I did with—not censorship or anything like that—but *monitoring* and being accountable to my parents.

Like many students, this young woman found that her family's influence could outweigh culture to some extent. Her parents communicated to her a need to be different from the surrounding culture, to value different things, and to evaluate herself on different terms. This gave her a sense of security, even when she did not have a boyfriend.

Falling in Love with an Illusion

Much of unrequited love is not really love at all. It is a crush based not on knowledge but on illusion and imagination. We

2. *Cinderella* (Columbia/TriStar, 1965); and *Cinderella* (Wide World of Disney, 1997).

do not love a real person; we love the imaginary person we have created. Perhaps this imaginary person has been given the face and mannerisms of a real person we have seen from afar, but the person we love is the person we have invented.

Sometimes we do this on purpose. We are in love with the idea of love, and in the absence of a real lover, we create an ideal for whom to long. Remember the character Marian, the librarian, in the musical *The Music Man*? She sang her good-nights to "her someone," the person she had not yet met but the one she was sure was destined for her. In a similar way, it is common for Christian young people to pray for their not-yet-known future mate, confident that God already knows that person's identity.

Sometimes people are less aware of what they are doing. Greg had been dating the same woman for several years. He knew she was wonderful, but he was always unwilling to make a commitment to her. Somehow things did not seem quite right. The woman said she knew why. "All his life," she explained, "he's had an image in his mind of the woman he would marry some day. I don't look like that image." An unreal image was separating Greg from a valuable and real love with a remarkable woman. It was not until he was able to let go of the image that he was able to embrace what was real, love the woman who was right in front of him, and build a life with her.

The imaginary loved one may not always be someone we have invented. We may build an imaginary relationship around a real person we have never met or know only from afar. Adolescents often develop infatuations with movie stars or musicians they idolize but do not really know. Some truly unhealthy people carry such infatuations with them into adulthood. Think of the mature woman for whom Elvis or 007 remains the ideal of manhood. Clearly, such a woman has no actual knowledge of Elvis Presley or Sean Connery,[3] and her fantasy about her idealized and unreal hero may well be a barrier to a healthy relationship with a real person. We may also become obsessed with a coworker we watch from afar or a student who sits across the aisle from us in a class.

3. Or the other 007s since Sean Connery's time.

One woman admitted to having this sort of crush on a young man she knew in high school. "I made him out to be somebody that I really wanted, this person who was in my head." He was a quiet, reserved boy, which allowed her to imagine him as anything she wanted him to be. "I kind of made my own formula," she said, "made this person in my head. I just loved this idea, this dream I made. I thought about him a lot. It became a distraction."

If you have ever been on the receiving end of such love, you know how disturbing it can be. I remember getting a letter from a fellow student when I was in graduate school. This man was someone I had nodded at in the hallway a few times, but we had never had a conversation. Yet he wrote me a note telling me that it was his firm conviction that God meant for us to be together, that he had been led to that school at that time in order to meet and marry me. I was horrified and at a loss as to how to respond. Everything he saw and thought he knew about me existed only in his imagination, a place to which I had no access.

In *Star Trek: The Next Generation,* the ship's engineer, Geordi LaForge, has such an imaginative relationship. In the course of trying to solve an engineering problem, he creates a holodeck program that includes Dr. Leah Brahms, the woman who designed the engine he is trying to fix. The computer generates this woman's character based on her personnel file. The basic data about her height, appearance, and voice are accurate, but the personality she is given is not. Geordi falls in love with this holodeck image. Later, he meets the real Dr. Brahms, who does not conform to any of his imagined assumptions about what she would be like. He has fallen in love with someone who does not exist, and until he can let go of that imaginary woman, he cannot become friends with the real woman.[4]

One young woman tells of being pursued by a man she had met while on spring break. They spent a great deal of time together during this fun week, but she was not attracted to him and did not see anything serious in their relationship.

---

4. The holodeck encounter with Dr. Brahms is in "Booby Trap," season 3, episode 6, air date October 30, 1989. The real encounter with Dr. Brahms is in "Galaxy's Child," season 4, episode 16, air date March 11, 1991.

Then the letters started coming, and these made everything clear to me. The first one he wrote was right after he got home from Spring Break, and it told me how much he missed me, and that he was going into withdrawal from not seeing me. He said he almost cried when leaving on that last night. I could not believe this. I really did not expect to read this all—much less from a guy I knew for a week. He continued to tell me in that letter that he had very strong feelings for me, and he had never felt this way toward anyone before. He said he always thought about me and wanted to see me again. I really didn't know what to do at this point, because I did not have any of these feelings. It was especially difficult because he wanted to know how I felt about him. The way I felt about him? Well, I thought he was a nice guy and I enjoyed having him as a friend, but I did not feel any romantic attraction toward him. He was not my type. I was not attracted to him physically, and I knew we differed a ton concerning our beliefs. He was not a devout Christian. Though I can't remember the details of my answer, I was honest with him. I think he was hurt by it, but we continued our correspondence. I don't believe I ever led him on to believe that I was attracted to him and wanted something more than a friendship. I think he just read into my signals a whole lot more than I ever intended.

She did not know how to respond because he seemed to be acting out of an experience utterly unlike her own. In the future, she will probably be more guarded when interacting with unattached men she does not want to attract. But even if she had been guarded, he still might have behaved in the same way. Imaginary love can feed on very little.

Often we do not recognize that we are loving an imaginary person. We think we really love someone when in fact we do not know that person at all. In our entertainment culture, it is particularly easy to spend time with someone without having conversations of any depth. If dates consist of sitting next to each other while watching a movie or going to a club where the music is too loud for conversation, a couple may go out for a long time without discovering anything about each others' faith, values, convictions, or commitments. This is doubly true when couples rush into a sexual relationship soon after they begin to date. The excitement of physical attraction fills the times they spend alone, making meaningful conversation unnecessary. Then a decision needs to be made or a crisis arises in one of their lives, and each person is startled to discover a dissonance between their commitments or presuppositions.

Even in a society that encourages conversation and discourages physical intimacy before marriage, this lack of knowledge is possible. In Jane Austen's novel *Mansfield Park*, Edmund, the hero of the novel, wastes most of the story being infatuated with Mary Crawford, a vulgar and shallow woman whose true nature is veiled by a façade of sophistication and charm. They spend countless evenings together making polite conversation, playing cards, and enjoying music. Yet they do not come to know each other until, near the end of the novel, Mary's brother has an adulterous affair with Edmund's sister, bringing disgrace on both families. Mary's morally insensitive reaction to this crisis allows Edmund to see her true self. The scales fall from his eyes, and he exclaims that he has been in love with "a creature of my own imagination, not Miss Crawford."[5]

Sometimes when we think we are experiencing unrequited love, we are in fact experiencing infatuation with an imaginary person. The solution is not convincing this other person to love you but rather realizing that you are not in love yourself. One test to determine the difference is to check your responses to unexpected revelations about this person. Do such revelations produce delight or dismay? Love is based on knowledge. Infatuation is based on ignorance. When we are infatuated with someone, that infatuation is fed by fantasy and is based on little or no true knowledge of the other person. In fact, reality will interfere with infatuation. When we are infatuated, we expect the other person to speak according to the script we have devised in our mind, and when the other person does not follow our preconceptions, we are struck by the dissonance.

It is possible to treat people we know quite well in this same way. Whenever we meet someone for the first time, we are obliged to fill in the gaps in our knowledge with assumptions about this person. We start with assumptions, and then we correct those assumptions as we go along, as our knowledge deepens. "Oh," we say, "you grew up in the same town I did. You must be . . ."

5. Jane Austen, *Mansfield Park*, vol. 3 in *The Oxford Illustrated Jane Austen*, 3rd ed. (Oxford: Oxford University Press, 1966), 458.

and then we fill in the blanks with assumptions. Many of those assumptions will be correct. Many of them will not be correct. Getting acquainted with another person is a long process in which simplistic preconceptions are challenged and a more complex picture emerges. However, if we are strongly attracted to someone early in this process, we may become infatuated with that person based on preconceptions that are largely inaccurate. It is possible to avoid real knowledge for a long time, especially if our interaction with the other person is superficial. It is possible to spend months or even years assuming that a person with whom we have regular but casual interaction shares our political convictions, our moral presuppositions, or our religious heritage.

Fantasy versus Reality

If you are infatuated with a person in this way and then have an opportunity for genuine knowledge, the experience will be disappointing. The other person's stubborn reality will not conform to the ideal fantasy created by your imagination, and the result will be a sense of having been cheated or duped. However, if you really love another person, that surprising reality is wonderful. The real person outstrips your dreams, hopes, and imaginings. One woman tells of just such an experience, of having her illusions shattered in a positive way in the midst of an experience of unrequited attraction.

> Every time I'm with him, who he is just blows me away. Who he is in my mind, I hate that person. But who he is really is just this nice, fun, interesting person that I feel comfortable with, who would never assume that anyone liked him this much. Who he really is, is great, and I love that. . . . So reality is definitely better, and it's definitely always just crashing every idea I have of him. I try to convince myself that he's a bad person, because then I'll feel better about him not liking me back, but then, every time I see him or talk to him, I can't think that because I know it's not true.

If your imaginary contact with a person is better than the reality, then you are not in love with a person; you are in love with a daydream of your own creation.

171

Loving a fantasy is the greatest barrier to loving a real person. Simone Weil explains that real love "consents" to the independent freedom of other people, whereas our imagination often leads us to live in a fantasy world in which we script and control a person's words and actions. Love is attentive to another person as purely *real* who has an independent existence not oriented to us. Weil writes of the common experience of writing to a friend and anticipating his reply. "It is impossible that he should not reply by saying what I have said to myself in his name."[6] Having scripted the response in advance and imagined a particular answer, we are startled and disturbed to encounter the other's independence. We act as though other people "owe us what we imagine they will give us."[7] But obviously they do not owe us anything of the sort. We each have the tendency to believe that the world is about us, to assume that other people's actions are designed with us in mind, but only a little reflection shows us that this is not the case.

It is especially difficult to let go of this "imaginary position as the center"[8] in instances of romantic love, when we long for our love to be returned. Imagining what it would be like for the one we love to love us back is almost irresistible, but doing so ignores the real other person and replaces him or her with an imaginary person of our own invention. This is not love, since love means paying attention to the independent reality of the other person.

In some sense, then, imagination is the opposite of love. Imagination is associated with possession, whereas love is associated with distance. Imagination is associated with illusion, love with reality.

> Love needs reality. What is more terrible than the discovery that through a bodily appearance we have been loving an imaginary being. It is much more terrible than death, for death does not prevent the beloved from having lived.
>
> That is the punishment for having fed love on imagination.[9]

6. Simone Weil, *Gravity and Grace,* trans. Emma Craufurd (New York: Routledge, 1987), 9.

7. Ibid.

8. Simone Weil, *Waiting for God,* trans. Emma Craufurd (New York: Putnam's Sons, 1951), 159.

9. Weil, *Gravity and Grace,* 57.

Most of us have probably had the experience of being disillusioned after an infatuation, of realizing that the person with whom we thought we were in love was merely the product of our imagination and that the real person is a disappointment. Most of us have probably not identified our fantasies in such instances as criminal, but that is how Weil defines them. She claims that such imaginings are an offense against reality and that they poison us for real love, which she elsewhere defines as "belief in the existence of other human beings as such."[10]

When you live in your imagination, you must live alone. No one else can join you there. If the person you love is only a product of your imagination, that unreal person can never love you back and your love will be forever unrequited. Even God cannot reach you in a world constructed out of your imagination, for God is completely real. The only place a creature can hide from God is someplace that is not real. In his fantasy *The Great Divorce,* C. S. Lewis theorizes that ultimately this is what hell is—an almost entirely imaginary place constructed out of the sterile and twisted imaginings of its inhabitants.[11] Only the imaginary can be truly separated from God, and when we prefer the imaginary to the real, we prefer our own creation to God's creation. We make ourselves divine.

Let me be clear. Imagination is a good gift from God. We need imagination to dream of things that are not yet real and to bring them to fruition. Imagination is required to create, to teach, to explore, to build. But like all God's good gifts, imagination can be twisted. Because it is a powerful gift, it is powerfully dangerous when used incorrectly.

Our experiences of romantic love are intimately connected with our imagination, both for good and for bad. Most of us have had the experience of meeting a new person and wondering whether this person, still unknown, may be our future spouse. This wondering is an act of the imagination, and in moderation it is a good thing. The imagination is the only faculty we have for thinking about things that are not yet real but that may become real some day. Without such imaginative wondering, we cannot change our lives or move into a new way of living. Imagination is the necessary precursor to change. Imagination is also the way in which

10. Ibid., 56.
11. C. S. Lewis, *The Great Divorce* (New York: Macmillan, 1946).

we check out our feelings and responses. Perhaps you have met someone interesting and attractive, but you find that you cannot imagine a life with this person. In our imagination, we play out possibilities and discover what we really want and what we really hope for.

On the other hand, we indulge our imagination in destructive ways when we turn other people into characters in our own inner drama. Most of us have probably done this at some point in our life. When imagination stops being a tool for wondering about real life and becomes instead an escape from real life, it is being used inappropriately. Some people construct elaborate imaginary worlds into which they escape each day, and often these worlds are populated by people who follow a script.

A friend once told me that she often had long imaginary fights with her husband during the day, and when he would get home at night, she would still be a little put out with him because of the things he had said to her during their imagined conversations. She laughed as she told me, realizing that she was being unfair to her husband. Where is the line between appropriate rehearsing of difficult conversations and an inappropriate scripting of another person's life? When imaginary dialogue, or an imaginary world, becomes so compelling that we cannot resist it, when we find ourselves taking refuge in it rather than confronting reality, the line has been crossed.

Keith Clark suggests a way that you can test the appropriateness of your romantic fantasy life:

> Follow that fantasy through to its realistic imagined consequences. If you acted out your sexual fantasy, what would it be like for you an hour later, or a day later, or a year later? The realization people often come to is that their fantasies may be pleasant at the point at which they are most enticing, but they are disappointing often in their consequences.
>
> If I acted out my sexual fantasy, for instance, the nature of many of the relationships in my life would be considerably different, and I don't want them to be different. . . . These impure thoughts of mine are not about sex as sex really is, because they don't include the consequences of sexual behavior.[12]

12. Keith Clark, *Being Sexual . . . and Being Celibate* (Notre Dame: Ave Maria Press, 1986), 121–22.

174

A disciplined imagination that considers consequences may be a corrective for an undisciplined imagination that dreams of sexual behavior without consequences.

There appears to be a conflict between two truths here. On the one hand, we all know the truth of the saying "Love is blind." People in love are often blind to the real nature of those with whom they are in love. On the other hand, there is another old saying, traceable to the twelfth-century monk Richard of St. Victor: "Only love sees." Irving Singer refers to such bestowal love, the love that sees the value and the glory of another person. It is a "valuative gesture" made by the imagination in which even the foibles of the one we love become somehow dear to us.[13]

> The lover's glance fixes upon the sheer presence of the beloved. In that extreme condition sometimes called "falling in love," such attentiveness often approaches self-hypnosis. . . . The lover's glance illuminates the beloved. He celebrates her as a living reality to which he attends. As in celebration of any sort, his response contributes something new and expressive. He introduces the woman into the world of his own imagination—as if, through some enchantment, she were indeed his work of art and only he could contemplate her infinite detail. As long as they intensify her presence, the lover will cherish even those features in the beloved that appraisal scorns. Does the lady have a facial blemish? To her lover it may be more fascinating than her baby blue eyes: it makes her stand out more distinctly in his memory. Does she have a sharp tongue and a biting temper? Her lover may come to relish these traits, not generally but in this particular woman. They make the image of her vivid and compelling. . . . They show him with unmistakable clarity what she is.[14]

Singer goes so far as to define love as "a subspecies of imagination."[15] Singer appears to believe that the lover's positive vision of the beloved is to some extent the lover's creation. I would argue that if the vision is generated by the lover, then this is a case of infatuation, not love. But if the vision is a result of the

13. Irving Singer, *Plato to Luther,* vol. 1 of *The Nature of Love,* 2nd ed. (Chicago: University of Chicago Press, 1984), 18.
14. Ibid., 19.
15. Ibid., 16.

lover paying close attention to the reality of the other person in order to see and draw forth the wonder and the glory that God has placed there, then such love reflects God's love for us. God creates the goodness of the particular person, which love then enables the lover to see.

This is the sort of love that is celebrated in the Song of Solomon. The bride says of herself, "I am a rose of Sharon, a lily of the valleys" (2:1), describing herself in terms of common flowers that grow in abundance in the land of Israel. She sees herself as commonplace, indistinguishable from any other young woman. But her bridegroom replies, "As a lily among brambles, so is my love among maidens" (2:2). She is the one woman to whom he is giving all his loving attention, and so she stands out for him as unique and marvelous. His love does not create her beauty; rather, his love draws out the beauty that is already there.[16]

Earlier I referred to Charles Williams's romantic theology. Like Singer, Williams takes a positive view of imagination and its role in the romantic experience, but Williams supports the idea that God is the source of the wonder that love perceives. For Williams, God's beauty and glory are most clearly and naturally apprehended in the experience of love—not just love in general but specifically the experience of romantic love. Williams thinks it is the faculty of imagination that allows us to see the glory of a loved person, a glory that is invisible to casual observers but is part of the person's God-given potential, which will ultimately be realized in heaven. This is why the person that we love can show us something of God's nature. Williams explores this theme in his first book of poetry, a cycle of eighty-four sonnets written for his wife as part of their courtship. In one poem, he explores the various meanings behind his love for his wife and concludes that the first meaning is "The steep / Whence I see God."[17] For Williams, falling in love is a source of knowledge and revelation. His love helps him to know God and to find stability, purpose, and self-knowledge.

16. For this reading of the Song of Solmon, I am indebted to Marion Snapper of Calvin Seminary.

17. Cited in Alice Mary Hadfield, *Charles Williams: An Exploration of His Life and Work* (Oxford: Oxford University Press, 1983), 18.

Williams is optimistic about discovering positive knowledge of God through daily experience and the created world. Because of the incarnation of God in Christ, we may confidently look for God in our experiences of the world, expecting that there is evidence of God in the world he has made and that God wants to communicate with us through the creation and our everyday experiences. As noted in chapter 1, Williams thinks that all people *could* give us a vision of the beauty and glory of God, but because of God's mercy, we are able to see that glory only in the ones we love. Love empowers the imagination to see a beauty that is not visible without the presence of love. That beauty is divine insofar as it reflects and obeys God, but it also reflects the essential nature or form of the person we love. Since no one in this life fully expresses his or her essential nature, we need imagination to see it. It is potential within the person in that it is not yet fully actualized but is in the process of becoming.

In traditional Christian philosophy, God is understood as pure actuality. There is nothing potential in God, nothing emerging, nothing not yet realized, nothing waiting to become. God *is*—fully, completely, and perfectly. This does not mean that God's existence is static. Quite the opposite. It means that all of God's nature is expressed, real, in action. Since there is nothing about God that is potential, imagination is not appropriate or necessary when perceiving God. In fact, imagination gets in the way of an accurate vision of God by distorting our perception.

People, however, are a mixture of actuality and potentiality, being and becoming. Some of what God has designed us to be is already actual, but most is not. Since our essential nature is not fully actualized, we have not yet come into our own. To see another person's full beauty requires seeing not only what is actual but also what is potential—what that person may become. Seeing such potential requires imagination, since it cannot be directly experienced as actual or real. An example of such vision is the way parents look at their children. A parent will say, "My child is special, gifted, and brilliant; my child is going to be a great artist, an athlete, or a scholar." The parent is not simply fantasizing. Rather, he or she has the ability to see beyond what is to what may be, to recognize potential attributes in the child as well as actualized attributes.

Clearly, there is a danger of imagining something illusory rather than a potential reality. Consider, for instance, parents who imagine their own frustrated aspirations fulfilled in their children. Such children may wish their parents had less imagination. The key seems to be the combination of imagination and love. Williams would agree that love celebrates another's independence. Therefore, loving imagination never seeks to use a person as an extension of ourselves but rather sees the potential of the other's essence realized. This ability to imagine the beauty that is coming as well as the beauty that is present is activated by love and made possible by imagination. Love lets us see one another as we may someday be. Love gives us insight into the divine spark in another. A loving vision sees potentiality fully actualized.

Although I am drawn to Williams's positive view of romantic imagination and its role in leading us to God, I also believe Williams is too trusting, too uncritical. As C. S. Lewis says in *The Four Loves*, "But Eros, honoured without reservation and obeyed unconditionally, becomes a demon."[18] In his affirmation of romantic experience, Williams is not sufficiently on guard against the ways in which that experience may mislead us. Indeed, late in his own life, he came to understand this danger more vividly when his own marriage was threatened by his friendship with a female coworker. He did not have an affair with her, but the temptation to do so made him aware of the potential danger of trusting romantic attraction.

Even though romantic attraction is a good gift from God, it can lead us astray when we elevate it to a position of excessive importance. In his book *A Severe Mercy*, Sheldon Vanauken talks about the strong romantic love that he and his first wife, Jean (known as Davy), experienced. They were committed to preserving their sense of "inloveness" and did so by decreeing that their love was their most absolute commitment. Anything that could interfere with their love for each other, anything that could separate them in any way needed to be rejected. They decided, for instance, that they would not have children because children tended to distract a husband and a wife from their love for each other and the care of children was not usually shared fully between a husband and

18. C. S. Lewis, *The Four Loves* (New York: Harvest Books, 1971), 154.

a wife. When the Vanaukens became Christians, this absolute commitment to romantic love was challenged. By the end of the book, Vanauken recognizes that this absolute commitment to love as "the sole criterion of all decisions . . . was in violation of the Law [of God]; for what was best for our love might not be in accordance with our love and duty to our neighbour."[19] In fact, he comes to see that his wife's death was God's "severe mercy." Given the idolatrous foundation of their relationship, it would have disintegrated under the pressure of their growing Christian commitment if she had lived.

In *The Four Loves*, C. S. Lewis makes the point that, although God is love, we may not therefore assert that love is God. Peter Kreeft expands on this idea:

> [One] misunderstanding about love is the confusion between "God is love" and "love is God." The worship of love instead of the worship of God involves two deadly mistakes. First it uses the word God only as another word for love. God is thought of as a force or energy rather than as a person. Second, it divinizes the love we already know instead of showing us a love we don't know. To understand this point, consider that "A is B" does not mean the same as "A equals B." If A = B, then B = A, but if A is B, that does not mean that B is A. "That house is wood" does not mean "wood is that house." "An angel is spirit" does not mean the same as "spirit is an angel." When we say "A is B," we begin with a subject, A, that we assume our hearer already knows, and then we add a new predicate to it. "Mother is sick" means "You know mother well, let me tell you something you don't know about her: she's sick." So "God is love" means "Let me tell you something new about the God you know: he is essential love, made of love, through and through." But "Love is God" means "Let me tell you something about the love you already know, your own human love: that is God. That is the ultimate reality. That is as far as anything can ever go. Seek no further for God." In other words, "God is love" is the profoundest thing we have ever heard. But "love is God" is deadly nonsense.[20]

19. Sheldon Vanauken, *A Severe Mercy* (San Francisco: HarperSanFrancisco, 1987), 212–13.

20. Peter Kreeft, "Love," in *Fundamentals of the Faith* (SanFrancisco: Ignatius Press, 1988), http://catholiceducation.org/articles/apologetics/ap0019.html (accessed January 8, 2003).

We may not make an idol of our own romantic experiences. Because romance is such a good gift from God, it makes a particularly powerful idol.

Romance is especially dangerous when we believe ourselves to be strong enough to handle it. An interesting example of such danger is seen in the journals of Thomas Merton. Merton had been a priest and a monk for decades when he fell in love with a young nurse (whom he calls M.) who cared for him during a brief hospitalization. He first mentions her in his journals when he gives an account of his stay in the hospital.

> I got a very friendly and devoted student nurse working on my compresses, etc. This livened things up considerably. In fact, we were getting perhaps too friendly by the time M. went off on her Easter vacation, but her affection—undisguised and frank—was an *enormous* help in bringing me back to life fast. I realized that though I am pretty indifferent to the society of my fellow monks . . . , I do feel a deep emotional need for feminine companionship and love. Seeing that I must irrevocably live without it ended by tearing me up more than the operation itself.[21]

In light of what eventually happened, his initial recognition that they were "perhaps too friendly" is telling. Merton's vocation included a vow of celibacy, and yet he ignored the warning in his own initial discomfort with this relationship. In the following weeks, he received a letter from M. in which she asked if she could come to see him. Apparently, her letter (which is not included in his journals) suggested that she was in need of spiritual guidance. Merton wanted to respond positively, though he recognized that his own "tenderness" for her made that risky.[22]

In his journal, he frets about the constraints on contact his monastery has put in place (for instance, about the possibility that his letters will be read) and admits, "I can do her little or no good as long as I am emotionally attached to her. I must try to be more free and more sure of what I mean by love in Christ—and

21. Thomas Merton, *The Intimate Merton: His Life from His Journals*, ed. Patrick Hart and Jonathan Montaldo (New York: HarperCollins, 2001), 275 (April 10, 1966).
22. Ibid., 277 (April 19, 1966).

not kid myself."[23] Yet he does kid himself. His self-deception is painfully obvious in the entries that follow. After he arranges to meet with M. during a doctor's visit, he observes:

> More than ever I saw how much and how instantly and how delicately we respond to each other on every level. I can see why she is scared. I am too. There is a sense of awful, awesome rather, sexual affinity. Of course there can be no hesitations about my position here. I have vows and I must be faithful to them. . . . Apart from that, though, we had a very good talk, and once again it was clearer than ever that we are terribly in love, the kind of love that can virtually tear you apart. She literally trembled with it. . . . I do so much want to love her as we began, spiritually. I do believe such spiritual love is not only possible but does exist between us deeply, purely, strongly, and the rest can be controlled. Yet she is right to be scared. We can simply wreck each other. I am determined not to give in to this, . . . but I can see I don't know how to handle this if it ever breaks loose. I have been imprudent. . . . My response has been too total and too forthright. We have admitted too much, communicated all the fire to each other, and now we are caught. I am not as smart or as stable as I imagined.[24]

Within weeks their feelings do "break loose," and their romance moves to an intensely physical level. Merton tells of celebrating mass one morning "soberly aware of myself as a priest who has a woman. True, we have done nothing drastically wrong—though in the eyes of many our lovemaking is still wrong even though it stops short of complete sex. Before God I think we have been conscientious and have kept our love good."[25]

Despite this last assurance, within days he is writing about the need to end the relationship in order to be true to his vows. Ultimately, one of the other monks listens in on a forbidden phone conversation Merton has with M. and reports it to the abbot, who then intervenes to end the relationship. Merton is somewhat relieved, writing, "I have to face the fact that I have been wrong and foolish in all this."[26] But he continues to write

23. Ibid., 278 (April 21, 1966).
24. Ibid., 281 (April 27, 1966).
25. Ibid., 287 (June 9, 1966).
26. Ibid., 288 (June 14, 1966).

about his love for her as a great good thing. It is not until August 1968, more than two years after their relationship began, that he writes in his journal, "Today, among other things, I burned M.'s letters. Incredible stupidity in 1966!"[27]

This account is striking because of the capacity it reveals for self-deception. At the time of this romance, Merton was in his early fifties and an acknowledged authority on spiritual practice. He imagined that he could control his physical attraction for this young woman and that their relationship was built on a deep spiritual connection. He tried to convince himself that he was keeping his vows as long as he did not have sex with her, even though he knew he was leading her into a relationship he had no intention of finishing. He dismissed his own commitments and choices, made in response to God's call on his life, writing, "I feel that somehow my sexuality has been made real and decent again after years of rather frantic suppression (for though I thought I had it all truly controlled, this was an illusion). I feel less sick. I feel human."[28] But the sickness did not lie in the vows he had made; the sickness (as he ultimately realized) was in being tempted to violate those vows.

We are particularly vulnerable to such self-deception when we spiritualize our sexual impulses. Romantic love can be a way in which God shows us his image, reflected in another human being. Romantic love can be a tool God uses to pull back the veil on that image, allowing us to see his glory clearly reflected in another person. But such an understanding of romance can also be a convenient way to justify and camouflage less exalted experiences, such as lust or illicit attraction. If Thomas Merton can fall prey to this, so can the rest of us.

27. Ibid., 336 (August 20, 1968).
28. Ibid., 285–86 (May 20, 1966).

Part 3

Rejecting, Pursuing, and Recovering

Let goods and kindred go,
this mortal life also.
The body they may kill;
God's truth abideth still.
His kingdom is forever.

Martin Luther,
"A Mighty Fortress"

For I am convinced that neither death, nor life, nor angels, nor rulers, nor things present, nor things to come, nor powers, nor height, nor depth, nor anything else in all creation, will be able to separate us from the love of God in Christ Jesus our Lord.

Romans 8:38–39

8

Rejecting Love

There must be fifty ways to leave your lover.

Paul Simon,
"Fifty Ways to Leave Your Lover"

For the whole law is summed up in a single commandment,
"You shall love your neighbor as yourself." If, however, you bite
and devour one another, take care that you are not consumed
by one another.

Galatians 5:14–15

Imagine that you are sitting in a movie theater watching the
opening scenes of a new romantic comedy. Assume that you have
not seen any trailers or read any reviews, and so you know nothing about the plot. In the opening scene, you are introduced to a
man and a woman who, for rather flimsy reasons, take a violent
dislike to each other. What do you expect will happen next?

If you are in the habit of going to romantic comedies, it will be
immediately obvious to you that these two people are destined to
be together. As the plot unfolds, one of the two main characters
will probably discover that he or she finds the other attractive
but will see little hope for a relationship since the other continues to treat him or her with dislike. Yet by the end of the movie,
this dislike will be overcome, and the two will acknowledge their
love for each other and will live happily ever after. How many
movies can you list that conform to that plotline?

It is not a new plotline, and it is not found only in movies. It is a staple of romantic novels as well. The humorous writer P. G. Wodehouse parodies this convention in his novel *Summer Moonshine*. His hero, Joe, has fallen in love with Jane, a woman he barely knows who is already engaged to someone else. But Joe used to work for a publisher of popular romantic fiction and has learned not to let such details deter him.

> "And now," said Joe, "to a more tender and sentimental subject." . . .
>
> "Are you really going to start that all over again?"
>
> "I don't know what you mean by 'start all over again.' I've never stopped. Haven't you noticed how I keep on asking you to marry me? Every day. As regular as clockwork."
>
> "And haven't you noticed how, every time you do it, I tell you I'm engaged to someone else?"
>
> "That has not escaped me, but I don't pay very much attention to it. In the manuscripts I used to read . . . the heroine was always engaged to someone else at the start. . . . From a man steeped in their contents as I am, no method of ensnaring the female heart is hidden. I know just how it's done. I shall rescue you from a burning house, or from drowning, or from bulls, or from mad dogs, or from tramps, or from runaway horses. Or I might save your kitten. . . . I tell you, young Jane, it is hopeless for you to try to escape me. You are as good as walking up the aisle already. You shake your head? Just you wait. A time will come—and shortly—when you will be doing so in order to dislodge the deposits of rice and confetti which have gathered in your lovely hair. If I were you I'd cease to struggle."[1]

Not surprisingly, Jane eventually comes to love Joe, and they live happily ever after. That, after all, is how the story is supposed to go.

Surely it is true that in many cases romance blossoms after two people have known each other for some time. Surely it is true that in many, perhaps most, cases one person falls in love before the other. Surely it is even true that sometimes initial dislike gives way over time to romantic feelings. Nonetheless,

---

1. P. G. Wodehouse, *Summer Moonshine* (London: Penguin Books, 1966), 148–49.

the prevalence of this plotline has had a destructive influence on people. Because we have all been indoctrinated into this story, in which initial dislike gives way to romantic love and commitment, we are tempted to hope that romantic rejection is only temporary and that if we persist in showing love to the object of our affections, eventually he or she will give in and love us too.

This makes it difficult to be a rejector. Most of us can find the courage and the words to reject someone once, but what are we to do if that rejection has no real effect, if the person to whom we have just said no keeps coming back? In real life, Jane would almost certainly find Joe's daily proposals more and more exasperating, and their friendship would almost certainly deteriorate into animosity.

Most love stories ignore the possibility of genuine rejection and focus only on the possibility that love will elicit love, leading social psychologists Roy Baumeister and Sara Wotman to label this story line a "script" we receive from our culture about romance. They tell the story of Nicholas and Alexandra, the czar and czarina of Russia. Nicholas loved Alexandra for ten years before they married and persisted in proposing for two years, despite her clear refusals. After ten years, she relented and came to love Nicholas as devotedly as he loved her. They had a long and happy marriage. Commenting on this story, Baumeister and Wotman note:

> What must two people think when they find themselves on opposite sides of an unreciprocated passion? To the would-be lover, it is clear that one must persist and strive despite setbacks. Even if one's beloved is unresponsive, perhaps some great effort . . . will finally succeed. One must never allow oneself to be discouraged by the other's unwillingness, lest *both* people be deprived of a supreme love. Meanwhile, the rejector must wonder if he or she will indeed come to love the other in return. For rarely is one loved by someone whom one hates or despises; usually there is some degree of positive feeling toward the other. It is hard for the lover to know whether these unspectacular feelings might someday blossom into a devoted love like Alexandra's.

The story of Nicholas and Alexandra also offers an ominous hint about another problem for the rejector. Just as Nicholas disregarded Alexandra's rejections, so do many aspiring lovers in today's United States disregard the rejections of their intended partners. That is what the culture teaches, that is what the great love stories show, and so aspiring lovers feel quite justified in persisting. The problem is that this pattern leaves the rejector in an almost helpless situation. . . . Many people *don't* end up reciprocating the other's love, and in those cases they find it painfully unpleasant and remarkably difficult to get rid of the other person.[2]

Such stories of lovers who persist in the face of rejection, only to elicit love in return, may make those who are in love feel entitled to have their love returned. After all, that is how the story is supposed to end. If you love someone, that person is supposed to love you back, if not immediately, then once you have proven your love through persistence. And why shouldn't you persist, since the loved person would be so much happier if he or she would only give in and love you too? It is in everyone's best interest for you to keep hoping and pursuing.

The community is also typically on the side of the pursuer. When I was a college student, I had some friends who had been high-school sweethearts and were still dating after several years of college. Everyone thought their marriage was inevitable, but the woman decided that marriage was too important to be entered into out of inertia. She broke off the relationship and transferred to another college for a year, wanting to discover who she was without this man and wanting to test her feelings for him. A year later, she came back, renewed her relationship with her former boyfriend, and soon thereafter they were engaged. When I told her that I thought her decision to break things off for a year had been very wise, she told me I was one of the few people who thought so. Her family members all loved her boyfriend and were upset at the idea of losing him. Her girlfriends were for the most part angry. Who did she think she was to break up with such a great guy? Her decision was seen as arrogant.

In Christian circles, this is a fairly typical reaction to a woman who rejects a nice Christian man. Women are supposed to be grateful for the offer of love from such a man, especially since

---

2. Roy F. Baumeister and Sara Wotman, *Breaking Hearts: The Two Sides of Unrequited Love* (New York: Guilford Press, 1992), 21–22.

there is a perceived shortage of them. Other women are especially vicious when a woman is uppity enough to say no. In my teaching, I have sometimes shown the movie *My Brilliant Career*, in which the heroine, Sybylla, an eccentric and rather homely woman, rejects a wealthy and very attractive suitor.[3] Students' reactions range from discomfort to anger. Who does she think she is?

Christians should not buy into uncritical support for the pursuer in romantic relationships because of the biblical presumption that singleness should be the default option. The Christian community needs to support that presumption. We should not feed the sense of entitlement that pursuers already have. The problem of how to reject someone clearly and yet kindly is exacerbated when the Christian community does not support such rejection.

One woman told of her experience living in a small town where a single professional man began to pursue her. Since they worked together, she refused to date him. He informed her that, given the size of the town, there was no one else for her to date. She needed to recognize that he was the best thing going. She failed to find this argument convincing and was frustrated by his apparent belief that he had a claim on her.

This sense of entitlement is examined in Shakespeare's play *Twelfth Night* when Viola tells Olivia, "What is yours to bestow is not yours to reserve."[4] She suggests that Olivia is obligated to give her love to someone, that she has no right to hold that love back from a suitor. But then, Viola is not an impartial advisor. She is speaking to Olivia on behalf of such a suitor, her master Count Orsino, and is attempting to convince Olivia to return his love. Olivia is unconvinced, saying:

> Your lord does know my mind; I cannot love him.
> Yet I suppose him virtuous, know him noble,
> Of great estate, of fresh and stainless youth; . . .

---

3. *My Brilliant Career* (UK Cinema Club, 1979).

4. William Shakespeare, *Twelfth Night, or What You Will*, in *The Complete Works*, ed. Stanley Wells and Gary Taylor (Oxford: Oxford University Press, 1988), act 1, scene 5, line 181.

But yet I cannot love him.
He might have took his answer long ago.[5]

Count Orsino has already been rejected, and yet he continues to pursue Olivia, especially through his messenger Viola, who comes repeatedly to Olivia to plead her master's case. Viola expects her master's love to elicit love on Olivia's part, but Olivia insists that it has not worked and that returning the duke's love is not within her power, even though she recognizes his merits.

Eventually, Viola comes to see the foolishness of her errand, but she finds that, even so, her master is difficult to convince. He seems to believe he has a right to Olivia's love. When Viola reports on Olivia's rejection, he says, "I cannot be so answered." Viola points out that if the roles were reversed, Orsino would expect his rejection to be taken as final.

Say that some lady, as perhaps there is,
Hath for your love as great a pang of heart
As you have for Olivia. You cannot love her.
You tell her so. Must she not then be answered?[6]

In response to this good sense, the duke replies that the sort of love he feels for Olivia is too strong ever to be felt by a woman for a man. Even as he claims to love Olivia, he dismisses her capacity to return his love. Even as he hopes she will return his love, he suggests that she is incapable of doing so. Here entitlement is combined with a disregard for the independent reality of another person. This is the sort of "love" professed by a man in a recent news story who killed his ex-wife when he found out she was seeing another man. This is love understood as the ownership of an object, not as a relationship with a free and independent other.

Even when the claims of entitlement are not so extreme, persistent attention can quickly become annoying. Such attention may feel manipulative, constricting, or intrusive. It may actually cause the person being pursued to lose respect for the one doing the pursuing. Here is one of many such examples:

5. Ibid., act 1, scene 5, lines 246–52.
6. Ibid., act 2, scene 3, lines 88–91.

It started off two years ago, at the beginning of my junior year. This guy told me he liked me, and I as politely as possible said no, but I thought it was as clear as can be. Then he said: I would still like your friendship, and I still want to keep in touch with you. I said: Well, let's just give it some time. This has happened a few times before, and I know from experience that I'm not very good at getting back to being friends. . . . Well, the guy's idea of giving me some time was like two weeks, and then he calls me up and says: Would you like to get together and do this? We had never had a group of friends, and whenever we would do something it was just the two of us. I did not want to be by myself with him after what had happened. . . . I tried to keep my distance from him, and he never backed off. That just made me feel more uncomfortable. And I had to have the same discussion with him over and over again, and he would always bring it up again. I'm just like, you know, this is the last time we need to talk about this. But it still went on. He actually just emailed me recently, and he's like, I'm sorry, but blah blah blah blah, and I think I'm a failure, and I messed everything up. I'm trying to tell him: No, you aren't. It wasn't your fault. It just was never meant to be, and I'm dead certain of that. But he's obviously having a very difficult time getting over it. It makes me feel guilty sometimes, but when what he says never matches what he actually does then I get frustrated. For instance, although he says he's over it, he sent me a dozen yellow roses on Valentine's Day without his name on it. So I'm guessing it has to be from him because he's the only person who does this kind of stuff. . . . So I asked: Did you send me these yellow roses? And he said: Yes, but they were only meant as friendship, because yellow is a symbol of friendship. I know that, but they're still roses! He says it's friendship, but . . . I've asked girlfriends about it, whether I'm reading this wrong, but I don't think that I am. It's very frustrating sometimes. . . .

This has been going on for two years. I try not to give him any encouragement. So sometimes he says he thinks I hate him, and I tell him: I don't hate you, but if I give you any encouragement whatsoever, I think you're going to get the wrong idea, because even without any encouragement you're still doing these things.

This young woman is not amused by her suitor. She is frustrated, exasperated, and annoyed. The more he persists, the less likely she is to say yes. She is trying to be kind, but he is making kindness very difficult.

One thing that is interesting about this story is that the pursuer thinks he has a right to claim her friendship, even though he does not have a right to claim her romantic feelings. She does not believe his intentions are merely friendly, and from time to time he reveals that they are not. He is being dishonest and manipulative in seeking to spend private, intimate time with her under the guise of friendship. Their shared assumption is that if he can establish that his pursuit is only friendly, then she is obligated to receive that pursuit with kindness and encouragement. But why? This young woman does not question the claim to friendship, but in this case friendship is not possible.

Even friendship is not a relationship of entitlement. We have no such claim on one another, and when a pursuer stakes such a claim, he or she is making an illegitimate assumption. One of the convictions of the Christian faith is that we have been set free in Christ. Such freedom means that we belong to no one but Christ. We are part of the body of Christ, the church, but that shared community is not a basis for making exclusive claims on one another, whether claims of friendship or claims of romance.

We need to be honest about the terms of the relationships we enter. If we have agreed to be "just friends," then we should act as friends. Friendship is by its nature a nonexclusive relationship based on shared interests. Friends are naturally hospitable, enlarging their group to include others. It is not appropriate to try to get your romantic desires met under the pretense of being friends. One woman told of the moment when she realized that she was doing exactly this. A man she had been seeing in a casual, friendly way confessed to her that he was in love with her. That was when she realized:

> Just for my own vanity, I had been allowing this person to heap all these compliments upon me. I hadn't been careful of his feelings in the way I usually demand of myself, because I had been so intent on receiving his flattering and his attention and feeling good because he was somebody who responded to my flirtatious behavior. And it was a real eye-opening experience for me.

She was recovering from a romantic breakup of her own, but when she had to respond to his declaration, she realized how inappropriate it had been to seek healing for her own hurt by toying with someone else.

The "Scriptlessness" of Rejection?

Whereas loving someone who does not love you can be painful, being the one to say no is usually more awkward. The one in love often has a bittersweet experience in which pain is mixed with the excitement of romance and daydreams about a happy life. The one saying no has no such compensatory pleasure, and if the pursuer is persistent, the rejector's experience will probably be one of growing anger and exasperation.

Given that culture teaches lovers to persist in their pursuit, even when rejected, Baumeister and Wotman say that rejectors are often reduced to "scriptlessness," when the initial efforts to reject a person have not been taken seriously and have had no effect. The one being pursued feels increasingly helpless and at a loss as to what to say. What are the magic words that will make this person go away?

Finding the words to say no can be a challenge. One man told of developing a script for saying no to women who are romantically interested in him.

> One of my excuses was always I'm just not ready for any kind of relationship. This is what I said a lot in college, and this is what I said to people about why I didn't date. "I'm just really focused on school, my friends are important to me, and I feel like if I have this dating relationship, I'm going to have to lose all my friends or I'm not going to be able to devote myself to school as much as I want." 'Cause I was kind of a study-aholic. I was driven. It was a way of hiding, I think, but I used that as a reason why I didn't have time to be dating, or have a relationship.

This was not an entirely truthful statement of why he did not want to date. Eventually, this man identified himself as gay, but while he was in college, that was still unclear to him, and it certainly was not something he felt it would be safe to share widely. We do not owe full disclosure of our inner life to every acquaintance, but rather than spinning a fictional story, it would be better simply to say no thank you. Remember, the burden of proof in any dating relationship is on the decision to say yes, not the decision to say no.

One young man was clearly experienced in the art of saying no. He talked about the importance of rejecting women in the least painful way possible.

> The best policy for me is being truthful. Now there are a variety of ways to be truthful. But I think if you do it right, it's not all that painful. The degree of pain can be diminished a whole lot by how you say it. For me, it's all about tact, really. . . . I'm not a smooth talker or anything like that. I think that my biggest appeal is that I'm honest with them, and they understand I'm not trying to pull anything over their eyes.

But when asked, "Are you really always honest? Do you say, 'I just don't find you all that attractive?'" he laughed and said, "Tact." When asked, "Does that mean saying 'It's not you, it's me'?" he answered:

> Well, so often that is true. I mean, I say: I am waiting for who I'm waiting for, and I'm pretty sure that's not going to happen for a good long while because I am not allowing it to happen, really, for another five, ten years. So really, I'm like, you're not it. It's not anything necessarily about you, but I am not allowing myself to even give you a chance. . . . I will not do this person justice if I get into a relationship with them and they want my all and I'm not going to give it, and so it's better in the long run that they know where I'm coming from, so that there are no surprises. I just had this conversation earlier this week, actually. I think everyone deserves to find their king or their queen, and I am not going to be that for anyone that I've met so far. So that's it; I'm not going to do you justice. I don't want your emotions to get heated up because I cannot do justice to those emotions, and because of that very thing I am limiting myself and I am saving myself.

It was clear that he had had this conversation many times and was remarkably effective in extricating himself from unwanted pursuit without hard feelings. Not all rejectors feel lost, confused, and "scriptless." The more often you have this conversation, the more likely you will discover ways to express rejection that are clear, definite, and firm without being cruel.

One woman admitted that she enjoyed being in the position of rejector, that it gave her a feeling of power after years of being the one who was rejected. "It's kind of cool. I kind of like it. The past couple years I have realized I can have power over this. Which is kind of bad and kind of good." She told a story of a "real nice guy" whom she rejected because he would have wanted a serious relationship and she "just wanted to have fun." She was pleased with the final outcome of that relationship, saying that "it was cool afterwards," once she had told her suitor "to take a hike." Since she enjoys the power of saying no and seems to have little concern about hurting those she rejects, this woman does not find saying no terribly difficult. In her case, it should probably be more difficult than it is.

Even those who do not take pleasure in rejecting someone may be flattered—at least initially—by the attention of romantic pursuit. After one of the most famous rejection scenes in English literature—Elizabeth Bennett's rejection of Mr. Darcy's initial proposal—Elizabeth sits thinking in amazement about the fact that Mr. Darcy is in love with her. Although she continues to dislike him, she has to admit that "it was gratifying to have inspired unconsciously so strong an affection."[7]

Another woman admits that she used to take pleasure in being in the rejector role, but since falling in love with someone who does not love her, she no longer enjoys rejecting others. In the future, she promises:

> I wouldn't take any sort of sick enjoyment in it whatsoever. I think I always did before, because it's flattering when someone likes you. But I don't think I would feel flattered any more. I would feel sad. But I wouldn't lead them on.

One of the values of having experienced unrequited love is that you develop more empathy for those who are in that situation, especially those who may be in love with you.

---

7. Jane Austen, *Pride and Prejudice*, vol. 2 in *The Oxford Illustrated Jane Austen*, 3rd ed. (Oxford: Oxford University Press, 1965), 193.

Of course, such empathy may simply make it more difficult to say no. One man spoke about trying to end a painful and disordered relationship for three months without success, although he had "emotionally detached." When asked why he had been persuaded to stay in a relationship he wanted no part of, he answered:

> Because I'm a sucker. No, because I'm too nice. . . . And I don't trust my own feelings in these kinds of situations. You know, in a business situation I have instincts, and I go with them. I know, and I feel good about it. In these relationship areas I'm much less sure whether what I'm feeling is what I should be doing, or whether what I'm feeling is somehow connected with something screwy going on with me and that I should be saying we're going to work against it. So I wasn't 100 percent grounded in what my feelings were telling me I needed to do. . . . But, for whatever reason, I said, okay, you know, we'll give it a shot. Because I was not sure of myself enough, and because I have a really hard time hurting people, and so I'll do almost anything to avoid doing that. It's really hard to break up with people because I'm not good at hurting or rejecting people. I feel really bad.

Saying no to the offer of love is hard for many reasons. Most of us like being liked, and if there is no better offer on the horizon, it is tempting to use this person to meet some needs for affection pending the arrival of someone more interesting. These difficulties are exacerbated if our rejection is simply brushed aside or not accepted, forcing us to become more and more firm. For someone not grounded in his or her decision to say no, such firmness may not seem possible. Self-knowledge is a first step toward making this easier, followed by an awareness that ultimately truth is kindness.

It is usually less painful for all concerned when rejection comes early, although then the rejector must face the pressure to give the relationship a chance. How can you know that it won't work between us, the pursuer will ask, if you haven't given it a try? Again, this line of reasoning presumes that the rejector needs a reason to say no, when in fact a Christian needs a reason to say yes to a relationship. If you *do* say yes in response to this line of reasoning and then try to end the relationship later, you will probably find yourself confronting the logic that to break up now would be a waste of all the time you invested in the relationship.

One way to avoid saying no is to force the other person into the role of rejector, playing saboteur in a relationship until the other person cannot take it any more. This is common for people who are afraid of confrontation. They simply make it untenable for the other person to stay in the relationship. One woman recounted such a story.

> He liked to go away with his buddies for the weekend, and he would go away for the weekend every weekend. I sat down with him, and I said, "You know what? I work all week. You work all week. I'm looking to be in a relationship with someone that I can spend time with on the weekend. So," I said, "I don't need to spend every weekend with you. Why don't we make an agreement? How about, like, you go away two weekends, you stay home two weekends?" He said, "Yeah, no problem, no problem." And then he went away for the next six weekends. So I said, "Obviously, you're telling me you don't really want . . ." "Oh, no, no, I really . . ." And I was like, "No, you really don't want this, and I don't really feel like going through this any more." So I ended it. But was I the one rejecting? I don't really think so.

Although this man probably thought he was being kind by avoiding a painful conversation, he was actually being irresponsible. He was not owning up to his own feelings, nor was he communicating honestly with a woman he claimed to care about.

Another man told a similar story but from the other side. "I ended it passively by not being there emotionally for her, which made her angry enough to say, 'If you can't be there for me then let's stop being friends.' So in the active role, she actually cut it off, but . . ." He recognized that he was the rejector in this relationship, even though she said the necessary words. In subsequent relationships, when he was the pursuer, he admits that he was much less passive. "When you're pursuing, you know what you want, what the next step *should* be, what the other person *ought* to do, and why it's good for them that they should do it. It all makes perfect sense." He also saw himself as having more control when he was pursuing than when he was rejecting. Yet those relationships in which he felt control all ultimately ended in rejection. He concedes that he prefers to be rejected clearly, with a "firm no," since that "gives you a sense of closure," and he recognizes that his own passive style of rejection may allow the person being rejected to feel hope when there should be no hope. But to this day he remains passive in rejecting people, although he no longer allows himself to be drawn into deep relationships where he will have to say no. Instead, he does his rejecting early, sidestepping the situation.

> There's that confusing thing about wanting to be . . . the gener-
> ous Christlike person that doesn't hurt other people that drives
> some of the mistaken behavior when it comes to not honestly and
> quickly terminating some relationships. I think, in my spiritual
> development and growing up in the church, I got no tools for
> dealing with relationships in a Christlike manner, other than the
> broad generalizations of be loving, be giving, think about others
> first, and put yourself last.

The Christlike thing to do is first to see the situation from the other person's perspective. Most of us have a limited ability to do this and are much more likely to be sensitive to what another person is experiencing if we have already been in a similar situation. Therefore, having been rejected tends to make people better at giving rejection gently. Having been a rejector tends to make people better at accepting rejection graciously.

The Christlike thing to do is *not* to be "nice" (in the sense of saying what the other person wants to hear) but to be truthful. Stringing someone along for months because you lack the courage to say no is not Christlike; it is cowardly. Christians are called to "let your word be 'Yes, Yes' or 'No, No'" (Matt. 5:37 NIV), which means that we must be honest and straightforward with one another, even while we are also gentle and gracious. This young woman's story illustrates the failure to be honest in this way.

> My roommate suggested that I go out with this guy Tom. And I
> said well, I don't know, whatever. . . . They finally talked me into
> it, and I went out with him a couple of times, and it was okay. I
> really didn't know him that well, so that was a little bit uncomfort-
> able in a way. Then I tried giving him subtle hints, but that didn't
> seem to work—things like not agreeing to do things with him if
> he'd call. I wouldn't try to carry on a conversation for very long.

I admit now that some of those things, well, I didn't do them in a very graceful way. I probably should have been more sensitive to that, but I honestly didn't know how or what else to do. Then he went away for break, and he kept on emailing me. So finally I just had to email him back and say, well, I think that your idea of our relationship is quite a bit different from my idea, and that was that. He finally got the hint.

If this young woman would have known how to say no to her friends and how to say no to a persistent young man, the experience would not have been, in her words, a "fiasco." As a result of experiences like this, she believes that being the rejector in a relationship is harder and more awkward than being the one who is rejected. She now says:

I guess I've learned that I need to be more gracious and more understanding. Even though something may be uncomfortable for me, as much as that was, I should have just been truthful right from the beginning and saved a lot of grief.

By "being more gracious" she does not mean going out with him longer. She now realizes that the kind thing to do would have been "to talk about it more freely instead of just hoping that it would all go away."

In ancient Greek mythology, the god Apollo, god of the sun, became enamored with a nymph named Daphne. He pursued her unrelentingly, despite her lack of interest in him. Nothing she said or did discouraged him. Sister Wendy Beckett comments on Bernini's sculpture of this story.

Bernini shows the last moment of the story, when Apollo has caught up with her and reaches out with ardent hand to clasp her to himself. We can just see his face beginning to change, to lose its rapture, because Daphne's father, the river god, has answered her prayer and she is being transformed into a laurel tree.

Her slender fingers are sprouting leaves, and around her body bark is already appearing. She is lost to her would-be lover even as he exults, and all that will be left to him is the laurel wreath to be used as his emblem. Bernini has made the drama visible and tangible. We can see her flesh, soft and human, drying into vegetation. We can see intense fear relaxing, intense joy disappearing.[8]

The only way Daphne could say no was through self-destruction. Myths such as these usually express common human experiences, and the experience of relentless romantic pursuit as a destructive force is common indeed. Although real human beings do not have the power to change themselves into trees, it is common enough for someone who is being relentlessly pursued to express dismay at the sort of person he or she has had to become in order to say no effectively. It often seems necessary to eradicate the appearance of kindness, to stop smiling, to stop showing basic courtesy, to become aloof and distant and even cruel before rejection is taken seriously. This is especially the case when one is inexperienced at giving rejection and when one's pursuer is inexperienced at hearing it.

Owning up to one's failures is also appropriate behavior for a Christian. A major study of unrequited love behavior done at a large public university suggests that most rejectors deny any responsibility for the pain of those they reject.[9] Christians should be willing to accept responsibility for their thoughtlessness, either in leading the other person on or in being less than forthcoming when they were rejecting another's romantic advances. Many of us handle these situations in ways that are less than ideal. We should be willing to confess our faults and learn from them.

Saying No

One young woman's account of resisting a romantic advance includes many complicating factors. This experience happened while she was participating in an off-campus semester in another country, and therefore she was particularly vulnerable. She was

8. Wendy Beckett, *My Favorite Things: Seventy-five Works of Art from around the World* (New York: Abrams, 1999), 24–25.
9. Roy F. Baumeister and Sara Wotman, "Unrequited Love: On Heartbreak, Anger, Guilt, Scriptlessness, and Humiliation," *Journal of Social and Clinical Psychology* 9 (1990): 165–95.

meeting many new people from different cultures, and indeed part of the point of the semester was to meet people and to interact with them. We will call her Beth.

> He told me I was beautiful . . . and that he thought we were coming from the same place (i.e., that we would have a lot in common). I blushed, not used to such an advance from a guy. I'd never been flirted with before.

Being found attractive is often disorienting, especially for those who are experiencing romantic pursuit for the first time.

> The next week before he left to go to school in the United States we spent many hours talking. I was very aware (through his room-mate—my friend) that he was romantically attracted to me, yet I did not feel the same way. However, I really enjoyed my brief time with him and actually was quite sad that he was leaving, thinking of what might have been (that is, a good friendship—he was very deep and mature and enjoyable to talk to). . . . He left. We had exchanged email addresses, and so, being interested in how he was finding the U.S., I emailed him regularly, often telling him about my experiences as well. Emails soon included "I miss yous" and "wish you were heres." An emotional attachment was growing on both ends.

There is something intoxicating about emotional intimacy, especially when you are lonely. Beth was away from her normal friendship structure, and intense experiences away from home tend to accelerate intimacy. As another interviewee said, "In a place like summer camp, with little distraction and a strong commitment to the Lord, a person can really start to see a person in a different light." Another student observed that such experiences are "a sort of vacation from life, since you're geographically removed from home, and so you can do things you wouldn't normally do and not suffer consequences." Unfortunately, as Beth shows, a sense of freedom from consequences is an illusion. There are always consequences associated with actions.

> Emails turned into letters and gifts and even phone calls on his end. He soon started proclaiming how much he liked me. This made me very uncomfortable for a number of reasons. For one,

I did not feel the same way. Secondly, he sounded really serious. He even discussed marriage and children! He kept talking about coming out to see me. . . .

I started "dating" someone else and felt really torn between these two guys. I felt I had some obligation to tell him about this new guy, even though we weren't dating, and I felt guilty for pursuing other relationships. I didn't want to hurt him. But I dated other guys, and he didn't date anyone else because he was waiting for me (even though I asked him not to). He confided in his roommates that he planned to be engaged (to me) soon. I guess I was too ambiguous in my response to him—I did like the attention, the letters, the affection, etc., yet I still wasn't attracted to him.

Beth then agreed to pay this man a visit.

I also went to spend time with some other friends, but my main purpose for going was to determine once and for all that I did *not* like him (I think it is easy for me to confuse emotional attachment for romantic feelings) and also to show him I wasn't perfect.

So I spent about a week with him, and he was very into me, and it was very obvious that he was attracted to me. He tried to kiss me about eighteen times, but I wouldn't let him. We spent a lot of time talking, praying, and having fun. We were usually in a group, so that reduced the pressure. By the end of my time there, I was confident that I wasn't romantically attracted to him (however, I did falter at one point—okay, at a few points! and kissed him. Stupid move, I know.) I guess I really did love the feeling of being liked, and I did care about him—I don't know why I let it happen though. He told me he loved me (which I obviously didn't return). No one had said this to me before, so it was pretty shocking. I didn't feel like he knew me well enough to say that, and I also had a hunch he had idealized me. Both of us are pretty romantic, emotional people, and with the whole distance thing, emotions were brought up unnaturally early on.

Beth was sending ambiguous messages throughout her encounters with this man. She entered into an intense email correspondence. She accepted his gifts and phone calls. She got on a plane and flew to the city where he was studying, spending a week there visiting him. It is not surprising that he was encouraged. Although she may not have said the words "I love you," she gave him ample reason to think he was making progress with her. By her own admission, she "loved the feeling of being liked." She also wanted to keep his friendship, and the terms on which that friendship was offered were romantic.

Part of Beth's problem with this offer of romance was that it did not seem real to her. She sensed that he was in love with an illusion rather than with her true self. There is something a bit insulting about this sensation. She found his declarations of love more shocking than appealing.

> By the end of the week I knew nothing would happen with us, so I told him—in a letter and in person. He didn't seem to get it. I flew home. I sent him another email being even more clear that nothing would ever happen (it might even have been perceived as rude—but I seriously cared about him and didn't want to see him waiting for me if I wasn't interested). He didn't write back for about a month (a very long time for him). I was hurt when he wrote back a very distant, unemotional email, not dealing with anything I had said (but he'd obviously gotten the point this time). The only other email I've gotten from him since was a brief, again distant email which casually mentioned his new girlfriend (less than two months after he'd wanted to marry me!).
>
> I was very hurt and upset by this. I was mad and told him he should not tell someone he wants to marry them if he can go on to a new girl in such a short time. I realized I had no place to be upset about a new girlfriend because of my decision (which I still believe was the right one), yet I was saddened that he didn't want to be my friend or as emotionally close anymore, just because there was no longer a prospect for romance. I haven't heard from him since.

Beth realized that it was irrational for her to feel possessive about a man she had rejected, yet her feeling is actually quite common. Think of the popular movie *My Best Friend's Wedding*, in which Jules decides she is in love with her best friend only when he gets engaged to someone else.[10]

Beth believed this experience changed her by making her more wary and more distant in her friendships as well as in potential romantic relationships. Although she may not see

10. *My Best Friend's Wedding* (Columbia/Tristar, 1997).

it, she has also gained wisdom. She will never again lead someone on in this way, unintentional though it was. She will never again assume that she can maintain a friendship with an unmarried man without doing the hard work of maintaining boundaries.

Another young woman tells of an encounter when she was seventeen years old. She and another girl were out for the evening and met a carload of young men.

> We ended up going to a park with them, and my friend went off with one of the guys. I talked with the other two or three, I forget how many. Thinking back this was all very unsafe. After hanging out with them for a while, maybe half an hour or forty-five minutes, my friend came back. At this point one of the guys asked for my phone number. I gave it to him, thinking that he would never call me. The next day he called. I was completely shocked. . . . He then began calling more often, or everyday. After a few days, he came to my work. I worked at a store where I was usually alone. I remember that I was shocked he came to the store. I think we talked for a little while, but it was pretty awkward. We didn't talk very much after that, but one day he came to my house. I know it hadn't been that long since I initially met him, and it was really weird that he came over. I remember that he didn't tell me he was stopping by. At this point I thought he was creepy, so I know I didn't talk to him anymore. A few weeks maybe months passed by, and I was driving in a car with a friend, and I received a page. It was him, and he was drunk or acting drunk. He tried to explain why he paged, and I know he said he loved me. I'm pretty sure he was drinking. Anyway, I basically hung up and never talked to him again.

One of the interesting things about this story is that the narrator is constantly surprised, even though the results of her behavior are not surprising. Even though she finds this man's behavior unacceptable, she does not communicate that to him directly. Eventually, she stops speaking to him, but there is no indication in the story that she ever told him she thought he was pushing the boundaries, probably because she had never established any boundaries.

A couple things may be at play here. One is that this young woman was too young to realize the risks involved in her behavior. Telling the story several years later, she realizes that going to a park with a carload of strange men was not safe, but at the time she did not seem to be aware of the danger. She also should have known how to say no when asked for her phone number. According to her account (and assuming that she is being truthful), she did not expect or want this man to call, and yet she gave him her number. Giving your phone number to someone you have just met is almost always a bad idea, and sometimes it is a dangerous idea. Yet Christian young people are often brought up to respond truthfully to requests for information and find that they do not know how to refuse such a request. It is a good idea to practice what you will say if asked for personal identifying information—such as a phone number, an address, or even your last name—in a situation when wisdom suggests keeping such information to yourself. No one you have just met is entitled to such information, and you have every right to keep it private. Refusing to give your phone number to someone you have just met is not rude; it is showing appropriate modesty and discretion.

As we grow more experienced in these sorts of encounters, we may communicate expectations, hopes, and discouragement in less direct ways that allow all parties to save face. One woman makes a habit of talking incessantly about a man she is in love with when she is out with male friends in whom she is not interested. I am not sure how sincerely in love with this man she is, but she finds that speaking of it forestalls unwelcome advances. Another friend of mine is quick to speak about his calling to celibacy when he first meets eligible women whom he wishes to discourage. Experience also helps us to read subtle body language and to understand the difference between friendliness and romantic interest.

Over time, the script becomes clearer, as is evident from my interviews with never-married adults between thirty-five and fifty. These people all laugh at the idea that there is no script for rejection. "Would you like to hear the script?" they ask. "It's not you, it's me." "I'm not ready for a serious relationship." And of course, "Let's just be friends." Over time, they learn to believe these lines when they hear them and in fact to avoid having the conversation in which the lines might be delivered.

But even older people do not find rejection easy. The introduction quoted a never-married woman in her forties who said that the pain of being rejected and having to reject others is the worst part of being single. At some point, many people decide that it is wiser to embrace their singleness as a good life than to continue this heartbreaking process.

9

Pursuing Love

Charlie Brown: I thought being in love was supposed to make you happy.
Linus: Where'd you get that idea?

Charles Schulz, *Love Isn't Easy: Passionate Peanuts*

"I will arise now and go about the city
in the streets and in the squares;
I will seek him whom my soul loves."
I sought him, but found him not.

Song of Solomon 3:2

In the popular series of young adult novels beginning with *Anne of Green Gables,* Gilbert comes to like Anne while they are quite young, and he persists in courting her despite repeated refusals. Each refusal is less harsh, and he continues to hope. At the end of *Anne of Avonlea,* Gilbert and Anne have become good friends and are having a conversation about a couple in their village who are planning to be married, a conversation that Gilbert invests with significance by the way he looks at Anne.

For a moment Anne's heart fluttered queerly and for the first time her eyes faltered under Gilbert's gaze and a rosy flush stained the paleness of her face. It was as if a veil that had hung before her inner consciousness had been lifted, giving to her view a revelation of unsuspected feelings and realities. Perhaps, after all, romance did not come into one's life with pomp and blare, like a gay knight riding down; perhaps it crept to one's side like an old friend through quiet ways; perhaps it revealed itself in seeming prose, until some sudden shaft of illumination flung athwart its pages betrayed the rhythm and the music; perhaps . . . perhaps . . . love unfolded naturally out of a beautiful friendship, as a golden-hearted rose slipping from its green sheath.[1]

Anne discovers that she has loved Gilbert all along, but her feelings have for some reason been "veiled" to her conscious perception. The way Gilbert looked at her at that moment provided a "sudden shaft of illumination" so that the veil was pulled aside, letting her know her own feelings. The plotline is the same as that of most contemporary romantic comedies.

Eliciting Love by Loving

So how long should you persist in pursuing someone? What is the difference between a love that elicits love in return and a love that is simply annoying and unwelcome? We need to balance our desire to pursue with a commitment to kindness. We need to treat a person as we would want to be treated, to respect and believe another's statements rather than second-guessing or presuming to know better.

Sometimes such patient graciousness can bear fruit. Songwriter Felicia Brady sings about a woman who has finally gotten up the courage to allow a man to love her.

> A little while ago you offered me a ride.
> I averted my eyes and graciously declined.
> You know me well by now, you can spot my defense
> And the grand entrance of Ice Princess.
>
> I've had one foot out the door because,
> well, because of things.
> I could come up with reasons.
> I could come up with nothing.

1. Lucy Maud Montgomery, *Anne of Avonlea*, in *Anne of Green Gables: Three Volumes in One* (New York: Avenel, 1986), 446.

But you've been constant, you've found me fine.
Becoming has taken me some time.
And I've decided to let you move me.

I am over here, and I am over there.
You stand upright while I flutter around you.
I stay in motion so you can't stir me.
But now I'm ready to come in for a landing.
And I've decided to let you move me.[2]

Sometimes we reject love for the wrong reasons—fear of being known, fear of being pinned down, fear of being hurt. Then we are like the woman in this song, fluttering around, staying in motion so we cannot be caught. Such a person, who is rejecting love out of fear, may eventually come to love his or her pursuer if loved with patience and without pressure.

Being loved by someone can be very seductive. Given that in most mutual relationships one person was attracted before the other, one common way for attraction to become mutual is through the power of love to elicit love in return. There is something powerfully attractive about being admired and appreciated. It is also possible that knowing you are loved will make it possible for you to trust the other person enough to offer love in return. One woman says candidly about a man she had a brief relationship with:

My interest in him was simply that he was interested in me, and this was a new experience for me. I did not have a lot of self-confidence at the time, and his interest made me feel special. I was not romantically attracted to him, but he gave me the attention I wanted.

Telling someone of your love for him or her may elicit love, but it can also be dangerous. Instead of eliciting love, you may leave yourself open to being taken advantage of or even abused. A young man tells about the transformation of a friendship into a dating relationship in just this way.

2. Felicia Brady, "Move Me," *Magazine Street* (Cambridge, MA: Magazine Street Music, 2001). Used by permission.

We became good friends, particularly because we both worked similar hours and could therefore spend a lot of time together. We played video games together and rode bikes together—two fun things. I still remember the first time I met her—it was not love at first sight. She ended up telling me that she liked me. I was not even thinking like that, but since I had never dated anyone before, I decided to go for it.

Although she has gotten him to go out with her, his motivation is not based on attraction. Instead, he wants to have a dating experience, and he now knows that she will not reject him. So he takes advantage of her to have someone to date.

Another possibility is that love will evaporate once it is returned. Some people only fall in love with those who are unattainable. One woman tells of the pain created in her life by a man who wooed her then lost interest when she said yes:

> Over the next year or two we were friends. He would tell me how much he liked me, and I was uneasy about it all. I didn't know if I was attracted to him; I was too young. But he would tell me that he cared for me, and then he would turn around and start dating someone else. I remember being turned off by his personality and his insecurities. But I think what is most amazing about it all is how I got strung along into thinking I was attracted to you.[3] It was as though my "needy" self who longed to be in a relationship where we would share, love, learn respect, etc. would rationalize that maybe he would suffice. Maybe he would be good to me, and maybe I just need to let myself go. So I would tell myself that I would give this a try. And when I would come to that conclusion, then he was no longer interested in me, leaving me hurt and crushed, especially because he was the one who was so interested in me, and my attraction to him fell out of his attraction to me.

Some people are able to love only those who are unattainable or at least uninterested, perhaps because loving someone who might love them back is too frightening. If you are being pursued by such a person, your surrender to the appeal of being loved will result in that love being quickly withdrawn. Christine Lavin

---

3. The student really did write "you" here, not "him." Clearly, while writing, she found herself addressing him in her mind.

sings about this tendency in her song "Attainable Love" about a middle-aged man who is always in love with "serious actresses" and other women who are unattainable. Lavin's diagosis is that "he is afraid of attainable love, afraid it will envelop him, swallow him up." She sings of the frustrations of this man's many female friends, saying, "They wonder if he's gay, but the truth is he's not; he just won't settle for whatever it is he's got."[4]

One woman tells of loving a man like this who never loved her back.

> I do think that there's something "wrong" with him, or at least something that most people in our society would think is wrong, since he just can't get into a serious romantic relationship. I saw how he was with me, and I've heard stories of how he's been with other women, and I've even watched him pursue one woman since we broke up—which was pretty painful for me to see! I think I see the pattern now. He's very drawn to a woman that he's just met, and he asks her out for coffee, and there's all this great conversation. His great gift is getting people to talk to him, to open their hearts to him, and so women are always completely charmed and tell him their whole life story. I know I did. Which means that things start to feel intimate and serious very quickly. At which point, he backs off. Always. I've come to think that there's something about that deep sharing, getting to know one another seriously, which triggers something inside him so that he stops being attracted. It's sort of as if you've suddenly been recategorized as his sister, you know? He can only feel romantically attracted to women who are far away. As soon as you get close, this weird trigger goes off and all his attraction to you evaporates. Or maybe a better image then evaporates—a door slams on it, so it's locked away. He's still sweet and funny and kind, but he doesn't acknowledge feeling any romantic attraction.

Most of us would probably agree that such a man has some problems that he needs to confront. At the very least, he needs to stop asking women out and leading them to trust him with their deepest thoughts. The attention he offers women is often interpreted as romantic, even if that is not his intention, which means he needs to become very good at maintaining appropriate

---

4. Christine Lavin, "Attainable Love," *Attainable Love* (Cambridge, MA: Rounder Records, 1990).

boundaries. Perhaps this woman is wrong in thinking that his intentions were ever romantic, but he clearly stirred up unfair expectations. She, however, has another more generous explanation for this man's behavior.

> Now on the one hand, it seems kind of clear that such a trigger is a psychological malfunction, right? I'm sure that's what most therapists would think. But on the other hand, it's a great device for keeping yourself chaste. It's only because he's developed this response that he's been able to live a godly, celibate life for all these years. He's in his mid-forties, and he's a virgin, not because he doesn't experience sexual desire but because his self-control is so developed. It's precisely this spiritual discipline, this real *virtue*, that makes me love him as much as I do, so how can I be upset when one consequence of that disciplined virtue is that he can't love me the way I wish he could? These things are two sides of one coin. If I love his virtue, then I have to love—or at least accept—his inability to love me romantically. They're one package.

Perhaps. But if this reaction of retreat when he begins to know a woman well is a strategy for keeping himself chaste, then why is he leading women into such relationships to begin with? A mature Christian man in his mid-forties should know better.

Yet this woman is surely right in seeing that an unwillingness to enter into deep, emotional commitments is not inherently a problem. Our therapeutic culture is quick to label such unwillingness an inadequacy, but that would be true only if each of us had an obligation to enter into a romantic relationship and pursue marriage. Christians cannot affirm such an obligation. Even those Christians who do enter into deep committed relationships recognize that their commitment to God is higher and more important. All human relationships are at best secondary.

When Augustine thought about his life, he saw that excessive commitment—not only to things but also to people (friends, family, and a woman he was in love with)—were threats to his commitment to God. Contemporary readers of Augustine's *Confessions* tend to think this shows he was hung up about sex. But isn't it a sign of wisdom to know our weaknesses and to fight against them? Isn't it a sign of wisdom to insist on placing God first in our life, even if it means giving up things that people around us think they cannot possibly live without? It is appropriate for Christians to give up romantic intimacy, but we need to be honest with others when we do so. A virtuous man should not have led a woman to believe he cared about her only to draw back from that suggestion without accepting responsibility for having made it.

Moving from Friendship to Romance and Back Again

Someone who loves us has a stronger claim on our attention when he or she is already a good friend than when that person is a new acquaintance or even a stranger. At the same time, the cost of exploring a romantic relationship with a good friend will be high if the romance does not work. One woman pointed out:

> There are different kinds of rejections. There's the person you care about so you try and love them and you still want to be friends with, and they're still going to be in your life and so you have to at least be sympathetic and stuff. But there's the kind of rejection that's just the random guy you meet somewhere, and he's a cool guy and you go out on a couple dates and then you're just like, I don't feel like doing this anymore. It doesn't really matter because you'll never see him again. So it really depends. Going into a relationship, it depends what kind of person it is.

When people say, "I don't want to jeopardize our friendship," they are often being completely sincere. Moving from friendship to romance and then back again is much more complicated than starting to date someone you have just met and then breaking up.

If a close friend really loves you, this is not a gift to be lightly discarded. I had a friend in graduate school who was very happy in his marriage. I remember asking him how he had met his wife and how he had decided to marry. He told me he did not feel he had the right to turn away from love when it was offered to him. At first, I was rather taken aback by this answer, wondering whether that was a good reason to marry. However, I appreciate that he saw the offer of love as something precious. He saw that he should take that offer seriously and treat the woman who loved

213

him with tenderness and respect, whatever his own feelings. Out of such tenderness and respect, mutual love has grown.

One woman tells about the time she spent wondering about a possible romance with a good friend only to find that he had never seriously thought about that possibility. The romantic relationship that had been so important to her had been largely imaginary.

I liked him for a year. I really thought that we were headed in the direction of a romantic relationship. . . . So many things were really pointing toward his interest in me, toward the fact that he was interested in developing a relationship. Then suddenly he just sort of stopped talking to me. I was really very confused. I really felt that we were moving in this direction and suddenly just communication seems to be sort of lacking. We would talk in public situations but never together. We would never do things together, and that was really confusing to me. I got angry with him, and I told him, what's up, what's the deal? Why are you not calling me, talking to me? He was really sorry about that, but he never answered my question. We went into the summer sort of tense, with a tenseness in our relationship. Throughout the summer we wrote each other a little bit, but it was very difficult. I really still was interested in him; I really liked him a lot. He was just what I thought my ideal would have been.

In the fall, when he came back, he talked about the girl he had met over the summer at camp who he really felt was *his* ideal, and suddenly I was just so hurting. Then we did talk. Finally, it all came out; everything came out—my interest in him and his non-interest in me. For all this time that I spent thinking about it and analyzing it and wondering, does this mean he's interested in me, are we headed in that direction, what's going to happen next, when is he going to ask me out?—all this time I spent, and he said that he thought about it once walking to my dorm. He walked from one dorm to the next thinking, would it ever work between us? No. And that was it. That was the extent of his thought process. That just boggled my mind because I had thought about it so much, and I had seen it as such a sure thing. But we did talk about it, and it was very helpful. It took me a long time to heal from that, but I think we came out of it on top because he and I remain friends, although he admits he had no idea how much he was leading me on and leading me to have these feelings and being so unaware. That has been something I have been able to help him with in his relationships now, asking him, What are you saying? What sort of message are you sending by doing this? That has been really good for him, and he has been helpful to me in lots of areas too, not just romantically, teaching me about not assuming things.

In this (rare) case, the friendship was strengthened by the woman's decision to talk about her feelings. Why? Because she spoke the truth in love and continues to do so. Now, both she and her friend are more likely to read relationships accurately. She will be less likely to invest friendly gestures with romantic weight, and he will be less likely to lead other women on in the name of friendship.

Often, however, the ending is more painful. When men and women are close friends, they often decide not to pursue romantic possibilities because they do not wish to jeopardize their friendship. This is not just a line. It is difficult to return to friendship after trying to have a romantic relationship, and even if some sort of friendship is achieved, it is seldom as close as it once was. Entering into a romantic relationship with a close friend, therefore, is potentially costly.

Because this situation can be so painful, men and women become increasingly wary as they grow older about developing close friendships with those of the opposite sex. It is easier to have a close friendship with someone who is obviously and unambiguously off-limits romantically—such as someone who is married—than with an unmarried person of the opposite sex. Yet such friendships usually have elements of romantic tension to them, and it is necessary to be careful and intentional about maintaining appropriate boundaries.

James Taylor points out that sexual sin is all about "overstepping bounds." Our problem is not that we have sexual desires but that we fail to recognize where those desires may and may not be met. He explains, "It's no coincidence, I believe, that the traditional wording of the Lord's Prayer, as it is used in most churches, defines our sins against each other as 'trespasses.'"[5] As we grow older, we are more aware of trespassing and more aware of those who trespass against us.

---

5. James Taylor, *Sin: A New Understanding of Virtue and Vice* (Kelowna, BC: Northstone, 1997), 91.

To Tell or Not to Tell?

All of this leaves us with the question of whether we should tell of our love. Given the possibilities of creating offense and of bringing more pain on yourself, is it wise to let your feelings be seen when you fall for someone who has not fallen for you? There is the possibility that you will elicit love by showing love, but there is also the possibility that you will drive the one you love even farther away.

There is something admirable about being honest and forthright. One young woman expressed her admiration for a boy who had written her a letter in high school, stating his love for her.

> That letter was so bold. I totally respect that. I kept that letter for a long time just because it was so . . . wow! It was really amazing that somebody would have the guts to do that.

His boldness elicited not love but a similar bold honesty on her part. After reading the letter, she promptly called him on the phone and told him she had no feelings for him.

> I said, "I am very, very flattered by the letter, but I don't feel the same way. I'm really sorry. I don't want to do this over the phone. I'm really sorry." He said, "No, no, I completely understand." Even though he said that, I still felt really, really bad. And in the back of my mind I was thinking, you know, maybe I could like him, make him feel better. But then I thought, I have no feelings for this person. None. Then, as the phone call ended, I said the dreaded line: "We can still be friends!"

Despite the line, they did not remain friends. Yet this woman did not regret confronting her former friend in this straightforward way rather than ignoring the letter or sending a more equivocal message. This early experience led her to form a policy of truth telling in relationships. She said, "I'm not going to pursue anything that would make him hurt more or play him or anything like that, because that would be mean." She was consistently committed to telling the truth in love, even though that was initially less comfortable for her.

Later in high school, this same young woman was on the other side of a relationship, and she credits the boldness of her early suitor with making her bold when she was attracted to someone. "I think that gave me the guts to do what I did. . . . I respect a person who can do something like that." Regarding her own decision to tell the young man she was attracted to about her attraction, she claims that it made her "a stronger person." At the same time, she sees the decision as one that resulted in severe embarrassment.

> We'd become pretty close friends in a nonromantic way. We would just talk a lot, and hang out, and talk on the phone. Other people were saying stuff about us—Are they going out?—we weren't, but I really thought it was going to happen. . . . I let this go on for three-fourths of the school year, and I was really scared to do something because I just wasn't sure. Then finally I thought, "You have to! You have to live in the moment, and do something now! Seize the day!" . . . I remember we were in the back hall at school between classes, and no one was there. The hallways were empty. I said, "Hey, I have to tell you something. . . . I just really have to get it off my chest, because you're ready to go to college, and I don't know what's going to happen to you. I really like you a lot. I don't know where I want this to go, but I just wanted you to know that." He said, "Wow, that's great." I was waiting for something more, and he said, "Well, I don't know what to say." I said, "I know, I know. I don't really know what I want you to say." He said, "This is really hard for me. I don't know if I feel the same about you." I said, "Oh. Okay. Well. Okay." The whole time I was just saying "Okay" I wasn't really listening to him because I was just freaking out. He said, "I don't really like you, not that way." I said, "I understand," and, you know, I really *didn't*. Then he said, "I like somebody else, and I was going to ask you to set me up with her." I said, "Oh, who is this?" He said the name, and it was one of my friends at the time. He said, "I'm really sorry, I'm really sorry." And I said, "No, you don't have to be sorry." I meant don't be sorry for your feelings, you know, but I wasn't really convincing. . . . He said, "Well, can you call her for me?" And I was like, "Come on!" . . . I actually ended up hooking those two up together, even though it was very, very painful.

Despite the heart-wrenching nature of this story, even seen from several years distance, this woman does not regret sharing her feelings.

It could have been a lot worse. I really think I learned a lot from that experience, even though it hurt a lot. I think I learned what I *was*. I gained a better sense of vocalizing my emotions and just being able to say, "This is how I feel about you." I can say that so easily to other people, in platonic relationships and everything. I had never really dated anyone seriously, so this was all very new to me, and I guess I wanted to take the experience, take the situation strongly. I want to be a strong woman. I don't want to see myself be weak like all these other girls I know. So I think I learned how to be stronger. Or I learned that I was strong enough to do something like this. That's important. It's important to be able to just say how you feel, even though you know rejection is the other side of the coin. . . . When I told my friends what happened, they said, "Oh my gosh, I can't believe you did that! That's amazing!" And I was like, "I know!" I think having that experience really taught me a lot.

It is certainly true that telling is generally the braver action, in the sense of confronting our natural fears and insecurities. So it is not uncommon to find that people are quite pleased with themselves for expressing their feelings, even if the end result may not be what they wanted. One woman described herself as "a chicken," saying, "That's one of my flaws: I don't think I could ever tell anybody unless he told me first." However, as a result of her reticence, she has no embarrassing tales to tell of being rejected. She always saved face, even when she was attracted to someone who was not attracted in return. Silence may often be the more self-protective decision.

Despite such common perceptions, silence may also be a courageous option. In the play *Cyrano de Bergerac*, the hero, Cyrano, who is a man of great physical courage, is asked by Roxanne, the woman he loves, to be her intermediary with a young man she finds attractive. Cyrano stifles his own expressions of love for her, which he had been preparing before their meeting, and agrees to help her. As she prepares to leave, she commends him for his courage in facing down one hundred armed men the night before. "I have fought better since," he answers, referring (though she does not know this) to his battle with his own feelings, which he has suppressed out of care for her.[6]

6. Edmond Rostand, *Cyrano de Bergerac: A Heroic Comedy in Five Acts*, trans. Louis Untermeyer (New York: Heritage Press, 1954), 70 (act 2).

Whether or not it is the bravest decision, expressing your love is probably not the kindest decision if you are reasonably sure your feelings will not be returned. Over time people get better at communicating this and at picking up the message, making painful scenes of self-revelation less necessary. Thinking about the encounter from the perspective of the person receiving the revelation will help you see that being placed in such a position is awkward at best. The truly loving act may be not to tell. After all, honesty does not require total self-revelation. You do not owe the revelation of your deepest feelings to everyone you know. It is legitimate to keep some feelings hidden and private. More than that, it is both wise and kind to do so.

You should not tell of your love when it would be wrong to enter into a relationship with the person to whom you are attracted. Keith Clark suggests that when we make a decision to express our feelings, we are stepping into the area of personal responsibility. We may not be responsible for the feelings themselves, but we are certainly responsible for choosing to share them, which is a first step toward deciding to act on them. Therefore, you should not share your feelings if you have fallen in love with a non-Christian or someone you know you could not marry. You should not share your feelings if you have fallen in love with someone who is married, or if you are married but have fallen in love with someone else, or if you are convinced that God has called you to a celibate life. Clark says that although there is no guilt in falling in love, since that is not under your control, talking about your love is another matter, since that is something you can choose. Once you start talking about a love you should not act on, it becomes harder not to act. Pretty soon you will find yourself taking what Clark calls a "roadblock" approach to romance, saying, "Well, at least I didn't do such and such."[7] This is what happened in the case of Thomas Merton, considered in the last chapter. He comforted himself that at least he had not had sex with M., a minimalist approach to keeping his commitments. Rather than share feelings and then try to keep yourself from acting on them, you should not share feelings on

7. Keith Clark, *An Experience of Celibacy: A Creative Reflection on Intimacy, Loneliness, Sexuality, and Commitment* (Notre Dame: Ave Maria Press, 1982), 167–69.

which it would be inappropriate to act. Clark does suggest that you share your feelings with someone you can count on to hold you accountable to your primary commitments, someone who will help you see the implications of your feelings and will give you an outlet for expressing them.[8]

However, if you are not going to express your feelings to the person who is the object of them, you should also refrain from expressing them to many others. One trusted confidant is one thing, but gossiping about your feelings with all your friends is a poor idea. A common problem is that people share their feelings with friends who then share those feelings with others. Here is one woman's account:

> Bob was/is a very nice guy, and I just fell for him. . . . However, I never directly said anything to him about wanting to date, so in retrospect I really think he was oblivious. Now it was a pretty well-known fact among my circle of girlfriends that I had a crush on Bob. And due to the ironclad laws of gossip, it was inevitable that this news would leak into the public, sooner or later. And it did when both Bob and I were on a bus to a softball game. Somehow news of my crush traveled to the guys' part of the bus, and someone asked Bob if he liked me. Bob said no, not like that. When it was revealed that I liked him, Bob became more adamant in not liking me.
>
> News of this traveled back to me, and I was absolutely crushed and ate a whole bag of Doritos. . . . After the double-header, Bob came up to me and basically said what amounted to "no chance." Although at the time I didn't realize it, Bob had a crush of his own, and it wasn't on me. He's been engaged for a year now, and I think the wedding is this summer. Anyway, I was completely crushed after this whole episode, and the worst part is that Bob and I will never be good friends again.

Because she did not tell Bob her feelings herself yet told many others, the news was broken to Bob in an uncomfortable way, leading to the breakup of their friendship. It takes discipline not to gossip about your feelings. Such gossip, even if not vindictive, can be hurtful. By gossiping in this way, you turn the other person into an object for speculation, undermin-

8. Ibid., 165.

ing his or her dignity. You turn love into a game rather than treating your feelings and the other person's feelings with care and gentleness.

Karen talks of the exhaustion she experiences because her consuming love cannot be expressed. Her tendency is to talk about it with all her friends, since she cannot talk about it with the man with whom she is in love. Recently, she has decided that this is not such a good idea. One wise friend suggested a better outlet. "One of my friends just told me that maybe I should just pray for him, and then that is how I can express it without getting anything back from him. . . . That's helped." Talking to God is a better idea than talking to all your friends, both because prayer is more discreet and because it is more helpful. Praying for the person we love helps us to express that love in ways that are neither demanding nor resentful. Bringing our loneliness and need to God allows us to experience our dependence on God's love, recognizing that our ultimate identity is found in him rather than in any other relationship.

No matter how sure you think you are that your love will not be returned, there is an impetus to share love. Remaining silent can be almost physically painful. Returning again to *Twelfth Night*, Viola (who, incidentally, is hiding from her father's enemies by masquerading as a man and has fallen in love with the duke, whom she is serving, although he has not figured out that she is a woman) talks about the damage that may be done by holding in one's feelings of love. She responds to the duke's assurance that a woman cannot love as much as a man by telling him of a woman's great love:

> My father had a daughter loved a man. . . .
> She never told her love,
> But let concealment, like a worm i' th' bud,
> Feed on her damask cheek. She pined in thought;
> And, with a green and yellow melancholy,
> She sat like Patience on a monument,
> Smiling at grief. Was not this love indeed?[9]

9. William Shakespeare, *Twelfth Night, or What You Will*, in *The Complete Works*, ed. Stanley Wells and Gary Taylor (Oxford: Oxford University Press, 1988), act 2, scene 4, lines 107, 110–15.

Love naturally wants to declare itself, and concealment feels most unnatural. Given this inner compulsion to share one's feelings, what really shows more courage: to share or to conceal? Given the estrangement that almost always results when feelings are shared but not returned, what shows more concern for the other person's feelings: to share or to conceal? Might it be possible to maintain a true friendship by not sharing everything you feel? Or is such a friendship simply too painful? In her song "I Love You," Sarah McLachlan sings about the pain of not expressing love, a pain that feels like grief. It is hard for her to be around the one she loves because "there's too much I can't say."[10] Silence brings its own grief, different from the grief of outright rejection but also painful.

Dana Gioia's poem "Unsaid" reminds us that this painful silence is not just about romance; much of what is important in our life is not expressed externally.

> So much of what we live goes on inside—
> The diaries of grief, the tongue-tied aches
> Of unacknowledged love are no less real
> For having passed unsaid. What we conceal
> Is always more than what we dare confide.
> Think of the letters that we write our dead.[11]

Part of this silence is a result of loneliness in the world, but part of it is the inadequacy of words. Most of us are simply not sufficiently eloquent to express what we feel without confusion. This is another reason why prayer is the best outlet for our self-expression, for in prayer the Holy Spirit helps us to transcend the limits of language and to bring the fullness of our selves to God (Rom. 8:26).

Ultimately, it is an insult to the one we claim to love if we persist too long. The clearest illustration of such insult is Mr. Collins's proposal to Elizabeth Bennett in *Pride and Prejudice*. At first, even though she finds Mr. Collins repellant and ridiculous, Elizabeth responds to his proposal politely, saying, "Accept my

10. Sarah McLachlan, "I Love You," *Surfacing* (New York: BMG, 1997).
11. Dana Gioia, "Unsaid," in *Interrogations at Noon* (Saint Paul, MN: Graywolf Press, 2001), 69. Used by permission.

thanks for the compliment you are paying me, I am very sensible of the honour of your proposals, but it is impossible for me to do otherwise than decline them." However, she finds that Mr. Collins is undeterred.

> "I am not now to learn," replied Mr. Collins, with a formal wave of the hand, "that it is usual with young ladies to reject the addresses of the man whom they secretly mean to accept, when he first applies for their favour; and that sometimes the refusal is repeated a second or even a third time. I am therefore by no means discouraged by what you have just said, and shall hope to lead you to the altar ere long."
>
> "Upon my word, Sir," cried Elizabeth, "your hope is rather an extraordinary one after my declaration. I do assure you that I am not one of those young ladies (if such young ladies there are) who are so daring as to risk their happiness on the chance of being asked a second time. I am perfectly serious in my refusal. You could not make *me* happy, and I am convinced that I am the last woman in the world who would make *you* so. . . . You must give me leave to judge for myself, and pay me the compliment of believing what I say. . . . This matter may be considered, therefore, as finally settled."
>
> And rising as she thus spoke, she would have quitted the room, had not Mr. Collins thus addressed her, "When I do myself the honour of speaking to you next on this subject I shall hope to receive a more favourable answer than you have now given me; though I am far from accusing you of cruelty at present, because I know it to be the established custom of your sex to reject a man on the first application, and perhaps you have even now said as much to encourage my suit as would be consistent with the true delicacy of the female character."
>
> "Really, Mr. Collins," cried Elizabeth with some warmth, "you puzzle me exceedingly. If what I have hitherto said can appear to you in the form of encouragement, I know not how to express my refusal in such a way as may convince you of its being one."[12]

Elizabeth's advice to those pursuing romance is good: "Pay me the compliment of believing what I say." Whether you respond to rejection with an indulgent smile or indignant protests, it is

---

12. Jane Austen, *Pride and Prejudice*, vol. 2 in *The Oxford Illustrated Jane Austen*, 3rd ed. (Oxford: Oxford University Press, 1965), 107–8.

not loving to disbelieve the other person's representation of his or her feelings.

Mr. Collins should serve as a warning to all who continue to pursue love in the face of clear and forthright rejection. The hope that the love we show will elicit love in return is not without foundation. However, our cultural script encourages us to persist, in hope if not in active pursuit, long past the point of being flattering, so that our very persistence comes to hurt our pursuit. Austen labeled such persistence "willful self-deception," but it is a self-deception in which popular culture cooperates. It is this self-deception that can make rejecting someone very daunting.

First Corinthians 13 tells us that love "bears all things, believes all things, hopes all things, endures all things" (v. 7). Some Christians believe this means we should never stop loving someone, no matter how our love is received. In one sense, this is obviously true. We should never give up on the overwhelming love of God in which we are invited to share. But that is different from saying we must continue to believe and hope for romantic fulfillment, even after we have been rejected. How do we move on from rejection in a way that still honors the commandment to love our neighbors as ourselves? This is the challenge of the next chapter.

10

Aftereffects

Happiness comes more from loving than being loved; and often when our affection seems wounded it is only our vanity bleeding. To love, and to be hurt often, and to love again—this is the brave and happy life.

J. E. Buckrose[1]

Love is patient; love is kind; love is not envious or boastful or arrogant or rude. It does not insist on its own way; it is not irritable or resentful; it does not rejoice in wrongdoing, but rejoices in the truth. It bears all things, believes all things, hopes all things, endures all things. Love never ends.

1 Corinthians 13:4–8

A painful experience of unrequited love can have lasting effects. One possible effect is that a person who has been hurt will avoid being hurt again. One man said:

I had one huge rejection, and now I'm always the rejector. Which is how it goes, you know. . . . I take it to the extreme, I think, as far as safe-guarding myself. . . . I go into relationships very skeptical, and I'm very, very cautious, which is a problem. I'm

1. J. E. Buckrose is the pseudonym of Annie Edith (Foster) Jameson. This quotation is on dozens of Internet sites with no further source information.

overly cautious, overly guarding my heart. My thing now is that I do guard a lot of who I am.

Another man said, "When you get knocked off a horse, you learn to stay away from horses." Despite the conventional wisdom about needing to "get back out there," this cautious attitude seems reasonable, especially in the immediate aftermath of rejection.

Having been hurt can also make people less willing to hurt others. One man said, "I definitely don't like giving pain because I know how it feels, which is why I'm much more tactful." In fact, many people say this is the greatest value of going through a heartbreaking experience of rejection: you become a more sensitive and decent person.

Ultimately, most people think they have learned things through their experiences of unrequited love and that the experiences have been worthwhile, even though they have not led to a lasting relationship. As one woman put it:

> I think every relationship, every person I have been in a relationship with has had some impact on my life, and not just as learning for me, but as an end in itself. There's something good in each of those relationships, and I'm glad now to look back without pain at most of them. Because now from a distance you can say, you know, that was neat. This was neat about it; this wasn't.

The experience of unrequited love also helps us set aside our self-centeredness, reminding us that the world does not exist for our convenience. It teaches us to let go of what we expect in order to receive what we have been given. We need to be willing to grieve for lost hopes and open our eyes to new possibilities. One man said:

> If I'm going to live the Christian life . . . then I've got to put myself to the side and move my ego out of the way. I've got to say: God, this is who I am and what I want and need, but the world isn't here for me. I'm here to serve. I'm here to worship the Lord my Creator. So that's the tension, to know clearly what I want, but I also know that I need to put me on the back burner.

As Walter Trobisch says, "The task we have to face is the same, whether we are married or single: *To live a fulfilled life in spite of many unfulfilled desires.*"[2] The Christian life is not about the pursuit of happiness, the avoidance of suffering, or the meeting of desire. The Christian life is about being transformed into the likeness of Christ, from one degree of glory to another, by sharing in his death and surrendering our will to him (2 Cor. 3:18–4:18). The promise of the gospel is that the by-product of such surrender will be deep happiness: fullness of life and unending joy. But we can receive such happiness only when we stop pursuing it directly.

Love and Anger

It is not uncommon for unrequited love to mutate into something else: rage, hatred, loathing, even violence. Shakespeare wrote, "Hell hath no fury like a woman scorned." Women know that it is not only women whose fury may be triggered by rejection; scorned men can also grow bitter. Love may become "a jagged little pill," as Alanis Morissette so graphically puts it.[3] The experience of rejection will bring many of us to this point of anger. One man told of how a woman he broke up with "freaked out, poured catsup and bologna all over my van, all this acidic stuff that would eat the paint off. It was just an ugly, ugly time."

Many people suggest that this anger is healthy. Garrison Keillor, who wrote an online advice column for a few years under the name Mr. Blue, gave this advice to a woman who had just been dumped by her long-term boyfriend and had asked, "How do I salvage my dignity?"

The psychological advantage is with the abandoner, who steels himself to make the break, announces it, fends off all entreaties,

---

2. Walter Trobisch, "Love Is a Feeling to Be Learned," in *The Complete Works of Walter Trobisch: Answers about Love, Sex, Self-Esteem, and Personal Growth* (Downers Grove, IL: InterVarsity, 1987), 126.

3. Alanis Morissette, "You Learn," *Jagged Little Pill* (Burbank: Maverick, 1995).

and marches off into the night, a brave soldier who did what needed to be done. Meanwhile, the abandoned feels like [dirt]. But you are not without resources. Do not be pitiful; be [angry]. If you've been crying on your friends' shoulders, stop. . . . Get a haircut and buy some new duds. Cut out alcohol and put yourself on a diet of greens and fruit. Hurl yourself into profitable activity: Read a book a week, enroll in a French class, memorize poetry, go to the gym daily. Do this for ninety days, and at the end of it, sit down and ask yourself how you feel about your life. Ninety days of self-improvement fueled by anger should use up much of your anger, and then you can have the final revenge, which is to forgive the pitiful [jerk] and get on with your life.[4]

Although he does anticipate a time of forgiveness (of a sort), Keillor also suggests embracing anger as a short-term strategy for fending off despair and a loss of dignity. While Keillor is often a wise man, this intentional cultivation of anger is not the best idea. Anger is corrosive. Even if it never leads you to harm someone—and in many cases, people do resort to harmful, vindictive, even violent behavior as a result of their anger at romantic rejection—it will harm you.

Ann had a very different attitude toward anger, one which—on the whole—is more healthy.

Bill and I went to the same church, and when he dumped me I gave some thought to switching churches. I had been so seriously in love with him, even though we had only dated for a short time, and I really thought that he had led me on. . . . So I figured I had a right to be angry, but I also really liked this church and knew that I was going to have to forgive him in order to stay there. I remember the pastor calling me up and asking me if I would help serve communion one Sunday right after Bill had told me he just wanted to be friends. I wasn't scheduled to serve that Sunday, but the pastor thought he might need one more person. The upshot of the conversation was that I'd be on stand-by to serve if I were needed, and I remember catching myself hoping that I wouldn't be needed, because I knew that if I served communion, I'd have to *take* communion. And if I were going to take

4. Mr. Blue, "If Love's Not There to Begin with, Is It Ever Gonna Be?" July 28, 1998, http://archive.salon.com/col/keil/1998/07/nc_28keil.html (accessed November 5, 2004).

communion, I would have to forgive this guy. When I realized what I was thinking and hoping, I was just horrified with myself. I mean, think about it. Hoping that you wouldn't have to forgive someone! What kind of Christian am I? So I prayed a lot about it, asking God to help me let go of all the anger I was experiencing. When I went to church the next Sunday, it turned out I didn't have to serve after all, but I knew that didn't let me off the hook. So I found Bill before the service and went right up to him—he looked a little nervous when he saw me coming; I'd been pretty obviously annoyed with him when we'd had our little talk, and I think he expected a scene—but I went up to him, and smiled, and put out my hand, and just said, "Before I take communion today, I need to know: Are we all right?" He seemed kind of startled but relieved too, and he smiled back a little more than was quite natural and shook my hand, stammering something like, "Sure, we're fine."

So I was pretty pleased with myself about having forgiven this jerk, when a few weeks later I was at a party with a bunch of church folks, and Bill was there along with his best friend who was visiting from out of town. I'd been very careful not to let anyone from church know about the tension between Bill and me, both for his sake and for mine. No one knew that we'd dated for a couple weeks, and no one knew about the breakup. But I figured that his best friend probably knew, and even if he didn't I didn't feel any particular need to keep him in the dark. I found myself talking to Bill and his friend quite a bit, without any other people really being in our conversation, and I kept making the most cutting, nasty jokes at Bill's expense. I didn't make any explicit references to the breakup event, but there was definitely a subtext, which I didn't usually allow to come through when I saw him at church. The friend thought it was really funny, and so did Bill actually. I think, in retrospect, that he found that sort of anger preferable to maudlin, weepy neediness. I was just starting to learn that he'd gone through those sorts of scenes with some other women in the church, so I suppose my response of discreet, controlled anger was kind of a relief to him. I was too proud to act hurt or wounded, so I just ripped into him. When I went home that night I realized that I had *not* forgiven this man. Not at all. I had to start working on that project all over again. It took me months of prayer and self-examination and repentance and starting over before I think I had really forgiven him. Which, of course, was painful in a whole different way, because then I had to admit to myself that I was still wildly in love with him. In fact, the process of forgiving him made me more in love with him, and letting go of the anger meant I didn't really have any defense against that emotion.

Ann recognized that anger was a defense against the pain of loving this man, and when she let go of the anger, she found herself defenseless. This is one reason it is so tempting to give in to anger and hate: it is a form of protection and self-defense. But it is a protection that exacts a great cost. Although it may feel like a way to restore lost self-esteem, it is a poisonous and improper way.

What gives rise to this response of anger, a response that is so difficult to resist or change? Partly, this feeling is based on the false assumption that our feelings have some sort of normative weight with the other person, that he or she is ethically obligated to love us because we feel love for him or her. Partly, it is the humiliation of having offered what is most precious in ourselves to someone and having had it devalued. The more we offer, the more the pain. Being turned down when you invite someone to go to the movies does not hurt as much as when you have told someone you are in love with him or her. The pain is intensified if someone else is preferred to you. One man was rejected by a woman after telling her he loved her. He said, "The thing that I really, really got disillusioned with is that, less than a year later, she got engaged to somebody she had known from high school. So it's not that she was against the concept of marriage or romance or commitment, just with me."

Romantic rejection is inescapably personal. In the movie *When Harry Met Sally*, the character Sally appears untroubled and serene when her long-term boyfriend breaks off their relationship. She has convinced herself that he is simply immature, incapable of commitment, clinging to his boyish irresponsibility. This story of the breakup allows her to continue thinking well of herself. However, she goes to pieces some months later when she hears that he is engaged to marry someone else. The story she has been telling herself—that she was not the problem in the relationship, he was—is suddenly revealed as untrue. Once he makes a commitment to someone else, she can no longer believe her story. Suddenly, she has to face the fact that he had not rejected marriage; he had rejected her.[5]

5. *When Harry Met Sally* (MGM, 1989).

This is why love most often turns to hatred not when we are rejected but when someone else is preferred to us. We can accept rejection without too much bitterness as long as we can believe it is rooted in a quality of the other person: an inability to make commitments, unresolved pain over a past relationship, religious differences, a fear of marital failure. Our therapeutic culture offers us many ways to rationalize being rejected without ever having to look at ourselves. But once the person who has refused to love us turns to love someone else, all those reasons are exposed as illusions. The real reason we have been rejected now appears to be that we are not worthy. It is much easier to become angry than to face that painful possibility.

Lauren Winner writes about the experience of discovering that her ex-boyfriend Steven was engaged less than six months after they broke up. She confesses, "It shakes me, their pending nuptials. I just don't get it." She thinks of the letters that Steven wrote her, begging her to marry him. How can she understand such letters now, in light of his decision to marry someone else so quickly? And why did she have to hear about his engagement from someone else rather than from him directly?

> I am a mean and petty person, and a terrible Christian to boot, and I spend all weekend hoping that Steven and his bride will be miserable, that his brilliant dissertation will turn to straw, that his roof will leak and his car will die and he'll be stuck in a loveless marriage in that god-forsaken town in Arkansas for the rest of his natural life. I hope, too, that she is not a Christian, that she'll lead him down a path of sin and restlessness, away from church and straight toward debauchery. I hope he forgets to baptize the baby all my friends imagine she's carrying.[6]

But Winner has one friend, Sam, who does not reinforce her indignation and anger. He tells her that she should pray for Steven and his bride. He says, "Mouth the words even if all you feel is anger. Remember that the Spirit does our praying for us." Winner notes:

6. Lauren Winner, *Girl Meets God: On the Path to a Spiritual Life* (New York: Shaw Books, 2004), 141.

This advice at first sounds nauseatingly pious. But then somehow it doesn't. I am annoyed when I read his note, because I know he is right. It hadn't occurred to me to pray for them. But Sam is wise, and I pray for Steven and Tiffany, not so much for their sake, but for mine.[7]

Rather than trusting her own words for this difficult prayer, Winner uses a collect for families found in the Book of Common Prayer. It is a hard prayer for her to say, and she cries as she prays, but she keeps praying, using the words of the church and trusting the power of the Spirit. The tears are a good sign. Rather than taking refuge in anger, she is acknowledging her pain.

Feeling Unworthy

If you have ever had to go through an evaluation or performance review at work, you know that this process is nerve-racking. Sometimes a supervisor will make a totally unwarranted criticism, but sometimes criticism helps you to see things about yourself that need to change. Knowing the difference between these two sorts of criticism requires openness to correction, a teachable spirit, and a certain level of detachment. You may not be able to work through the valid criticisms on the day you receive them, but eventually—if you want to improve at work—you will have to confront your failings as well as your achievements.

Romantic rejection requires some of the same skills of discernment, the same ability to distinguish between criticisms that tell you something about the problems of the critic and criticisms from which you need to learn. After romantic rejection, in addition to the work of forgiveness, you may need to do the even harder work of self-examination. Maybe the truth is that this other person was not sufficiently mature or discerning to see your real worth. That is doubtless what all loyal friends will tell you. This person was not worthy of you. This was his loss, or hers, and you are well rid of such a person.

But what if that is not true? Maybe the truth is that this other person was very mature, very discerning, and saw your real worth

7. Ibid.

all too clearly. Could it be that the judgment of this person was correct? Maybe there are things in your character that need to be changed. Perhaps you are often unkind, or domineering, or self-absorbed. Perhaps your eagerness to please makes you anxious, creating anxiety in other people. Perhaps this person who was such a spiritual help to you did not find you spiritually helpful.

Sometimes unrequited love saps the confidence of a person whose confidence should not be sapped. But sometimes we really are unworthy. If I am an unpleasant, bitter, carping person, why should anyone love me? Might this rejection be the necessary impetus for an overdue self-improvement campaign? Might it be the prod I needed to allow God to make me a more righteous person? One woman had just this reaction to romantic rejection.

> I know that I'm still not where he is spiritually, and so in a way I think he's right not to love me. I don't deserve him. I can't say that to any of my friends because they immediately think I have some kind of self-esteem problem and start lecturing me about how I'm too good for him. I don't have any problem with my self-esteem. In fact, my tendency is to think far too well of myself, to avoid looking at my faults. This process of loving him and learning to love him without expecting anything back, to love him freely—it's made me look at my faults and admit to them.

Becoming a better person is a difficult project. There are easier ways to deal with our sense of unworthiness. Rather than becoming more virtuous, more loving, more gracious, we try to alter superficial things about ourselves that do not hit quite so close to home. We try to become someone we are not in order to win love from someone who has rejected the person we are.

Linda admitted that for years whenever she left her apartment she checked around to make sure it would be ready to receive company should she be surprised into bringing someone home with her. After all, while at the grocery store or in the park, she might run into *him*, a man she was infatuated with but who had insisted on being just friends. She might persuade him to come back to her place for dinner or coffee. So there had better be some food for dinner, and some coffee, and some sort of dessert. And the place had better be welcoming and clean, just in case.

233

Linda admits she is not naturally domestic. She is absorbed with her career, and when there is no man in her life, there is also no food in her refrigerator, except perhaps leftover Chinese takeout. But Linda believed this man whom she adored wanted a domestic woman, a homemaker, a good cook, someone to tend to his comfort. She was determined to become that woman. She hid her true self and tried to develop a new self in her efforts to win his approval. His initial rejection had led her to believe that she was inadequate as she was and needed to be remade. But even if Linda's changed patterns made her acceptable to the man she loves, what would that mean exactly? Would he be loving her or a role she was playing for his entertainment?

Jean was on the other side of that equation. She was dating a man she had not known well when they first started seeing each other. The first months of dating were filled with one startling revelation after another, each followed by a radical change on his part. First, it came out that he was not a Christian, indeed, not religious in any way whatsoever. She said this was a problem. Within days he claimed a significant religious experience and gave his life to Christ. He had a long-term drug habit, but to please her he quit cold turkey. He listened only to R&B, but she liked classical music, so soon he did too. He eventually told her he had always been sexually promiscuous, but when he first decided to ask her out, he gave up other women and was reconciled to waiting for sex until he could convince Jean to marry him. She was deeply flattered by all this attention and quite infatuated for several months, but ultimately she broke free. She said that even though his willingness to change for her was intoxicating, she found it difficult to trust that the man she thought she was in love with was the *real* person. Would he change again if she became less important to him? Was he just playing a part? Jean has not stayed in contact with this man, so we have no way of knowing if any of these changes were permanent. It seems unlikely, motivated as they were by his hope of winning her.

Being motivated to genuine self-improvement does not mean making superficial changes or insincere changes in order to satisfy someone else's requirements for your life. It means opening yourself to the transformation that God wants to work in your life, transforming you into a holy and virtuous person.

It means resisting the temptation to excuse your behavior or to blame the one who has rejected you. It means becoming a person who is unafraid to be alone and quiet, to face up to who you are before God.

The Search for a Cure

People are often ambivalent about their feelings of unrequited love. On the one hand, there may be a desire to stay in love, even if the other person will never love you back. When you are deeply in love, the suggestion that you should move on may be distasteful and offensive. Your love for another person may have become so important to you, so much a part of who you think you are, that it is inconceivable to let go. The singer Dido expresses this feeling in her song "White Flag," in which she sings, "I will go down with this ship, and I won't put my hands up and surrender." By "surrendering" she means moving on, giving up her love. Instead, she defiantly announces, "I'm in love and always will be."[8] Her concession to the pressure to move on is that she will keep her love a secret, unexpressed and interior. But she has no real intention of moving on. She is embracing the drama and the pain of loving from a distance.

At the same time, there is usually at least some desire to let go of this love, since it can be a source of deep and real pain. U2 advises letting go in the song "Walk On," in which they counsel, "You can only take so much" heartbreak, and you need to "walk on; leave it behind."[9] But is love, even unrequited love, the sort of thing that should be left behind?

Karen expresses this ambivalence, wanting to stay in love and wanting to get over it at the same time, an ambivalence that now colors her prayers:

> I've prayed that I would get over it, because I thought that, even though I don't even want to get over this, I need to. I thought, maybe this just isn't healthy for me, so I prayed that I would

8. Dido, "White Flag," *Life for Rent* (New York: Arista, 2003).
9. U2, "Walk On," *All That You Can't Leave Behind* (Santa Monica, CA: Interscope Records, 2000).

get over it, and it just got worse. So then I was thinking, Okay, I guess all I can do is pray for strength to deal with it. Maybe it's because I don't want to get over it that God wouldn't let me. I prayed, "Even if I really don't want to get over it, can't you just make me get over it? I mean, even if every inch of my being says I don't want to get over this yet, but can't you just make me?" But it's not happened.

Some of the pressure to move on comes from most people's discomfort with being in the presence of emotional pain. Some people will urge you to move on because your unhappiness makes them uncomfortable. Those who care for you are especially unhappy at the sight of your unhappiness, and forgetting about the painful situation seems like the quickest path back to a happy life. In the face of such pressure, Dido's reaction of keeping her feelings private seems appropriate.

But most of the pressure to move on is based on the assumption that everyone ought to be about the business of finding a life partner and that pining after someone who has rejected you is simply a waste of time. This was exactly the lesson of *He's Just Not That into You,* cited in the introduction. Given the understanding that Christians should embrace singleness as their default way of life, this seems like a poor reason to get over love. Still, when a Christian experiences heartbreak, it is common for other Christians to advise moving on as quickly as possible on the assumption that "God has someone out there for you." Clearly, this failed relationship "wasn't meant to be."

This reaction to a broken heart is flawed for several reasons. First, it is an easy way to avoid considering our own responsibility for the relationships in our life that do not work. If we believe that God himself reached into the relationship and ended it, despite our continued feelings of attraction or even love, then we do not need to own up to the ways we may have sabotaged the relationship by mistreating the person we claimed to care for, or the ways we may have alienated the other person by our excessive jealousy or neediness, or any other way in which we may have contributed to the relationship's breakdown.

Second, attributing another person's rejection of us to God's will fails to recognize the genuine agency of the other person. Such an attitude assumes that the other person would not have made a free choice to reject us but was prompted to reject us by God. Given the full agency of other people, there is also something wrong with the idea of praying that a particular person will come to love us. Such a prayer is a way of asking God to override another human being's free will in order to gratify us and treating the other person as a means to meet our own needs. It is a prayer that in our heart of hearts we know God must refuse to grant. It is a prayer that, if we *really* love the person we are praying about, we do not actually want God to grant. We do not want another person handed to us as a prize for our faith. We want to be loved freely. This should not surprise us. God makes the same choice, preferring to risk our rejection by giving us free will rather than by forcing us to turn to him as loving puppets. Why would God override another person's freedom to give us the love we long for when he refuses to do this for himself?[10]

Finally, assuming that rejection means God has some other relationship in mind for you fails to recognize that your love for the person who has rejected you might very well have been a gift from God. It may be that God pulled back the veil on the other person's glory to give you a vision of his own image in this human form, to teach you something about loving him. It may be that this love is a great gift to be enjoyed in a nonpossessive, openhanded way without being concerned about being loved in return. Maybe part of your job is now to get up every morning thanking God for the existence of such a person in this world. Maybe that remains your job even if your love is not returned. If you assume that God has someone else for you, you may well be missing the *actual* gift God has sent you: the vision of this particular person's glorious true nature.

If you have decided that it is time to get over your love or infatuation, what can you do? It is not like you can just turn off a switch and suddenly stop having feelings for someone. Here are some possible strategies.

10. My understanding of free will is shaped by the Westminster Confession, which presents free will and predestination as complementary truths. I am not denying God's providence as the primary cause of everything that occurs, but I also affirm the liberty of secondary causes, including human free will.

First, we can seek help in prayer. C. S. Lewis once said that the point of prayer is not to change God but rather to change ourselves.[11] We pray to bring our will into conformity with God's will, to bring our mind into conformity with God's mind, to bring our hopes into conformity with God's hopes. We pray to cultivate contentment and to learn confidence in God's goodness. Such prayer is especially important in cases when we feel most helpless, when there is nothing we can do that would be the right thing. One of the most frustrating aspects of unrequited love is that, eventually, you run out of things to do and are left waiting, pondering, thinking—all internal actions that do little to satisfy the restless sense that there must be something you can do to advance your cause. At such a time, we are driven back into our inner life, making it especially vital that our inner life conforms to God.

Second, we need to confront reality. If the love you are experiencing is based on fantasy or illusion, getting to know the person you think you love will probably cure you. If you are living through a painful breakup, don't remember just the beautiful times but face the painful, hurtful times as well. It is always tempting to idealize the past, but by consciously disciplining your memory, you may avoid that.

Third, if the love you are experiencing and trying to get over is based on knowledge, not illusion, you should try distance and lack of exposure. Most love will die away quickly enough when it is not nourished by exposure to the loved person. This can be difficult when you have friends in common. You may need to weigh the importance of seeing your friends against your need for distance. Ann decided she was unwilling to give up her church to place distance between herself and the man she was in love with, but at least she created some emotional distance by holding her emotions inside and not talking about them with anyone at church.

Fourth, despite his advocacy for anger, Mr. Blue gave good advice when he suggested doing something positive and worthwhile to keep busy. Even better than learning French is helping someone in trouble. Being self-absorbed is not helpful. Immerse

---

11. For a fuller discussion of the effect of prayer on God and us, see C. S. Lewis, *Letters to Malcolm: Chiefly on Prayer* (New York: Harcourt Brace Jovanovich, 1964), 77–82.

yourself in something that puts your worries into perspective and reminds you how few problems you really have. You should be busy enough with meaningful activity that you are not able to spend hours replaying the past or dwelling on what might have been.

Fifth, learn how to enjoy being alone. Learn how to do things alone, such as going to the movies or out to dinner. Learn too how to be alone without distraction, without turning on the television or the stereo. Learn how to embrace your aloneness. In class discussion, many students are determined to defend an inability to be alone as a character trait common in more gregarious personalities, not as a sign of sin. Yet a spiritually mature person is capable of spending time alone, facing his or her thoughts, cultivating an inner life, and listening to God. Allow your loneliness to teach you dependence on him.

Sixth, cultivate Christian community and spend time with good Christian friends. During the time in church history when singleness was most highly valued, singleness rarely meant living alone as a hermit. It meant living with others in intentional Christian communities. Even if you do not choose such a community, you can reach out to people at church or in your family. Our culture teaches us that grown-ups need to disconnect from their parents and families to establish themselves as independent, but that idea is revealed as eccentric when put in the context of how most people around the world and throughout history have thought about adulthood. Adulthood does not mean running away from your family but being able to take your place as a responsible member. Spend time developing your relationships with parents, grandparents, and siblings. Reach out to members of your church—not just other singles but a variety of people.

Finally, cultivate a spirit of thankfulness. The bitterness and sense of entitlement that often accompany romantic rejection can best be dispelled by genuine gratitude. One man pointed out that romantic disappointment is not such a big problem in the great scheme of things.

> My faith puts things in perspective. As Paul says in Romans 8, I reckon that the sufferings of the present time are nothing compared to the glory that will be revealed to us. And I'm also quoting 2 Corinthians 12 to myself: My grace is sufficient for you.

If the worst thing that ever happened to me is getting dumped by college women, then that's really not the worst thing that could happen to somebody. Other than romance, practically everything else in my life has just fallen into my lap, and I'm thankful for that.

The loss you may feel after romantic rejection is real, but the other blessings in your life are real too.

Some people advocate dating other people to get over inappropriate love. In *Persuasion*, Jane Austen says that a "second attachment" is "the only thoroughly natural, happy, and sufficient cure" for disappointed love (although she also advises a "change of place . . . or novelty . . . or enlargement of society").[12] A young man who was suffering from unrequited love expressed a hope for just such an attachment.

I knew I loved her and knew none of her feelings for me were the same. I knew that I had to let go but couldn't. I realized that I had liked her (albeit on and off) for about five years, and my feelings for her ran very deep. She really did it for me. But not me for her. The previous year, I had decided that I needed to not like her any more because it did me no good. But she was now the standard that all other girls would be judged by. What I needed was for someone to make me forget about her.

He felt the need for someone else. The previous year, he had dated a woman for three months, trying to forget about the woman he was in love with, but eventually he ended that relationship because he was not yet over this long-term love. Yet now he wants to try that approach again. The end of the story is that he has found someone new to think about, a woman he is not dating but who "is in [his] life in an interesting way," distracting him from his obsession with his old friend. He concludes, "Love hasn't really been all that successful for me. . . . Maybe I'll never get married and that's okay too." In a case like this, it is hard to avoid feeling sorry for the women who are being used as medicine in this way.

12. Jane Austen, *Persuasion,* vol. 5 in *The Oxford Illustrated Jane Austen,* 3rd ed. (Oxford: Oxford University Press, 1954), 28.

Many people move on too quickly, producing the common rebound relationship. Just as it is unwise for a recently widowed person to remarry quickly, it is also unwise for a recently rejected person to rush into another relationship. In both cases, grief is involved. It is far better to face your sense of loss squarely and honestly. One man who is a counselor offered the following advice:

> Learn to view yourself as a whole complete person, not as half of something waiting to be completed. . . . One of the things I recognized early on is that I had to have a full life of my own, and I wasn't going to defer things like having a nice place to live and taking interesting vacations and going places I wanted to see, even if it meant doing those things on my own, by myself. That was all part of having a full life and a lot of rich experience.

He went on to observe that loving, mutual relationships are far more likely to emerge for people who are living full lives and are not desperately looking for a partner. "The more rich and complete you are in yourself, the more you have to offer, the better your possibilities versus this whole relationship thing." Of course, if you are only pretending to have a rich, full life in hopes of attracting someone to date, you have missed the point.

Even better advice is to recognize that every life, even the most richly satisfying, includes some unmet desires. Some years ago, I caught myself being jealous of a colleague who seemed to me to have a perfect life: amazing talent, a great career, and a loving marriage. Less than a week after my encounter with jealousy, I heard about her divorce. I had been foolish to envy her. But my envy would have been foolish even if her marriage had been as wonderful as it appeared, for there would still have been unmet desires in her life. Longing, craving, and dissatisfaction are part of *every* life this side of heaven. The book of Ecclesiastes is all about the futility of trying to find satisfaction and meaning in this life alone. We are made for something more than the best this world can give us. When our lack is most clear to us, then we are most open to receive this something more—a relationship with God himself.

241

Love with Open Hands

In the middle of the Renaissance, a young man in Florence saw a young girl on the street and was overwhelmed with a sense that his life had changed forever. Her face was suddenly "terrible as a god" to him. To use the language of the Song of Solomon, she was "terrible as an army with banners" (Song of Sol. 6:4). He went home that day and started a journal, in which he wrote, "Here begins my new life." Beatrice never loved Dante back, and she died while still a young woman. But for the rest of Dante's life, he loved Beatrice. When, decades later, he wrote his masterpiece, *The Divine Comedy,* it was Beatrice who was his guide to heaven.

Culture teaches us that the only kind of love that matters or has value is mutual love. Unrequited love is simply a failed attempt to get to mutual love, and so it should be left behind as quickly as possible. But unrequited love has a value of its own. Ann's story, which we heard earlier in this chapter, illustrates this.

> He is *so* committed to God, it's the focus of his whole life. Can I really be upset that he refuses to be distracted from that in order to start gazing back at me? He has become a sort of window to God for me. I look at him and think that for him it really is true (or becoming true more fully than for anyone else *I* know) that he's no longer living his own life, but it's Christ who lives in him.

It would seem that Ann's love for Bill is of the Dantean variety, that Bill has become an icon of sorts through whom she sees an aspect of God's nature more clearly. She continues:

> Loving him has been the greatest spiritual experience of my life. And it's precisely because he doesn't love me back that it's been that. I've had to learn how to let go of my anger, how to face down my fears, how to love him freely, without demanding anything back. It's been so hard! But it's also been very, very good. . . .
>
> I still can't imagine that I'd want to marry anyone, or even *date* anyone, except Bill. My friends like to lecture me about the importance of "moving on" and "getting over him," and they say things about some other man being "out there" for me. But

why would I want to "get over" the best thing that's ever happened to me? I mean, I see God in this man! I don't want to stop seeing that. So where does this idea come from that I have some obligation to recover? I have no intention of trying to get over him, but I *have* learned not to talk about it. I do find that my feelings for him are less intense over time, more peaceful. I suppose someday they might just be a nice memory. But even then I don't think I'd ever be interested in marrying someone who doesn't hit me with the same force. Loving him has shown me how much I can love someone, and I don't want to settle for anything less than that.

In some cases, unrequited love may point us to God even more truly than mutual love. In mutual love, we may be distracted from God and lost in the experience of loving. Unrequited love includes pain and restlessness that prompt us to look beyond the person we love to the one toward whom that love points. This does not mean that unrequited love is the only way for another person to reflect God to us, but it is one of the most common ways.

It is possible to practice an asceticism of the spirit, to love without expectation of return, without the goal or even the hope of possession. This is a costly form of love, an emotional poverty that is not possible for everyone. This form of love is not the stuff of American popular culture. In fact, this form of love is profoundly counter-cultural, belonging to the city of God, which is an alternative to the city of this world.

Jim Monaco suggests the following questions if you are trying to love someone in this way:

Am I loving without anger?
Am I loving without possessiveness?
Am I loving without jealousy?
Am I loving without fear?[13]

If you can answer yes to these questions, then you are loving with open hands. These questions also teach us what to pray for in our romantic relationships. If you are attempting this path

13. Jim Monaco gave these to me in conversation. He is an administrator at two parishes in Buffalo, NY.

of loving without hope of return, pray each day for the ability to love without anger, without possessiveness, without jealousy, and without fear. Pray to love with open hands.

These questions are a good guide for prayer even if your love is returned. Anger, possessiveness, jealousy, and fear are forces that destroy many relationships, undermining the trust and the mutual submission that should characterize Christian marriage. These questions offer a wonderful, painful process for self-diagnosis. A love that is without anger, possessiveness, jealousy, or fear is certainly not a needy love. It is a love that imitates the self-giving of God.

In the case of mutual love, such openhandedness need not feel like emotional fasting, since one's love is returned. In the case of unrequited love, the decision to continue loving is a decision for emotional poverty, emotional asceticism. If you cannot honestly make such emotional poverty your goal, this path is not for you. An example of the choice for emotional poverty is found in the account of a young man who fell hard for a woman who worked with him at a Christian summer camp. She had a serious boyfriend back home.

> I know that I never tried to put moves on her or wanted to break them up . . . but if they would drift apart, in my mind I would be there. So I settled quite happily to be her friend. She is that wonderful. I even helped her calm her boyfriend's fears by offering advice on how to maintain trust when so far away. At the end of the summer, I reluctantly said goodbye to a great friend.
>
> One month later, I found out that she was engaged. At the end of that school year, I made the trip to go to her wedding. She looked wonderful and wonderfully happy. I was very happy for her—what else could I do?—but I still have a special place for her in my heart.

After having a conversation about openhanded, nonpossessive love, Karen said:

> In the loving with open hands thing—I think I'm getting there. But I don't feel like that's really romantic love any more, not once you reach it. The one thing that I'm worst at is that I'm very afraid. I'm not jealous, and I'm not really angry. But I'm really afraid where I'm going to end up. What is going to hap-

pen in a year when I graduate? I have no reason to think that this is going to go away. I'm just more afraid if I start to think about the future and how much I've staked in this, how much importance this has to me.

The problem with the idea of loving with open hands is that it can easily become an excuse for neurotic behavior rather than a helpful way to mine this experience for its spiritual value. Karen is clearly extracting spiritual value from her pain in a mature Christian way. When asked about the line between her approach and something less healthy, she said:

> I think that to avoid doing that, there has to be some sort of letting go. I think in a lot of ways I have let go. I think you can let go and still love the person. That doesn't mean having no hope. But it would be really hard, once you reached that point, if the person turned around and loved you back. I think it would be really hard to transition back to where you were before. It's almost like you've moved past them, you know? I think maybe I'm letting go in the sense that I don't need this for my life to be full. I don't need to have a relationship with this person to be okay. I'm just happy he's alive and that I see him when I do.

If you can get up every morning and say thank you for this person, then your attitude is one of gratitude rather than possessiveness. Praying for the person you love is a way to make sure your attitude is gratitude rather than possessiveness, since prayer requires you to acknowledge that this person belongs to God, not to you. Prayer may not change the situation, but it changes you, helping you to think in a nonpossessive way about this person, to put his or her good above your own desires.

The Path of Joy

A friend with whom I was talking about the idea of emotional poverty labeled it "emotional anorexia." There are certainly people whose emotional lives are barren, who have an unhealthy inability to receive or give love, who are fixated obsessively on an unattainable ideal person rather than loving the real people around them.

245

But surely not all forms of emotional poverty are so unhealthy, just as not all forms of material poverty are unhealthy. Any act of deliberate renunciation will appear strange in the light of our acquisitive culture, but Christians should be comfortable with the idea of poverty as a good thing, given the Bible's consistent message of God's love for the poor. The test of whether one is practicing a form of unhealthy self-denial or a Christian discipline of poverty (whether material or emotional) is whether the result is joyful.

I once heard a Franciscan professor lecture about Francis of Assisi's embrace of poverty as a way of life. He said, "Francis had an experience of God which was so overwhelming that he had to move everything else out of his life to make room for it. If you practice poverty as a legalistic discipline without having the overwhelming experience of God, all you're left with is a barren life."[14] The same analysis can be applied to emotional poverty, to a decision to turn away from pursuing intimate relationships. Such inner asceticism should be motivated by an overwhelming experience of God. It should result not in barrenness but in joy.

As mentioned in chapter 2, C. S. Lewis talks about the way in which all our desires in this life, all our yearnings, are actually pointing us to God. Lewis labels those desires and yearnings "joy," a longing that is in itself sweet and pleasurable, that stirs up in us a desire for God himself. In a similar way, Karl Barth says, "Most joy is anticipatory. . . . It normally has something of an eschatological character."[15] Joy points us forward to the next life, to the time when we will see God face to face, when all our desires will be met and exceeded. Barth sees the "limitation, fragmentariness, and frailty" of our desires and yearnings as a sign of the provisional nature of life and asserts that we need to experience joy even in the midst of suffering and pain, because this is how we enter into the death of Christ. We make the choice for joy through a process: first, by recognizing that our identity is found in our relationship with God, not in

14. Xavier Seubert, St. Bonaventure University, July 1997, Allegheny, NY.

15. Karl Barth, *Church Dogmatics: The Doctrine of Creation*, vol. 3/4, trans. A. T. Mackay, T. H. L. Parker, Harold Knight, Henry A. Kennedy, and John Marks, ed. G. W. Bromiley and T. F. Torrance (Edinburgh: T & T Clark, 1961), 377.

the incidental circumstances of our present life; second, by paying grateful attention to the beauty and the wonder of our present life in all its fragility, even when we are in pain; and third, by trusting God's loving, providential care for us, such that ultimately all things must work together for our good (Rom. 8:28). If we refuse to will joy while we are suffering, then we are evading the cross. It is only when we embrace our sufferings as Jesus embraced his that we will share in his glory (Rom. 8:17).

Barth points out that we belong to God, not to ourselves, and in our sinful state, it is "outside of our power . . . to discover . . . what constitutes the real pleasure of our real life."

> We think we should seek . . . [pleasure] here or there because this thing or that appears as light or alleviation, as warmth, benefit, refreshment, consolation and encouragement, promising us renewal and the attainment of that which hovers before us as the true goal of all that we do and refrain from doing. But do we really know this true goal and therefore our true joy? God knows it. God decides it. But this means that our will for joy, our preparedness for it, must be wide open in this direction, in the direction of His unknown and even obscure disposing, if it is to be the right and good preparedness commanded in this matter. It should not be limited by the suffering of life, because even life's suffering (or what we regard as such) comes from God, the very One who summons us to rejoice. He has given to the cosmos and therefore to our life an aspect of night as well as day, and we have to remember that His goodness as Lord and Creator is the same and no less in the one than the other.[16]

What this means in practice is that we need to say yes to what life brings us, even if it is not what we would have chosen, even if it is painful, because God is in charge of our life. Barth calls us to "a readiness to accept with reverence and gratitude and therefore with joy the mystery and wonder of the life given to us by God, its beauty and radiance, and the blessing, refreshment, consolation and encouragement which it radiates as the gift of God, even where it presents itself to us in its alien form."[17]

16. Ibid., 383.
17. Ibid., 383–84.

There is no question that unrequited love is a form of suffering, but it may also be a source of joy. It may be an "alien form" under which the gift of God comes to us. Karen reminds us:

> But I keep thinking that he's a Christian and I'm a Christian, and so someday at least we'll both love each other more than I can imagine loving him. At least I'm part way there already. And at least I know that some day he'll look at me and he'll love me, and it might not be here, but he will. And maybe even he'll know that I always did, or maybe he'll understand. . . . I need to trust that it's going to be okay, and no matter what happens we're still going to have a shared heavenly moment someday. As long as I can seek God first and realize that I'm seeking God, not this guy, it's going to be okay.

If the people we love are brothers and sisters in Christ, we may count on encountering them again in the New Jerusalem, where each of us will reflect the glory of God and we will be able to see that glory in one another and delight in one another in ways that make our present experience of romance seem pale.

Alfred Lord Tennyson famously said, "'Tis better to have loved and lost than never to have loved at all." I believe this is true. There is value in the experience of loving someone else, even if that love is not returned. Sometimes the value is the same as that of other experiences of suffering: pain turns our attention back to God. Sometimes the value is the renewed awareness that the world is precious. Sometimes the value is the realization that the world is not centered on us. Sometimes the value is a deepened perception of God's presence.

A poem by Christina Rossetti summarizes the themes of this book:

> Lifelong our stumbles, lifelong our regret,
>   Lifelong our efforts failing and renewed,
>   While lifelong is our witness "God is good,"
> Who bore with us till now, bears with us yet,
> Who still remembers and will not forget,
>   Who gives us light and warmth and daily food;
>   And gracious promises half understood,
> And glories half unveiled, whereon to set
> Our heart of hearts and eyes of our desire;

Uplifting us to longing and to love,
Luring us upward from this world of mire,
Urging us to press on and mount above
Ourselves and all we have had experience of,
Mounting to Him in love's perpetual fire.[18]

All of us stumble in our romantic life. We do things that we later regret. Perhaps we have merely been foolish. Perhaps we have been unkind or even cruel. Our hope is found not in our own ability to love well but in God's unchanging love for us. It is in his power that we may try to love again, in a better way.

God is good. He shows us his goodness by showing us "glories half unveiled, whereon to set / Our heart of hearts and eyes of our desire." Love is how we pay sustained attention to someone else in order to see the half unveiled glory of God's image. Such love—whether or not it is returned, or perhaps especially when it is *not* returned—helps us to escape the prison of self-centeredness, to "mount above ourselves," and in so doing to learn to love God more.

18. Christina Rossetti, Sonnett 11 in the sequence "Later Life," in *Poems of Christina Rossetti*, ed. William M. Rossetti (London: Macmillan, 1905), 302.

Appendix

A Word to the Church

Protestantism has done much to elevate the worth of marriage, understanding marriage as a covenant that contributes to the well-being of a Christian society.[1] However, in asserting the value of marriage, Protestants have often gone overboard. Martin Luther said:

> Whoever will live alone undertakes an impossible task and takes it upon himself to run counter to God's Word and the nature God has given and preserves in him. . . . Stop thinking about [marriage] and go to it right merrily. Your body demands it. God wills it and drives you to it. There is nothing you can do about it.[2]

It is a sad truth that Protestantism has consistently ignored the Bible's clear teaching on singleness. In contemporary American Protestantism, we actually see an underlying assumption that "family values" and "Christian values" are synonymous. Protestants have often argued that marriage is necessary for civil order and that Christians are thus obligated to maintain the creation order by preserving marriage as the norm.[3] Janet Fishburn has

---

1. Max Stackhouse, *Covenant and Commitments* (Louisville: Westminster John Knox, 1997), 26.
2. Martin Luther, *Letters of Spiritual Counsel,* trans. and ed. Theodore G. Tappert, Library of Christian Classics (Philadelphia: Westminster, 1955), 274.
3. Stackhouse, *Covenant and Commitments,* 27.

written about the American church's "idolatry of the family,"[4] and the expression does not appear to be too strong.

The Protestant church's assumptions about marriage have a sad side effect: they create unnecessary barriers between the church and the growing number of single people in society. For many years, social scientists in the United States have been talking about the trend of people marrying later in life. Whereas it was once common to marry for the first time in one's late teens, it is increasingly common to marry for the first time in one's early thirties. Now it also appears that more people are simply not marrying at all. Many of those who do marry do not stay married long. The U.S. Census Bureau reports:

> The median age at first marriage is rising for both men and women. . . . In 1970, the median age at first marriage was 20.8 years for women and 23.2 years for men. By 2000, these ages had risen to 25.1 years and 26.8 years respectively. . . .
>
> More young adults have not been married. . . . The proportion of women 20 to 24 years old who had never married doubled between 1970 and 2000—from 36 percent to 73 percent. . . . This increase was relatively greater for women 30 to 34 years old; the proportion of never married women more than tripled over this time period from 6 percent to 22 percent. Changes were similarly dramatic for men—the proportion of men 20 to 24 years old who had never married increased from 55 percent in 1970 to 84 percent in 2000. Men 30 to 34 years old experienced an increase from 9 percent to 30 percent. However, the vast majority of men and women in 2000 had been married by their 35th birthday (74 percent), and by age 65, about 95 percent of men and women had been married, indicating that marriage is still very much a part of American life.[5]

With all due respect to the U.S. Census Bureau, this last conclusion seems unfounded. Marriage is still very much a part

4. Janet Fishburn, *Confronting the Idolatry of Family: A New Vision for the Household of God* (Nashville: Abingdon, 1991). Note that, although I am fond of the name of this book, I am not in complete agreement with Fishburn about how we should respond to this problem.

5. Jason Fields and Lynne M. Caspar, "America's Families and Living Arrangements," *Current Population Reports* (U.S. Census Bureau, June 2001), http://www.census.gov/prod/2001pubs/p20-537.pdf (accessed December 10, 2002).

of American life for those who were sixty-five and over in the year 2000 (the group for whom the 95 percent statistic applies). There is no reason to believe that this will be the case by the time current college students reach age sixty-five.

The truth is that in the year 2000 35 percent of all Americans between the ages of twenty-five and thirty-five had never been married, and (an even more revealing statistic) 25 percent of all households in the United States were single-person households.[6] So why does the church persist in speaking as though marriage is the norm for everyone? People need help leading godly single lives, and instead the church for the most part continues to act as though everyone is married or soon will be, thereby guaranteeing that most never-married people will never darken the door of a church.

It is not surprising that many single people find the church irrelevant to their lives. One student, when confronted with the census statistics, expressed skepticism, saying that these numbers certainly did not reflect the makeup of the people *she* knew in those age brackets, people who were members of her church. It did not seem to occur to her that her local congregation may not be representative of the population at large.

In our society, marriage is the primary rite of passage into adulthood. It is when we marry that we typically set up our own home and are given the furnishings to make that possible. Since we have no analogous rite of passage for those who do not marry, many single people are treated as irresponsible adolescents well into mid-life. Single adults are more likely to be addressed by their first names, even by small children, in settings where married people are addressed as Mr. or Mrs. In many churches, single people are routinely skipped over for leadership positions. Singles are ghettoized in singles groups, which have the goal of getting people married rather than integrating them into the full life of the church as adult members. One woman says she always knows when the young men of her congregation will be nominated to be deacons: it happens within a year after they are married. A man who was not deacon material when he was single at the age of thirty-four is nominated to be a deacon a year later because he has (finally) gotten married

6. Ibid.

(i.e., demonstrated his maturity). Another woman recounts, "I have a vivid memory of sitting in my church some years ago, listening to my pastor pray for 'the sick, the lonely, the shut-in, the single.' He was completely baffled when I told him this made me angry." A conversation with any never-married Christian adult will undoubtedly yield more such stories.

In an essay titled "SWF Seeking King," Jennifer Holberg reflects, "I have decided that asking God for a husband is like the Israelites asking for a king: they only wanted one because everyone else had one and once they got one, it was all downhill from there." She goes on to tell of her experience with a church singles group that kicked people out once they reached the age of thirty-five, apparently assuming "that 'young' and 'single' are synonymous. . . . One can either be single or one can be adult."[7] Given such messages, it is hardly surprising that many singles use their singleness as an excuse to prolong adolescence indefinitely.

One more side effect of the Protestant church's disregard for scriptural teaching on singleness is that the church has no credibility when it tells homosexual brothers and sisters that they are called to celibacy. For more than four hundred years, Protestants have equated Christian life with married life. Not surprisingly, homosexual Protestants conclude that if they are to live Christian lives they need to be allowed to marry. Perhaps if we had been teaching a scriptural view of singleness as God's preferred way of life for Christians, homosexual members would believe us when we tell them that celibacy is an honorable calling and that it is possible to live a fulfilled and fruitful life as a single person devoted to Christ. For more than four hundred years, we have been teaching that celibacy is an exceptional gift, that most people cannot possibly be expected to exhibit the level of self-control required for celibate life, and that singleness is somehow unnatural and even anti-creational. These false teachings are now coming back to haunt us.

How is it possible that Protestant churches, especially those that claim to take the Bible seriously, have structured themselves in complete opposition to the clear teaching of the New Testa-

7. Jennifer Holberg, "SWF Seeking King," *Perspectives* (October 2002), http://www.calvin.edu/minds/volume01/issue01/swf-seeking-king.php (accessed November 5, 2004).

ment? If the Protestant church were to submit to the teaching of the New Testament on marriage and singleness, the majority of Christians would probably still marry. If my students were all to embrace the idea that singleness is their default life path and that they should consider marriage only if they have come to love and be loved by a fellow believer who helps them to be a better Christian, I suspect that most of my students would still marry. But such a paradigm shift would produce some changes. First, marriages would be entered into for better reasons—not out of fear but out of obedience—and would therefore be stronger, less likely to end in divorce. It should be a matter of deep shame to Christians that our divorce statistics are no better, and in some places are worse, than those of non-Christians. Second, single people would be recognized and respected as full members of the church, capable of leadership and supported by community, honored rather than pitied for their single state. If congregations ever begin to take the Bible seriously on this matter of singleness, we will be living toward our future instead of toward our past, looking forward to the New Jerusalem instead of looking back to Eden.

It is not only conservative Protestants who have defied Scripture on this matter. Liberal Protestants embrace the same assumptions about the need to be partnered but sometimes leave out the need to be married. One woman in her forties who attends a mainline Protestant church observes that among "progressive" Christians there is an assumption that everyone needs to be sexually active to be fully human, leading to a similar anti-single bias:

> Even though I've never been married and I've always been a Christian, there are people in my denomination, maybe even in my congregation, who just assume that I'm sexually active. When I tell them I'm celibate, they think that I must be warped in some way, I must be lacking something, that I am not a full person because I'm not sexually active. The prejudice is *so* strong against genuine singleness, celibate singleness, that I feel stronger pressure to be partnered from my liberal Christian friends than from my conservative Christian friends.

Another single adult, a man in his forties, makes a similar observation about his experience.

I think the fundamentalist church respects celibate singleness as an eccentric acceptability. It's not a norm, but if you are one of those poor unfortunates, for whatever reason, who can't find a wife or a husband—then that's your option. And as long as you conform to that you can be on the periphery of our life. We'll invite you along to some holiday events, but those are mostly family events, so you're going to be mostly on the outside, but you're still one of us, and we want you to be there. . . . Among the more progressive churches I think that there is generally a lack of solid sexual ethics, so that a lot of those churches don't assume their single members are sexually inactive. I think a great many people can't imagine somebody not being sexually active at all, and while they're certainly more comfortable with you being sexually active in a committed relationship they're going to assume that you're going to have sexual activity anyway, 'cause everybody's got to do it.

An example of such an approach to ethics is the PC (USA) statement *Keeping Body and Soul Together* issued in 1991,[8] though never ratified by the General Assembly. This statement is so completely out of touch with orthodox Christian ethical tradition that Camille Paglia, a self-described lapsed-Catholic pagan of "wavering sexual orientation" and a notorious provocateur, found the statement incoherent and offensive:

> The report is so eager to argue away the inconvenient facts of Christian morality about sex that one has to ask the committee members, Why remain Christian at all? Why not leave Judeo-Christianity for our other great Western tradition, the Greco-Roman, in which philosophic discourse about ethics is possible without reference to a transcendental deity?[9]

We Christians must bear witness to God's new design for our romantic lives, and one of the truths to which we must bear wit-

8. General Assembly Special Committee on Human Sexuality, *Keeping Body and Soul Together: Sexuality, Spirituality, and Social Justice: A Document Prepared for the 203rd General Assembly (1991)* (Louisville: The Committee, 1991). A record of the details surrounding the discussion and the eventual decision not to adopt the statement can be found in the minutes from the 203rd General Assembly.

9. Camille Paglia, "The Joy of Presbyterian Sex," in *Sex, Art, and American Culture* (New York: Vintage Books, 1992), 36. Originally published in the *New Republic*, December 2, 1991.

ness is that sexual activity is not necessary for life. We need to have social contact to live, but we do not *need* to have a sexual partner. Under the sanctifying power of the Holy Spirit, we are beginning to be restored to our created nature in place of our fallen nature, but we are also moving forward to a new creation in which we will be transformed again.

Index